The Image and Influence of America in German Poetry since 1945

This book focuses on the image of the United States in German poetry and the reception of American poetry in Germany since 1945. Gregory Divers examines poems by major figures in twentieth-century German literature — including Arp, Benn, Brecht, Bachmann, Jandl, Enzensberger, and Grass — and offers in-depth analyses of the work of poets who shaped America's postwar image in Germany. From the prisoner-of-war poems of Günter Eich and the 1950s travel poems of Rudolf Hagelstange to the jazz portraits of Jens Gerlach and Volker Braun and the pop poetry of Rolf Dieter Brinkmann and Peter Handke, Divers traces America's status in Germany from 1945 to 1970. And while the 1960s protest poems of Erich Fried, Yaak Karsunke, and others show how the Vietnam War tarnished America's image in Germany, 1970s travel poems by Brinkmann, Günter Kunert, and Reiner Kunze confirm the resiliency of that image. Finally, Divers looks at select poems by Harald Hartung, F. C. Delius, and Thomas Kling to illustrate the new heights reached by America's image within German literary circles during the 1980s, and to show nuances in the status of America in Germany after reunification.

Divers also shows how American influences are crucial to the understanding of German postwar poetry. Thus, besides surveying the reception of Walt Whitman, T. S. Eliot, Ezra Pound, and William Carlos Williams in postwar Germany, he examines the influence of such figures as Charles Olson and Robert Creeley, Allen Ginsberg and the Beats, Frank O'Hara and John Ashbery, and Robert Lowell and Sylvia Plath on German poetry since 1945.

Gregory Divers received a Ph.D. in German literature from Washington University in St. Louis.

Studies in German Literature, Linguistics, and Culture

Edited by James Hardin
(*South Carolina*)

Gregory Divers

The Image and Influence of
America
in German Poetry
since 1945

CAMDEN HOUSE

First published 2002
by Camden House

Camden House is an imprint of Boydell & Brewer Inc.
PO Box 41026, Rochester, NY 14604–4126 USA
and of Boydell & Brewer Limited
PO Box 9, Woodbridge, Suffolk IP12 3DF, UK

ISBN: 1–57113–242–2

Library of Congress Cataloging-in-Publication Data

Divers, Gregory, 1950–
    The image and influence of America in German poetry since 1945 /
Gregory R. Divers
    p. cm.
ISBN 1–57113–242–2
    1. German poetry—20th century—History and criticism. 2. United
States—In literature. 3. American poetry—Appreciation—Germany.
I. Title.

PT553 .D58 2002
831'.914093273—dc21
                                                              2001043195

A catalogue record for this title is available from the British Library.

This publication is printed on acid-free paper.
Printed in the United States of America

Contents

Acknowledgments

I WOULD LIKE to thank the Fulbright Commission for a travel grant for study at the Freie Universität Berlin and the opportunity to conduct research out of which this project grew. I would also like to acknowledge the assistance of the following libraries: Die Bibliothek des Germanischen Seminar an der FU Berlin, Die Stadtbücherei Dortmund, the Olin Library at Washington University in St. Louis, Harvard's Widener Library, the Archives and Special Collections at the Dodd Research Center of the University of Connecticut Libraries, and the Public Library of the City of St. Louis.

In addition I would like to thank my *Doktorvater*, Egon Schwarz, Professor Emeritus of German at Washington University in St. Louis, for his help in taking the manuscript from dissertation to book, and Jerry Glenn, Professor of German at the University of Cincinnati, for his suggestions and support.

Introduction

ON 23 APRIL 1945, as Soviet troops advanced on the capital of Nazi Germany, Albrecht Haushofer, who had been imprisoned for his role in the resistance movement, was shot and killed by the SS just outside the Gestapo prison in the Moabit district of Berlin. Discovered along with the body approximately three weeks later by Haushofer's brother Heinz were five sheets of paper bearing what have come to be known as the *Moabiter Sonette*. Of these eighty sonnets, number thirteen, "Maschinensklaven,"[1] begins with a listing of European cities — among them Salzburg, Munich, Genoa, Westminster, Cologne, and Antwerp — juxtaposed with the names of two other cities, Krasnoyarsk and Omaha. The intent is readily apparent as Haushofer contrasts the refinement of European centers of culture with the backwardness of cities in Soviet Russia and the United States. Even the sound qualities of the latter two city names strengthen the dichotomy: the Slavic strains of Eastern Europe backed by the trisyllabic Native American drumbeat of the New World. The judgment is all the more ominous as this sonnet, an apostrophe to "slaves of the machine," anticipates the nuclear arms race initiated by the two world powers emerging at the end of the Second World War. Within this context, Haushofer's sonnet marks a turning point in the long tradition of America in German poetry. His Janus-like assessment not only draws on the conventional cultural-elitist European view of the United States but also looks ahead to the latter half of the twentieth century and America's newly achieved status in its role on the world stage.

If Haushofer's "Maschinensklaven" provides a starting point for the study of the image of America in German poetry after 1945, then the 1946 release of his *Moabiter Sonette* in limited edition under the auspices of American military officials illuminates

---

[1] Albrecht Haushofer, *Moabiter Sonette*, 4th ed. (1946; Berlin: Blanvalet, 1953), 23.

the strict regulations controlling the publishing industry during the early postwar years. After the defeat of Nazi Germany anything cultural — art, literature, music — was secondary to basic matters of survival. New books were luxury items.[2] Almost everything, including paper, was in short supply and under the jurisdiction of the victorious armies of occupation. The lingering effects of twelve years of National Socialist ideology were countered by Allied attempts to establish a system of denazification and re-education designed to expose the crimes of Hitler's fascist regime. Publications were controlled by paper allotment, and all printed material had to be licensed by the military authorities. As a result, paper was available only to those furthering the prescribed re-education process.[3]

Haushofer, however, furnishes only a partial representation of the status of America in German poetry as of 1945. A more composite picture can be found in another early postwar publication, namely, Max Rohrer's anthology *Amerika im deutschen Gedicht*.[4] From Christian Friedrich Daniel Schubart's "Der sterbende Indianer an seinen Sohn" (1774) to Hoffmann von Fallersleben's "Heimatklänge in Texas" (1845) to Ernst Waldinger's "New York von einem Wolkenkratzer gesehen" (1945), Rohrer's selections highlight the image of America[5] through three centuries of Ger-

---

[2] See Bernhard Zimmermann, "Literary Criticism from 1933 to the Present," trans. Franz Blaha, in Peter Uwe Hohendahl, ed., *A History of German Literary Criticism 1730–1980* (Lincoln and London: U of Nebraska P, 1988), 390–91.

[3] See Volker Wehdeking, "Eine deutsche *Lost Generation*? Die 47er zwischen Kriegsende und Währungsreform," *Literaturmagazin* 7 (1977): 145–66, here 147.

[4] Max Rohrer, ed., *Amerika im deutschen Gedicht* (Stuttgart: Röhm, 1948). Five thousand copies were published with permission of the military authorities under license number US-W-1019.

[5] Secondary literature on America in German letters is voluminous. Among the more important works, see Harold Jantz, "Amerika im deutschen Dichten und Denken," in Wolfgang Stammler, gen. ed., *Deutsche Philologie im Aufriß*, 2nd ed., 3 vols. (Berlin: Schmidt, 1962) 3: col. 309–72; Hans Galinsky, *Amerikanisch-deutsche Sprach- und Literaturbeziehungen: Systematische Übersicht und Forschungsbericht 1945–1970* (Frankfurt am Main: Athenäum, 1972); Sigrid Bauschinger, Horst Denkler, and Wilfried Malsch, eds., *Amerika in der deutschen Literatur: Neue Welt — Nordamerika — USA* (Stuttgart: Reclam, 1975); Wolfgang Paulsen, ed., *Die USA und Deutschland: Wechselseitige Spie-*

man poetry. The significance of this anthology, however, lies not so much in the contents per se, but in the editorial choices determining how the selections are to be presented. Rohrer does not choose to arrange the poems chronologically, nor does he offer an alphabetical listing of poets accompanied by their representative verse. Instead the book is divided into three sections with each focusing on one specific aspect of America in German poetry. Part one bears the caption *Neue Welt — Neues Leben* and features such poems as Schiller's "Kolumbus" (1795), Goethe's "Den Vereinigten Staaten" (1825) with its frequently cited first line, "Amerika, du hast es besser," Nikolaus Lenau's "Abschiedslied eines Auswandernden" (1832), and Theodor Fontane's "John Maynard" (1857), the poem providing both title and point of departure for the one-act play *Noch zehn Minuten bis Buffalo* by Günter Grass.[6] Owing to the overriding theme of hope and promise associated with the opportunity for a fresh start in a new land, this section highlights the positive side of the myth of America.[7]

---

gelungen in der Literatur der Gegenwart (Bern: Francke, 1976); Richard Ruland, *America in Modern European Literature* (New York: New York UP, 1976); Alexander Ritter, ed., *Deutschlands literarisches Amerikabild: Neuere Forschungen zur Amerikarezeption der deutschen Literatur* (Hildesheim and New York: Olms, 1977); Manfred Durzak, *Das Amerika-Bild in der deutschen Gegenwartsliteratur* (Stuttgart: Kohlhammer, 1979); Anita Krätzer, *Studien zum Amerikabild in der neueren deutschen Literatur: Max Frisch, Uwe Johnson, Hans Magnus Enzensberger und das "Kursbuch"* (Bern and Frankfurt am Main: Lang, 1982); Paul Michael Lützeler, "Vom Wunschtraum zum Alptraum: Das Bild der USA in der deutschsprachigen Gegenwartsliteratur," in Lützeler, *Zeitgeschichte in Geschichten der Zeit* (Bonn: Bouvier, 1986). Of these texts, Alexander Ritter's is noteworthy for its detailed bibliography.

[6] See Günter Grass, *Theaterspiele* (Neuwied: Luchterhand, 1970), 131–50.

[7] Jantz, col. 311, delineates a fourfold myth of America as characteristic of the European concept of the New World from the early sixteenth century onwards: 1. the myth of golden primitivism, 2. the opposite thereof, the myth of a monstrous, harsh continent, 3. the historic myth of the westward migration of culture, 4. America as the promised land of the future, but sometimes with negative signs. Hans Galinsky, "Deutschlands literarisches Amerikabild: Ein kritischer Bericht zu Geschichte, Stand und Aufgaben der Forschung," in Ritter 4–27, here 19, contends that subsequent research has neither improved nor replaced Jantz's original thesis. See also Jantz, "The Myth about America: Origins and Extensions," *Jahrbuch für Amerikastudien* 7 (1962): 6–18, rpt.

Part two is entitled *Landschaften und Städte*, and its selections reflect the European fascination with America's picturesque landscapes as well as life in urban centers. Here we find Christian Friedrich Scherenberg's "Reisephantasien" (1830), Lenau's "Der Urwald" (1836), Alfons Paquet's Whitmanesque portrayal of New York City in "Die atlantische Stadt" (1905), and those excerpts from Max Dauthendey's *Die geflügelte Erde* (1910) that deal with his travels through North America. Most significantly, the poems in part two point to the long tradition of America as a travel destination for German writers.

Whereas sections one and two present, for the most part, a positive image of America, part three, with its heading *Versunkene Welt*, introduces a decidedly different attitude toward the New World. The focus here is on various Indian tribes of North America, but the poems closing the anthology are not simply songs in praise of the noble savage; more prominent are those selections questioning the authority of the U.S. government in its dealings with Native Americans. For example, Adalbert von Chamisso's "Rede des alten Kriegers Bunte Schlange im Rate der Creek-Indianer" (1829) is an exposé of the inhumane policy of President Andrew Jackson in driving the Creek Indians from their homelands in Georgia and Alabama. Thus, this final chapter indicates how historical realities act to displace the myth-oriented perspective otherwise dominating the subject of America in German literature. Moreover, the concluding section of *Amerika im deutschen Gedicht* provides a lasting impression reminding the reader not only of America's culpability but also of Germany's literary heritage in taking a highly critical stance while addressing such issues. Not to be overlooked is the absence of any army-of-occupation shadow cast over the anthology. Clearly evident is the latitude allowed Rohrer in both his selections and editorial comments, as there are no signs of efforts to eliminate criticism of the United States.

Of the poets included in Rohrer's anthology, Ernst Waldinger is worthy of special mention for he represents a distinctive category in the postwar era of German poetry. An Austrian Jew born in Vienna in 1896, Waldinger was forced into exile in 1938. Having

in Ritter 37–49; and *Sprache im technischen Zeitalter,* numbers 54 and 56 (1975), special issues on "Mythos Amerika" and "Amerika-Bilder."

published two volumes of poetry in the 1930s, he arrived in New York as an established writer; nevertheless, Waldinger lacked the reputation of other exiled authors such as Heinrich and Thomas Mann, Bertolt Brecht, Lion Feuchtwanger, and Alfred Döblin. Waldinger was one of eleven Austrian and German writers who founded the *Aurora Verlag* in New York in 1944, the house publishing his first postwar collection of poems.[8] The early years in exile produced a number of New York poems, and Rohrer includes "Ein Pferd in der 47. Straße," "Die Brücken New Yorks," and the sonnet "Im Rhythmus eines New Yorker Hochbahnzugs," poems documenting Waldinger's initial impressions of America in a trademark style blending Old World verse forms with New World subject matter. Unlike other writers driven into exile, Waldinger remained in the U.S., and his subsequent literary career underscores the unique challenges facing the German-language poet living and writing in America.

This book arose from research carried out in a 1990 dissertation, "America in West German Poetry: 1945–1975." Thus, those parts of chapters one through eight pertaining to West German poets and up to 1975 are based on the dissertation; all else is new. We shall consider both the image of America as expressed in selected poems and American influences on contemporary German poetry. With the end of the Second World War American influences rushed into Germany as never before. America was not only a military but also a cultural presence as American music, radio, theater, and film became staples of everyday life in the western sectors of Germany. The formal founding of the two German states in 1949 — and the ensuing cold war strategies — led to pivotal changes in German-American relations affecting, in turn, the literary climate. Hence, America as subject matter and the reception of American literature have carried pronounced cultural and political implications in Germany since 1945. This factor is all the more im-

---

[8] Ernst Waldinger, *Die kühlen Bauernstuben* (New York: Aurora, 1946). A. Sexl of Vienna brought out the continental edition of this collection in 1947, followed in 1949 by the Aufbau house of Berlin publishing the East German edition for book trade in the Soviet zone. In addition to Waldinger, the writers founding the Aurora publishing house were Brecht, Döblin, Feuchtwanger, Heinrich Mann, Eugen Bloch, Oskar Maria Graf, Wieland Herzfelde, F. C. Weiskopf, Ferdinand Bruckner, and Berthold Viertel.

portant due to the nature of literary criticism in the German-speaking world. In brief, Germans distinguish between literary criticism and literary scholarship: the former finding expression via the mass media (newspapers, magazines, radio, and even television) while the latter is confined to the university setting and scholarly publications.[9] With respect to this study the distinctions are crucial, for throughout the postwar era the subject of America in German poetry has produced a crossover effect between the public and academic spheres. Finally, twentieth-century advancements, especially a new age of international travel, have increased contact between German and American writers.[10] Taken together, these various factors illustrate how the second half of the twentieth century established entirely new parameters for German literature.

Aside from examining the image of America, this book will document the reception of American poetry since 1945 in order to illuminate America's role in the evolution of postwar German poetry.[11] Although matters of image and reception pertaining to America generally exist as separate entities during the early postwar period, image and reception begin to merge in the 1960s. Throughout the greater part of this study the spotlight will fall on what was known as West Germany for reasons relating to the political division of Germany following the war. First of all, American influences from 1945 to 1990 are much stronger in the literature of the Federal Republic of Germany than in that of the German Democratic Republic. This is primarily attributable to the Ameri-

---

[9] Peter Uwe Hohendahl, "Introduction," *History of German Literary Criticism*, 1–2.

[10] See A. Leslie Willson, from the editor's introduction, "Perspective: The Image of America," *Dimension* Special Issue (1983): 14.

[11] For a bibliographic overview of German poetry since 1945, see Hans-Jürgen Schlütter, ed., *Lyrik — 25 Jahre: Bibliographie der deutschsprachigen Lyrikpublikationen 1945–1970*, vol. 2 of *Bibliographien zur deutschen Literatur* (Hildesheim: Olms, 1983), and Rolf Paulus and Ursula Steuler, *Bibliographie zur deutschen Lyrik nach 1945: Forschung — Autoren — Anthologien*, 2nd ed. (Wiesbaden: Athenaion, 1977); as to the reception of contemporary European and American poetry in the German-speaking world, see Lothar Jordan, *Bibliographie zur europäischen und amerikanischen Gegenwartslyrik im deutschen Sprachraum: Sekundärliteratur 1945–1988* (Tübingen: Niemeyer, 1996).

can presence in everyday West German life after the defeat of Hitler's fascist state. Second, America often embodies the antithesis of East German ideology, not only politically but also culturally. According to the literary precepts of the GDR, American imports such as rock 'n' roll music and other forms of pop culture represent the "cultural barbarism" of the United States.[12] This, however, is not to suggest that GDR poetry presents a one-sided view of the country, as there is ample evidence to show how America provided an impetus for East German poets to push the envelope of socialist dogma. That postwar conundrum known as the German question, the East-West battle for the ideological high ground, plays a fundamental role in literary matters relating to America. Indeed, a certain tension results whenever America surfaces, either in terms of image or influence, in German poetry after 1945. In fact, an America-induced tension frequently serves as a driving force in the postwar evolution of German literature. Although this study will accord the greatest attention to German poets, contributions to the image of America by Austrian, Swiss, and German-American writers — as well those from German-language enclaves of Eastern Europe — will also be considered.

---

[12] See Zimmermann 422. Not until the late 1970s does East German criticism offer a positive evaluation of rock 'n' roll without sacrificing socialist dogma. Due to the uncontrollable influx of Western mass culture via television and radio a new official position became necessary, one that viewed certain forms of rock music not as a commercial exploitation of the ignorant masses.

1: Pfannkuchen, Coca-Cola, Hollywood, Harlem: America's Early Postwar Image

IN THE YEARS immediately following the war, one image of America in German poetry could be understood in terms of the contents of a CARE package. For example, Günter Eich's first postwar publication includes the poem "Pfannkuchenrezept"[1] with the opening lines:

> Die Trockenmilch der Firma Harrison Brothers,
> Chikago,
> das Eipulver von Walkers, Merrymaker & Co,
> Kingstown, Alabama

— that is, the start of a list of the ingredients for pancakes in a prisoner-of-war camp, rendered in Eich's distinctive inventory style of language.

"Pfannkuchenrezept" draws heavily on the image of America the bountiful in its benevolent provider-role during the early postwar years. Moreover, Eich follows the German tradition of celebrating indigenous American products such as tobacco, potatoes, coconuts, and other exotic plants and flowers, as well as the melodious names of American cities and states.[2] To be sure, Eich's "Pancake Recipe" features nothing melodious or exotic — the place names are as dry as the powdered milk and eggs distributed to the prisoners. Likewise the company name "Merrymaker" — in context — is only an ironic comment on the potential of these American consumer goods, and serves as a reminder of how the literary legacy is subjected to harsh postwar realities.

---

[1] Günter Eich, *Abgelegene Gehöfte* (Frankfurt am Main: Schauer, 1948), 34. Three thousand copies were printed "unter Zulassung Nr. 8 (Dr. Georg Kurt Schauer) der amerikanischen Militärregierung," rpt. in Günter Eich, *Werke I: Die Gedichte*, ed. Horst Ohde (Frankfurt am Main: Suhrkamp, 1973), 31.

[2] See Wilfried Malsch, "Einleitung. Neue Welt, Nordamerika und USA als Projektion und Problem," in Bauschinger, Denkler, and Malsch, 4.

Although Eich casts the United States in a positive light, Bertolt Brecht often takes the opposite approach in his poems with an American focus. During his exile years in California (1941–1947) Brecht fashioned a clear, sharp image of America, in particular that of Hollywood and the film industry. In poems such as "Nachdenkend über die Hölle," "Hollywood," and "Hollywood-Elegien"[3] he likens Los Angeles to hell, declares the film studios marketplaces where lies are sold, and exposes the machinations of the "dream factories" of Hollywood. These poems, along with his "Sonett in der Emigration,"[4] capture the bitterness, disillusionment, and powerlessness of countless Europeans in exile.[5] Although Brecht's American experience was mostly negative, there are scattered positive images, for instance his "Brief an den Schauspieler Charles Laughton"[6] concerning the actor's translation of and subsequent title role in the American production of Brecht's *Leben des Galilei*, and "Garden in Progress,"[7] a picturesque tour of Laughton's home high above the coast of Southern California. The cold war, however, brought new tensions and choices to the fore, and the poem "Stolz"[8] shows Brecht aligning himself, with pride, on the side of the Soviet working class:

> Als der amerikanische Soldat mir erzählte
> Wie die wohlgenährten deutschen Bürgertochter
> Käuflich waren für Tabak und die Kleinbürgertochter für
>   Schokolade
> Die ausgehungerten russischen Sklavenarbeiterinnen jedoch
>   unkäuflich
> Verspürte ich Stolz.

---

[3] Bertolt Brecht, *Gesammelte Werke in 20 Bänden* (Frankfurt am Main: Suhrkamp, 1967), vol. 10, *Gedichte 3*, 830, 848, and 849 respectively.

[4] Brecht, *Gedichte 3*, 831.

[5] For a documentation of exile in America during the Second World War, see Eike Middell, ed., *Exil in den USA*, vol. 3 of *Zu Kunst und Literatur im antifaschistischen Exil 1933–1945 in sechs Bänden*, gen. ed. Werner Mittenzwei (Leipzig: Reclam, 1979).

[6] Brecht, *Gedichte 3*, 938.

[7] Brecht, *Gedichte 3*, 883–86.

[8] Brecht, *Gedichte 3*, 940.

Finally, both Brecht's image of America and his stance on the German question can be gleaned from the poem "Der anachronistische Zug oder Freiheit und Democracy,"[9] with its thesis that the so-called Western democracies are just smoke screens for capitalistic war machines.

In spite of an increased American presence in everyday West German life after the Second World War, America as subject matter found surprisingly little expression in West German poetry of the 1950s. One explanation for this absence was a general trend characterized by Peter Rühmkorf as a mindless escape from the reality of the era.[10] As a result, West German poets tended either to seek refuge in a tradition-bound nature poetry or to choose the path of aestheticism. The one poet most responsible for this latter choice and the development of the esoteric absolute poem in the 1950s was Gottfried Benn. When America does surface in his poetry, the reference reveals a casual cynicism, as in the following excerpt from "Restaurant,"[11] a poem written in 1951:

> in einer amerikanischen Zeitschrift las ich sogar,
> jede Zigarette verkürze das Leben um sechsunddreißig
>   Minuten,
> das glaube ich nicht, vermutlich steht die Coca-Cola-
>   Industrie
> oder eine Kaugummifabrik hinter dem Artikel.

Here Benn's lyric persona, an incorrigible know-it-all, subjugates proposed scientific evidence to an insider understanding of American marketing techniques. For Benn, American consumer goods carry none of the potential as shown in Eich's poem. In fact, Coca-

---

[9] Brecht, *Gedichte 3*, 943–49, a poem modeled on Shelley's ballad "The Mask of Anarchy," stanzas of which Brecht had translated for his essay "Weite und Vielfalt der realistischen Schreibweise"; see Brecht, vol. 19, *Schriften zur Literatur und Kunst 2*, 340–49.

[10] Peter Rühmkorf, "Das lyrische Weltbild der Nachkriegsdeutschen," in Rühmkorf, *Die Jahre die Ihr kennt: Anfälle und Erinnerungen* (Reinbek bei Hamburg: Rowohlt, 1972), 96.

[11] Gottfried Benn, *Sämtliche Werke*, ed. Gerhard Schuster, 6 vols. (Stuttgart: Klett-Cotta, 1986), vol. 1, *Gedichte 1*, 245.

Cola and chewing gum stifle instead of stimulate the poet's imaginative powers. But even though Benn's skepticism attempts to discredit the forces that rule the American economy, his conclusion is as trifling as the products he ridicules.

Benn shows a similar attitude toward America in the poem "Der Broadway singt und tanzt,"[12] "Eine magnifique Reportage!" — as the ironic subtitle reads — on a variety of New York musicals, in particular one featuring Noah and the Ark. Here Benn turns a spotlight on the monstrous aspect of the myth of America where the young continent's primitivism is far from golden. Broadway's luster is revealed as the gilding of America, and musical revues are considered the sign of a society still in its infantile stages. Benn portrays America as a land where culture is geared for the masses, epic tales are condensed to a suitable time frame for the stage, and even truth must have an inherent entertainment value. Yet regardless of the travesty of a "Broadway-Noah," Benn's brand of cultural criticism is, no matter how accurate, timeworn. As early as the 1920s conservative European critics saw signs of cultural decay emanating from America in the form of jazz music, boxing matches, and the show business industry.[13]

A similar style of outmoded criticism can be seen in Rudolf Hagelstange's "Funeral Home,"[14] a poem that observes the stultified relationship of an average American man to the women in his world. The first two stanzas introduce Hagelstange's protagonist and his predicament:

> Mr. Barker wich aus dem Menschenstrom
> und bog in die Yellow-Street,
> zum letzten Male — im Funeral Home —
> Betty Simpson to meet.

---

[12] Benn, *Gedichte 1*, 287–88.

[13] See Jürgen Theobaldy, "Begrenzte Weiten: Amerika-Bilder in der westdeutschen Lyrik," *Akzente* 22.5 (1976): 402–17, here 404–5.

[14] Rudolf Hagelstange, *How do you like America? Impressionen eines Zaungastes* (Munich: Piper, 1957), 92–94. This book, a collection of poetry and prose, is based on Hagelstange's travels in America during the mid-1950s as an official guest of the U.S. State Department.

> Er war an die Fünfzig. Sie Dreißig vorbei.
> (Genaueres wußte er nicht.)
> Er war geschieden. Sie war immer noch frei,
> attractive — bis auf das Gesicht.

Mr. Barker is slow and shy, hence as a man a difficult case. Moreover, contact with the opposite sex seems restricted to his place of work, so that now — death having ended the possibility of a relationship with Betty Simpson — his thoughts turn to the younger Evelyne Dull:

> Die war stets gutgelaunt und saß auch im Büro,
> und die hatte ein hübsches Gesicht.
> Doch die anderen Dinge, die waren nicht so.
> (Genaueres wußte er nicht.)

Like Benn, Hagelstange offers little new in his portrayal of America. His Mr. Barker could just as well be a character from a Sinclair Lewis novel of the 1920s. Furthermore, the rampant irony, quatrain stanza form, and *abab* rhyme scheme suggest the influence of Heinrich Heine rather than innovative twentieth-century trends. The only element reflecting the times is the use of English words and phrases — a tendency that would later become even more pronounced in German poetry. Here, unfortunately, the English word does little more than fulfill a rhyme function or carries too obvious and heavy a meaning as in the name Evelyne Dull.

Hagelstange's American travel poems focus on topics unique to the host country. His function is like that of a journalist reporting to an uninformed public, as in the opening stanza of "Bei den Schwarzen Baptisten."[15]

> In Charlottesville,
> in Virginia,
> traf ich, bei den schwarzen Baptisten,
> seit längerer Zeit die freundlichsten Christen.
> An der Kirchentür sah ich schon einen warten
> auf mich und mußte eine der Karten
> ausfüllen: Name, Adresse, Herkunftsland —
> und was noch sonst auf der Karte stand.

---

[15] Hagelstange, 31–35.

> Dann brachte ein Mädchen in schneeweißem Kleid
> mich an einen Platz, nicht weit
> von der (gewissermaßen) Bühne,
> im Halbkreis geschwungen, vorn ein Podest;
> dahinter, erhöht wie auf einer Tribüne,
> drei Reihen des Chors, der eben erschien,
> bald gefolgt von Reverend Green.

The poem is a narrative account of events on a particular Sunday morning in Charlottesville. The Black Baptists are portrayed in most positive terms, as shown by the superlative adjective form in "the friendliest Christians." In addition to the hospitality of his hosts, Hagelstange notes the singular quality of worship practiced by this congregation. He makes no mention of an altar, referring instead to a stage, and the parenthetical addition "to a certain extent" is a not so subtle hint that the poet recognizes the theatrical features of this worship service. The remainder of the poem fixes on the sermon of Reverend Green,[16] and especially the spirited interplay between preacher and parishioners:

> Und es sprangen die Worte wie glühende Brocken
> von seinem Munde. Bald sprach er schnell;
> dann geriet er ins Stocken
> und suchte nach dem treffenden Wort.
> Und hatte er's, warf er es ihnen zu.
> Und sie fingen es auf.
> Oder riefen's ihm zu.
> Und sagten: Oh, Yes.
> Und: That's right, Sir. That's true!

Hagelstange's account concludes with Reverend Green bidding his congregation to greet their guest from abroad, a gesture eliciting stereotypical amazement "über den Mister aus Germany." Unfortunately what the poem may lack in literary merit is not offset by

---

[16] Hagelstange's fascination with Black American preachers is also reflected in his translations. See James Weldon Johnson, *Gib mein Volk frei* (Gütersloh: Mohn, 1961), excerpts of which were reprinted as "Gottes Posaunen" in Hagelstange, *Gast der Elemente: Zyklen und Nachdichtungen 1944–1972* (Cologne: Kiepenheuer & Witsch, 1972), 133–64.

the expository function of capturing the atmosphere of the worship service. This poem is a period piece reflecting a non-critical attitude of the 1950s that prefers pathetic tenderness over issue-oriented scrutiny. Hagelstange's maxim is simple: be not provocative. And his objective is just as basic: to depict and promote a seldom featured facet of German-American fellowship.

With a focus on the natural wonders of the land, Hagelstange's "Grand Canyon"[17] counts as one of his more traditional travel poems. The first of its two sections depicts less of the Grand Canyon itself than the tourist trade revolving around this geologic marvel:

> Grand Canyon Station. Es krümelt noch Schnee.
> Dreihundert Yards hanghinauf: El Tovar Hotel.
> (Man fährt dich im Bus, und das geht schnell.)
> Touristen wenig; meist Geld-Hautevolée.
> Du kaufst eine Karte »All expense day«:
> Breakfast, lunch, dinner; zwei Auto-Touren;
> einen Geologen auf Schöpfungsspuren
> und — nicht zu vergessen —: Indianertanzen.
> (Vierzehn Dollar im ganzen.)
>
> Ein gezähmter Hopi mit rotem Band
> nimmt den Mantel, öffnet Türen und Hand.
> Hinein (den Quarter)!

The primary purpose of these two stanzas seems obvious: to reveal the crass commercialization of a once pristine site.[18] However, besides this business aspect of "Grand Canyon" there are two lines from the poem serving to characterize Hagelstange's impressions of America. First, the allusion to "einen Geologen auf Schöpfungsspuren" implies an American scientific methodology ostensibly linking geology with biblical creation theory; and second, the choice of adjective in the reference to a "gezähmter Hopi" evokes a lingering image of Wild West days and the apparent need to tame the aggres-

---

[17] Hagelstange, 61–64.

[18] Max Dauthendey had noted the budding years of American tourism in the poem "Am Weltabgrund (Grand Cañon)" from *Die geflügelte Erde: Ein Lied der Liebe und der Wunder um sieben Meere* (Munich: Langen, 1910); this poem also appears in Rohrer, 87–91.

sive instincts of Native Americans. Although this adjective might also evoke its opposite, wild, as a desirable state of untamed nature corresponding to Jantz's notion of golden primitivism, the irony of Hagelstange's word choice lies in a clearly unintended oxymoron: the name Hopi, for members of a Pueblo tribe of Shoshone Indians, literally means "peaceful ones." Part two of "Grand Canyon" reads more like a nature study in verse. Its grandiose tone corresponds to Hagelstange's role as a well-traveled European man of letters undergoing a transformation in the face such magnificence. The grandeur of the language reflects not only the natural setting but also the poet's literary heritage. As a result, "Grand Canyon" reveals as much about the poet as the subject matter at hand.

Hagelstange did much to further America's place in postwar German poetry. The strength of *How do you like America?* is the wide range of subject matter in the various American travel poems. Hagelstange brings the German reader up-to-date with 1950s America, and his poetic sketches of the United States provide social commentary, an inside look at Black America, and veneration of geologic marvels. With respect to style, however, he remains tied to European conventions. Born in 1912, Hagelstange is a poet of his generation; even when he adopts a comparatively lighthearted tone, Old World formal structures tend to dictate New World content. As a contrast, let us consider two Austrian poets, Ingeborg Bachmann and Ernst Jandl, born in 1926 and 1925 respectively, and how they address similar topics. Whereas Hagelstange looks at rural America in his portrait of the Black Baptists, Bachmann turns to an urban setting in "Harlem,"[19] a poem associating the African-American experience with music:

> Von allen Wolken lösen sich die Dauben,
> der Regen wird durch jeden Schacht gesiebt,
> der Regen springt von allen Feuerleitern
> und klimpert auf dem Kasten voll Musik.

[19] First published as "Haarlem" in *Jahresring 56/57*, 3 vols. (Stuttgart: Deutsche Verlags-Anstalt, 1956) 3: 228; rpt. with title spelling "Harlem" in Ingeborg Bachmann, *Werke*, Vol. 1, ed. Christine Koschel, Inge von Weidenbaum, and Clemens Münster (1978; Munich and Zürich: Piper, 1982), 113. As to Bachmann's image of America and especially New York City, see the 1958 radio play *Der gute Gott von Manhattan* in *Werke*, Vol. 1, 269–327.

Die schwarze Stadt rollt ihre weißen Augen
und geht um jede Ecke aus der Welt.
Die Regenrhythmen unterwandert Schweigen.
Der Regenblues wird abgestellt.

Bachmann opts to establish a mood rather than a narrative line, and does so by hearing music in rainfall. The repetition of *Regen* in the first stanza corresponds to the repetitive sound of raindrops and provides a counterpoint to an otherwise silent setting. The sound quality of the verb *klimpert* initiates the musical motif, while in the second stanza the compound nouns *Regenrhythmen* and *Regenblues* literally bind the rain to music. Likewise adding to the mood, the first quatrain features attributive adjectives of superlative degree (*all* clouds, *every* shaft, *all* fire-escapes, *full* of music), thus spawning a sense of urgency. Stanza one having set the scene, stanza two employs personification to create an image functioning as an objective correlative. With this notion of the black city rolling its white eyes Bachmann not only offers an emotional response to the previous stanza but also intimates an attendant comment on black-white race relations in the United States.

In terms of subject matter alone, both Hagelstange's "Bei den Schwarzen Baptisten" and Bachmann's "Harlem" show postwar German poetry looking in new directions. Although employing a formal stanza structure, Bachmann pushes for new modes of expression, varying meter and relying more on off-rhyme than rhyme. The content is pared to essentials with the rain adding an impressionistic wash to the scene. All in all, Bachmann's "Harlem" is a transitional poem, traditional in its underpinnings yet still anticipating the freer verse forms of the coming decade. Just as Hagelstange takes a conventional approach in his scenic travelogue poems, a more novel, indeed experimental means of celebrating the natural wonders of North America in verse can be found in the early work of Ernst Jandl,[20] specifically the following poem from 1957:

---

[20] Ernst Jandl, *poetische werke*, ed. Klaus Siblewski, 10 vols. (Munich: Luchterhand Literaturverlag, 1997) vol. 2, *Laut und Luise & verstreute gedichte 2*, 78.

niagaaaaaaaaaaaaaaaaa

ra felle

niagaaaaaaaaaaaaaaaaa

ra felle

Any elucidation is superfluous if not detrimental; suffice it to say that Jandl explores new linguistic frontiers and displays his mastery of the tenets of concrete poetry by creating a refreshing word-picture of the Niagara River, as divided by Goat Island, and its twin falls.

In spite of a generally positive image in West Germany due to the Marshall Plan, America's standing as emergent world power carried threatening overtones. If development of the atom bomb capped off America's rise to superpower status, then Hiroshima and Nagasaki became code words denoting negative aspects of its world-wide reputation. Furthermore, cold war tensions of the 1950s heightened by the arms race served as a reminder that America had already twice deployed the atom bomb. The dawning of the atomic age became the focal point of a number of poems. Hansjörg Schmitthenner, for example, addresses the topic of "Hiroshima · Nagasaki"[21] in verse, but does so without mention of America. His poem expresses mankind's fear since that day when "aus dem Himmel fuhr Atomblitz" and enlists the aid of "Gottesmutter süße" to deliver "uns allen/ aus unsrer tiefen Not." Like Hagelstange, Schmitthenner avoids provocation, opting for a spiritual solution to what is, in essence, a political issue. Wolfgang Weyrauch voices similar apprehensions in "Atom und Aloe,"[22] a poem pondering the possibilities of a global nuclear war between the United States and the Soviet Union. Weyrauch likewise refrains from making any overt political statement and blames neither side for this imagined catastrophe.

---

[21] In Wolfgang Weyrauch, ed., *Expeditionen: Deutsche Lyrik seit 1945* (Munich: List, 1959), 25–27.

[22] In Hans Bender, ed., *Mein Gedicht ist mein Messer* (Heidelberg: Rothe, 1955), 22–34.

A closer look at 1950s America can be found in "Hiroshima"[23] by Marie Luise Kaschnitz, a poem that does not, despite its title, focus on the Japanese city or its inhabitants. Instead, "Hiroshima" marks a place in time and serves as the point of departure for a psychological probe of the pilot of the aircraft that dropped the first atomic bomb:

Der den Tod auf Hiroshima warf
Ging ins Kloster, läutet dort die Glocken.
Der den Tod auf Hiroshima warf
Sprang vom Stuhl in die Schlinge, erwürgte sich.
Der den Tod auf Hiroshima warf
Fiel in Wahnsinn, wehrt Gespenster ab
Hunderttausend, die ihn angehen nächtlich
Auferstandene aus Staub für ihn.

Nichts von alledem ist wahr.
Erst vor kurzem sah ich ihn
Im Garten seines Hauses vor der Stadt.
Die Hecken waren noch jung und die Rosenbüsche
    zierlich.
Das wächst nicht so schnell, daß sich einer verbergen
    könnte
Im Wald des Vergessens. Gut zu sehen war
Das nackte Vorstadthaus, die junge Frau
Die neben ihm stand im Blumenkleid
Das kleine Mädchen an ihrer Hand
Der Knabe der auf seinem Rücken saß
Und über seinem Kopf die Peitsche schwang.
Sehr gut erkennbar war er selbst
Vierbeinig auf dem Grasplatz, das Gesicht
Verzerrt von Lachen, weil der Photograph
Hinter der Hecke stand, das Auge der Welt.

Although the first stanza consists entirely of poetic speculation, the denial of the validity of these conjectures in line one of stanza two does not diminish their force. In effect, stanza one establishes the context on which the reality of stanza two builds a contrast, thus suggesting that the pilot should have at least occasional pangs of conscience. By identi-

---

[23] Marie Luise Kaschnitz, *Neue Gedichte* (Hamburg: Claassen, 1957), 25.

fying the photographer as "the eye of the world"[24] Kaschnitz emphasizes not only that the world has not forgotten Hiroshima but also that
the pilot's subsequent life is subject to public review. Hence, "Hiroshima" is as much an antiwar poem[25] as a censure of middle-class life
in 1950s America. The familial pleasures depicted here are projected
against the backdrop of Hiroshima and thus represent an isolationist
American attitude oblivious to the rest of the world. Moreover, with
the focus on the man "who dropped death on Hiroshima" these back-
yard antics create an image of American suburbia all the more crass.
Not only has the pilot found a means to forget, as Kaschnitz implies,
but he also has the audacity to pose for a world audience looking in on
his carefree life after Hiroshima. Whether or not he has found true refuge, however, is called into doubt by a "face/distorted by laughter" —
an intimation of internal unrest with appearances masking reality.

The advent of the atomic age brought new perspectives on the
role of the scientific community within society. The opening stanza
of Hans Kasper's poem "Nachricht (Michigan)"[26] reports a news
item seeming to proclaim science's gain as poetry's loss:

> MICHIGAN. John Claymans,
> geboren 1932,
> Lyriker,
> Hoffnung der jungen
> Poesie,
> hat sich entschieden:
> er
> studiert
> Astro-Physik.

---

[24] As Kaschnitz explains, "Ich sah in einer Illustrierten das Foto des Mannes,
der leben mußte, ein Kleinbürgerdasein." See Hilde Domin, ed., *Nachkrieg
und Unfrieden: Gedichte als Index 1945–1970* (Neuwied and Berlin: Luchterhand, 1970), 39.

[25] Among the more notable antiwar poems set in Hiroshima is Günter
Kunert's "Der Schatten" from the mid-1960s. The central image of this finely
crafted sonnet is the horrific "shadow" of a human being cast on the arch of a
bridge by the flash of the atomic explosion. See Günter Kunert, *Der ungebetene Gast* (Berlin and Weimar: Aufbau, 1965), 30.

[26] Hans Kasper, *Nachrichten und Notizen* (Stuttgart: Goverts, 1957); quoted
here from Weyrauch, *Expeditionen*, 52.

Kasper, however, does not follow the standard pessimistic line of cultural criticism proclaiming the demise of art in the dawn of a new technological age. Instead, he takes a positive view of the poet's decision by showing that in America it is possible to negate the separation between science and art. "Nachricht" is noteworthy, then, for its innovative treatment of the myth of America, specifically Kasper's presentation of an updated version of America's pioneer spirit in the mid-1950s: the process of westward expansion on *terra firma* having been completed, the U.S.A. will now strive to explore new frontiers in the stars.

Hans Arp, renowned early-twentieth-century dada poet, offers not only a change of pace to an otherwise staid decade but also an original view of postwar European politics in "Amerika,"[27] a poem combining elements of circus milieu burlesque with a surrealistic animal fable:

> Ein fadenscheiniger Clown
> steigt einem fadenscheinigen Clown
> auf den Buckel
> und diesem fadenscheinigen Clown
> steigt wieder ein fadenscheiniger Clown
> auf den Buckel
> und so fort.
> Dem letzten fadenscheinigen Clown
> steigt ein schwärmender Kolumbus
> auf den Buckel
> um nach seinen Karavellen Ausschau zu halten
> die inzwischen in See gestochen sind
> und zwar in der finsteren Richtung
> aus der es stöhnt röchelt und gurgelt
> und wo selbst die himmlischen Lichter
> vor Angst zittern.
>
> Ein Bettler mit einem Kopf wie eine Dörrbirne
> entdeckt im Kleiderschrank
> des schwärmenden Kolumbus
> ein tadelloses ungetragenes Amerika.

[27] Hans Arp, *Auf einem Bein* (Wiesbaden: Limes, *1955); rpt.* in Hans Arp, *Gesammelte Gedichte II: Gedichte 1939–1957* (Zürich: Schifferli; Wiesbaden: Limes, 1974), 177–79.

Nicht weit von der Höhle des Bettlers
in der weiten sandigen Ebene
erhebt sich täglich einmal ein Erdteil
ein noch unbeschriebenes Blatt.
Dieser Erdteil hat vier gewaltige Adlerbeine
mit mächtigen rotlackierten pedikürten Krallen.
Wie ein Raubvogel stürzt sich dieser Erdteil
in das himmlische Gewölbe
und schreit:
«Ich will das tadellose ungetragene Amerika
haben.»
Der Bettler zählt der Ordnung wegen
den Rest seiner Tage.

Ein brüchiges Clownsskelett
wird dick fett und reich
und kauft sich einen dressierten Esel.
Der Esel gerät unverhofft
in einen eigentümlichen Fall von guter Hoffnung.
Vier Beine wachsen diesem Esel über Nacht
aus dem Rücken.
Nun können sich die beiden
nicht mehr entschließen
auf welchen der vier Beine
ausgeritten werden solle.

Als der Bettler mit dem Kopf wie eine Dörrbirne
der Wehmut verfiel
versuchte der schwärmende Kolumbus
das Übermenschenmögliche.
Er versprach was die Sprache hergibt
und ließ noch während einer Woche
glattzüngige gleisnerische Onomatopoesien
folgen.
Er versprach dem Bettler
die wunderjauchzende massiv diamantene
selbstgeigende Zigeunergeige.
Vor dieser Wundergeige
müßten selbst die altbekannten Himmel
einpacken

die voller Geiger hängen.
Die Folge davon sei
daß beide
der Bettler und seine Wenigkeit der Kolumbus
hoch hoch oben
in den lichtesten Tiefen des Himmelsauges
mit allen fuchswild gewordenen Engeln
zu den jeder Beschreibung spottenden Klängen
der diamantenen Zigeunergeige tanzen würden
und aller Wehmut quitt wären.

Amidst this bizarre grouping of human characters and beasts, Columbus plays — as shown in repetition of the attributive adjective *schwärmend* — the pivotal role of a visionary linking Europe and America.[28] The opening stanza, with its sequential build-up of threadbare clowns forming a lookout perch for Columbus, concludes with a menacing portrait of the New World. Like a prologue establishing context, this stanza presents European history as time-worn and repetitive. Moreover, its concluding lines parody the medieval mind-set confronting Columbus, namely, the notion of America lying beyond a moaning, death-rattling realm of darkness where even celestial bodies tremble with fear.

Stanza two incorporates a fresh sequence of imagery appropriating Columbus for the twentieth century and casting America in new light. With the appearance of a beggar "with a head like a dried pear" and the discovery of "a flawless unceremonious America," Arp varies the clothing metaphor of stanza one in order to depict Europe, and specifically West Germany, as trying on America for size. Postwar Germany is presented as a "clean slate" with its future identity to be determined by the four former Allies, and the insistent cry — "Ich will das tadellose ungetragene Amerika haben" — suggests a greedy desire for material benefits accorded by the Marshall Plan.

Stanza three retrieves the clown figure as representative of Old World Europe now, however, growing fat and rich thanks to post-

---

[28] See Cecile Cazort Zorach and Charlotte Melin, "The Columbian Legacy in Postwar German Lyric Poetry," *The German Quarterly* 65.3–4 (1992): 267–93, especially 277–79.

war American beneficence. The remainder of the stanza reads like an animal fable with the trained donkey suggesting the stubborn yet dutiful conservatism of West Germany during the Adenauer era. The union of the clown and donkey leads to a grotesque pregnancy resulting in four legs growing out of the donkey's back, an image recalling the four powerful eagle talons of stanza two. Here, however, the indecision on the part of the clown and donkey as to how these legs are to function corresponds to cold war tensions following the division of Germany, specifically a crippling uncertainty resulting from the diametrically opposed forces guiding the two German states.

Absent in stanza three, Columbus returns in the final stanza to voice promises of a glorious future, a motif traditionally associated with America. The lyrical qualities of this stanza coupled with the clever neologisms stand as a testament to Arp's unique gift of language. Columbus, no longer the seafarer, is now a full-fledged visionary spouting "smooth-tongued onomatopoeia" intended to allay the cold war anxieties besetting the beggar in stanza two. Arp draws heavily on the German literary tradition in this stanza, adding a Nietzschean touch ("das Übermenschenmögliche") to the concept of America as the land of unlimited opportunity, and rephrasing the musical strains of Romanticism by changing Brentano's enchanted horn to a "Wundergeige." In the end, as Zorach and Melin point out, this poem transcends national boundaries locating itself in the land of angels and gypsies. As such, Arp's "Amerika" is less a political territory than a promised state of mind. In spite of its undeniable political thrust this poem is strictly nonaligned. Compared to other poems discussed in this chapter, Arp's "Amerika" is the one poem to face postwar political realities in Germany head-on without paying lip-service to political parties or armies of occupation. Moreover, the poem takes a vigorous approach in terms of language, conveying a deadly serious message by means of lively wordplay. And in this regard Arp maintains his dada tradition in the face of Adorno's proclamation on lyric poetry after Auschwitz and Hiroshima by letting language, not ideology, take priority.

These scattered examples of America in German poetry of the 1950s reflect both the literary norms and the social climate of the decade. The relative absence of America in early postwar German verse can be explained in terms of the lingering effects of the war and attempts to escape postwar realities. In West Germany the most dominant images of America in everyday life — from CARE packages to GIs in olive drab — served as reminders of a past preferably forgotten; in the East, America was strictly on the periphery. Just as citizens of the two newly formed German states sought to build countries of which they could be proud, postwar poets displayed a similar desire to regain international standing. To do so, they were faced with not only cleansing the German language of Nazi impurities but also relearning the world language of poetry.[29] Initially America played a minor role in this transition, as French standards established the prevailing mood. Although American film, music, prose fiction, and theater were exercising growing influence in Germany, American poetry had yet to make a serious challenge to European traditions. And geographically speaking, the United States was too distant a land to be a travel destination for more than a fortunate few.

Ernst Waldinger provides an interesting variant on this theme as the expatriate poet living in America and writing in German. His poetry of the 1950s finds its subject matter either in memories of a Europe left behind or impressions recorded during travels throughout America. Although he remains true to formal structures, in particular the Petrarchan sonnet form, Waldinger adopts a freer verse style in the travel poem "Betrachtung auf der Golden Gate Bridge."[30] His literary life in exile also brought him in close contact with American poetry, and throughout the 1950s he translated numerous American poets including Robert Frost, Robert Lowell, Archibald MacLeish, Marianne Moore, Edwin Arlington Robinson, and Allen Tate.[31] In 1958, twenty years after being

---

[29] See. Karl Krolow, *Aspekte zeitgenössischer deutscher Lyrik* (Gütersloh: Mohn, 1961), 13; and Hans Bender, ed., *Widerspiel* (Munich: Hanser, 1962), 10. See also Nicolaus Jungwirth and Gerhard Kromschröder, *Die Pubertät der Republik* (Frankfurt am Main: Fricke, 1978), 6.

[30] Waldinger, *Zwischen Hudson und Donau* (Vienna: Bergland, 1958); rpt. in Waldinger, *Noch vor dem jüngsten Tag*, ed. Karl Markus Gauß (Salzburg: Müller, 1990), 99–100.

[31] See Ernst Waldinger, *Gesang vor dem Abgrund*, selected and with an introduction by Ernst Schönwiese (Graz and Vienna: Stiasny), 1961.

forced into exile, Waldinger received the *Theodor Körner Preis*, and in 1966 on the occasion of his seventieth birthday he was awarded the *Goldene Ehrenmedaille der Stadt Wien.* These two honors, however, should not suggest that he enjoyed due recognition in Austria. An ardent patriot, Waldinger struggled to make Austrian literature better known in America while he himself gradually faded from memory in his homeland. In the end, Waldinger's life story coupled with the fact that the original editions of his eight books of poetry are long since out of print, accentuates the oftentimes cruel fate of the postwar poet in exile.

In review of America's image in German poetry of the 1950s, we see few poets following Eich's realistic portrayal of the American presence in Germany since 1945. Benn and Hagelstange, whether in disapprobation of or fascination with America, display outdated attitudes and modes of expression, hence little stimulus for innovative directions in poetry. Hagelstange, however, is noteworthy along with Bachmann for drawing attention to Black America. As with other poets of the decade, Kasper adopts a pose only partially representative of the times. Enamored of America's role in exploring new frontiers, he recycles a Whitmanesque visionary optimism that, in the end, falls victim to its own naïveté. As a model Marxist critique of America, Brecht's "Der anachronistische Zug oder Freiheit und Democracy" anticipates the literary side of cold war rhetoric. While most West German poets of the 1950s avoid political issues, Kaschnitz takes a clear stance with regard to America and the bomb. Her "Hiroshima" holds nothing back, and its forcefulness is enhanced by pitting the American way of life against a backdrop of atomic devastation (and implicitly the ruins of war-torn Europe) so to sarcastically evoke Goethe's line "Amerika, du hast es besser." Moreover, Kaschnitz sets a standard for the future as she foreshadows German political poetry of the 1960s. In spite of its apparent whimsy, perhaps the most honest and serious portrayal of America's postwar role is Arp's "Amerika," particularly with regard to the political complexities of postwar Europe. Finally, Jandl shows that German verse readily rejoins the world language of poetry by means of the visual-based principles of concrete poetry.

2: Prejudice, Problems, Fragments: Early Postwar Reception of American Poetry

THE RELATIVE ABSENCE of America as subject matter in early postwar German poetry does not obscure an otherwise strong interest in American literature. As Frey wrote in 1954: "Like the rest of Europe, postwar Germany has been extremely America conscious. And like most of Europe, she has shown an extraordinary receptivity toward American literature."[1] During the years 1945 to 1950 approximately seven hundred American books were published in German translation.[2] Of these texts, as Frey points out, nearly three hundred were works of fiction and about one hundred children's books; lyric poetry, on the other hand, was "not offered abundantly in German."[3] Although worthy of notation, these fig-

---

[1] John R. Frey, "America and Her Literature Reviewed by Postwar Germany," *The American-German Review* 20.5 (1954): 4; cf. Frey's article, "Postwar Germany: Enter American Literature," *The American-German Review* 21.1 (1954): 9–12, that begins: "In spite of their various prejudices toward the United States, since 1945, Europeans generally have taken an extraordinary interest in American literature. And to be sure, the role of American literature in postwar Germany constitutes a most interesting chapter in the annals of international literary relations."

[2] For a bibliographical documentation of the early postwar period see: Office of the United States High Commissioner for Germany, Education and Cultural Relations Division, *Verzeichnis amerikanischer Bücher in deutscher Übersetzung: Erschienen in Deutschland seit 1945* (Frankfurt am Main: Information Centers Branch, 1951); and Richard Mönnig, *Amerika und England im deutschen, österreichischen und schweizerischen Schrifttum der Jahre 1945–1949: Eine Bibliographie* (Stuttgart: Kohlhammer, 1951).

[3] "Postwar Germany," 9, 11. Frey notes that of the seven hundred American books in German translation, approximately forty were published in the "East Zone." The two above-cited articles in *The American-German Review* provide the pertinent background information for Frey's essay "Postwar German Reactions to American Literature," *Journal of English and Germanic Philology*

ures are not that significant, given the fact that poetry traditionally garners a tiny share of the publication market.

Immediately after the Second World War, American poetry did not enjoy the status of American prose and drama abroad. Whereas writers such as Steinbeck and Hemingway[4] served as models for a distinctively American prose style and Thornton Wilder's *Our Town* appeared as *Unsere kleine Stadt* on stages in West Germany and West Berlin,[5] contemporary American poets still suffered from European prejudice against literary developments in the United States. Attempting to counteract this bias, critic Hans Hennecke wrote a series of essays and monographs on American poets and poetry.[6] American poetry, he argues, features the interaction of two diametrically opposed forces, experiment and tradition, a distinction serving to explain its thematic and formal diversity. For Hennecke, verse in the U.S.A. is both young (as in the relative cultural age of the New World) and old (as reflected by its foundation of five centuries of English poetry). Likewise, he sees a definite polarity in the two standard bearers for American poetry at the midpoint of the twentieth century, Walt Whitman and Emily Dickinson.

54.2 (1955): 173–94, where he examines the interest of German writers in American literature "as a barometer of the mental climate among the creative minds of postwar Germany." All three articles concentrate on prose fiction with only passing mention of the influx of American poetry. See also W. B. Fleischmann, "Amerikanische Dichtkunst und deutsche, 1945–1965," in Horst Frenz and Hans Joachim Lang, eds., *Nordamerikanische Literatur im deutschen Sprachraum seit 1945: Beiträge zu ihrer Rezeption* (Munich: Winkler, 1973), 65–78, especially 67, where he writes that American poetry received scant mention in the German press during the first twenty years of the postwar period.

[4] See Frank Trommler, "Realismus in der Prosa," in *Tendenzen der deutschen Literatur seit 1945*, ed. Thomas Koebner (Stuttgart: Kröner, 1971), 216. See also the editor's preface to *Tausend Gramm: Sammlung neuer deutscher Geschichten*, ed. Wolfgang Weyrauch (Hamburg: Rowohlt, 1949).

[5] See Horst Frenz, "The Reception of Thornton Wilder's Plays in Germany," in *Modern Drama* 3.1 (1960): 123–37.

[6] See "Die nordamerikanische Lyrik der Gegenwart" (1946) in Hennecke, *Dichtung und Dasein: Gesammelte Essays* (Berlin: Henssel, 1950) 215–19, especially 216: "Vorurteile, die seit einiger Zeit dem Roman und der Novelle, und ganz neuerdings auch dem Drama Nordamerikas gegenüber, zu fallen beginnen, sind, was die Lyrik betrifft, bei uns immer noch völlig unerschüttert."

Whitman, according to Hennecke, remains a vital force in American poetry, indeed indispensable in terms of contemporary developments. In fact, as he goes on to say, without Whitman the poetry of Carl Sandburg, Edgar Lee Masters, Vachel Lindsay, and William Carlos Williams would be unthinkable. Dickinson, whom Hennecke labels an elfin sibyl comparable to Annette von Droste-Hülshoff, exercises a different brand of influence. Her poetry, he maintains, is inseparable from her life. Consequently, she is a model for such poets as Allen Tate, Yvor Winters, and Delmore Schwartz both in her reclusive lifestyle and in the fullness of her linguistically restrained inspiration. Thus, if Whitman epitomizes an unbridled poetic energy, Dickinson offers a balance with her disciplined style and choice of subject matter.

Recalling his original description of American verse, Hennecke deems Edwin Arlington Robinson and Robert Frost exemplary of that middle ground between experiment and tradition. The former rates as a master in his peculiar blend of pathos and satire, and the latter as one of the few remaining representatives of the Virgilian bucolic tradition. Other poets such as Marianne Moore and Archibald MacLeish feature a fusion of experiment and tradition, a trait most apparent in the work of T. S. Eliot.

At the beginning of the postwar era Eliot is, according to Hennecke, the most significant writer in the English language owing to his dual role as both poet and critic. His status as poet rests on both his early poetry, especially *The Waste Land* (1922), and later works such as *Ash-Wednesday* (1930) and *The Four Quartets* (1943) which, according to Hennecke, rank among the great spiritual poems of this century. Furthermore, Hennecke recognizes Eliot as the reference point for examining the work of his fellow countrymen. For example, Conrad Aiken echoes Eliot with a distinctive melancholic tone, and Eliot's spiritual poetry finds its sole complement in the meditative verse of Wallace Stevens, particularly in such poems as "Sunday Morning" and "Le Monocle de mon Oncle."[7] Hennecke concludes his 1946 view from abroad by al-

---

[7] See also Hennecke's 1956 essay "Einbildungskraft als Wert" in Hennecke, *Kritik: Gesammelte Essays zur modernen Literatur* (Gütersloh: Bertelsmann, 1958), 87–103. Not until 1961 did a book of Stevens's poems appear in translation: *Der Planet auf dem Tisch: Gedichte und Adagia*, ed. and trans. Kurt Heinrich Hansen (Hamburg: Claassen, 1961).

luding to the large number of women poets in America. In addition to
Marianne Moore he names Elinor Wylie, Louise Bogan, and Léonie
Adams as following the tradition begun in Puritan fashion by Anne
Bradstreet and then raised to artistic heights by Dickinson. In this regard
his overview is thorough and relatively complete. However, Hennecke
fails to mention one major figure of twentieth-century American poetry,
Ezra Pound, whose absence can be explained by his controversial politi-
cal activity during the Second World War.

Hennecke's knowledge of American poetry far exceeded the
norms of the day. Before contemporary American poets could find
a wider German audience, the American poetic tradition had to be
re-established. Hence, Germany's interest in American poetry following 1945 began with a Walt Whitman renaissance, an interest
that parallels the wave of Whitman reception after the First World
War when Germans learned democracy from The Good Gray
Poet.[8] Most significantly, attention to Whitman was strong in both

---

[8] Between 1946 and 1949 no fewer than six books of Whitman's poems appeared in translation. Three bore the title *Grashalme* and featured selections
from *Leaves of Grass* by various translators: new German versions offered by
Elisabeth Serelman-Küchler and Walter Küchler (Erlangen: Dipax, 1947) and
Georg Goyert (Berlin: Blanvalet, 1948), plus from the "East Zone" a re-issue
of Johannes Schlaf's turn-of-the-century translation (1907; Leipzig: Reclam,
1948). Also from the East came Whitman's *Hymnen für die Erde* (Leipzig:
Insel, 1947), translated and with an afterword by Franz Blei. Finally, Hans
Reisiger provided three collections of Whitman's verse, *Gesang von mir selbst*
(1946), *Salut au monde* (1946), and *Auf der Brooklyn Fähre* (1949). Selections from these volumes, all published in Berlin by Suhrkamp, are based on
Reisiger's earlier translations; cf. *Grashalme: Neue Auswahl* (Berlin: Fischer,
1919); and *Gesang von der offenen Landstraße* (Lauenburg/Elbe: Saal, 1922).
Reisiger eventually consolidated his translations and added an introduction to
complete the 501-page opus *Walt Whitmans Werk* (Hamburg: Rowohlt,
1956); an abridged version of this text appeared as *Grashalme* (Berlin: Aufbau, 1957) specifically for book trade in the GDR. In addition to poetry,
Suhrkamp also published Reisiger's monograph on Whitman (1946) as well
as translations of selected prose works, *Tagebücher 1862–1864, 1876–1882*
(1946) and *Demokratische Ausblicke* (1948), two essays written after the Civil
War in which Whitman examined the status of democracy in America. "Democracy" was published in the December 1867 issue of *Galaxy*, and "Person-
alism" in the same magazine in May 1868. In 1871 the two essays were
combined to form the volume *Democratic Vistas*. *Demokratische Ausblicke* is
especially significant for postwar German readers as here Whitman does not

Germanys. East German critics, who generally ignored American poetry, enthusiastically noted his revolutionary spirit and the energy he brought to the Puritan tradition of American poetry.[9] Whitman served as a model poet because of his political activity, identification with the working class, and manner of incorporating the language of the common folk into his verse. In fact, some of the highest praise came from East Germany.[10]

Edgar Allan Poe was also rediscovered by German readers after the Second World War but primarily for his short stories; only one volume of his verse appeared in translation.[11] Poe's *The Philosophy of Composition* (1846), an essay refuting romantic theories of artistic creation and serving as a foundation of modern poetics for its analytical explication of how "The Raven" was composed, likewise

---

extol the virtues of his native land; instead he focuses on the responsibilities of a democracy's citizenry: "I say we had best look our times and lands searchingly in the face like a physician diagnosing some deep disease." The postwar portrait of Whitman is completed by two biographies: H. S. Canby's *Walt Whitman, an American* (1943), translated by Georg Goyert as *Walt Whitman: Bildnis eines Amerikaners* (Berlin: Blanvalet, 1946), and Hans G. Cwojdrak, *Walt Whitman, Dichter und Demokrat: ein Lebensbild* (Hamburg: Christen, 1946). For a review of Whitman reception in Germany see Martin Christadler, "Autobiographen — Essayisten — Lyriker," in Frenz and Lang, 126–31.

[9] See Horst Frenz and John Hess, "Die nordamerikanische Literatur in der Deutschen Demokratischen Republik," in Frenz and Lang, 171–99, especially 173–74. As to how East German critics of the early cold war years viewed Whitman's humanistic, proletarian spirit as a corrective to McCarthyism, see Heinz Rusch, "Dichter der Zukunft," in *Börsenblatt für den Deutschen Buchhandel* 121.22 (1954): 487–88.

[10] See Karl-Heinz Wirzberger, "Einhundert Jahre 'Leaves of Grass,'" *Zeitschrift für Anglistik und Amerikanistik* 4.1 (1956): 77–87, who claims the entire body of modern poetry is unthinkable without Whitman's *Leaves of Grass*. This article is the text of a lecture held in Weimar in November 1955 commemorating the 100th anniversary of the publication of the first edition of *Leaves of Grass*. Wirzberger's address focuses on Whitman's humanistic spirit and anti-slavery politics, in particular his protests against the Mexican War of 1846 on the grounds that this war was waged in the interests of plantation owners in the southern states who sought to extend slavery into the newly conquered territories.

[11] Poe, *Der Rabe und andere Gedichte*, trans. Johannes von Guenther (Hannover: Hahn, 1947).

appeared in a German edition.[12] Henry Wadsworth Longfellow's *Evangeline*, a poem inspired by Goethe's *Hermann und Dorothea*, reappeared in German blank verse,[13] but did little to rekindle any lasting interest in the popular American poet. A limited edition of Emily Dickinson had been published near the end of the war; however, not until the latter half of the next decade did a more comprehensive collection of her poetry become available in German.[14] As can be seen, no poet of the previous century other than Whitman stirred much interest. Hence, *Das goldene Zeitalter* and *Die Harfe*, two anthologies with the subtitle *Nordamerikanische Lyrik des 19. Jahrhunderts*,[15] became all the more important as overviews of America's poetic heritage.

Eventually postwar publications began to feature contemporary American writers, most of whom were introduced by the anthology *Amerikanische Lyrik des XX. Jahrhunderts*.[16] A radically different approach was taken by Stephan Hermlin with *Auch ich bin Amerika*, the first German anthology devoted strictly to the work of black American poets.[17] The significance of this text, a collection featur-

---

[12] Poe, *Vom Ursprung des Dichterischen*, trans. Albrecht Fabri (Cologne: Staufen, 1947).

[13] Longfellow, *Evangeline*, trans. August Vezin (Heidelberg: Meister, 1947).

[14] Dickinson, *Ten Poems*, trans. Rosey E. Pool (Amsterdam: Balkema, 1944); *Der Engel in Grau: Aus dem Leben und Werk der amerikanischen Dichterin Emily Dickinson*, letters and poems selected and translated with an introduction by Maria Mathi (Mannheim: Kessler, 1956); and the bilingual edition of Emily Dickinson, *Gedichte*, trans. Lola Gruenthal (Berlin: Henssel, 1959). Paul Celan also contributed to Dickinson reception with his translation of "Acht Gedichte" in *Die Neue Rundschau* 72.1 (1961): 36–39.

[15] Kurt Erich Meurer, ed. and trans. (Heidelberg: Meister, 1948, 1949 respectively).

[16] The German title of selections from Harriet Monroe and Alice Corbin Henderson, eds., *The New Poetry* (New York: Macmillan, 1923), trans. Rolf Göhring (Waibstadt: Kemper, 1948). The gap in publishing dates — twenty-five years between the original compilation and the appearance of the German edition — reveals how lingering prejudices kept reception of American poetry far from up-to-date.

[17] Stephan Hermlin, ed. and trans., *Auch ich bin Amerika: Dichtungen amerikanischer Neger* (Berlin: Volk und Welt, 1948); rpt. in Hermlin, *Nachdichtungen*, 2nd ed. (Berlin: Aufbau, 1987) 227–73. The anthology title is from

ing the work of Countee Cullen, Langston Hughes, Claude McKay, Jean Toomer, and others, is that it was published in East Germany. Adding to its value as a cultural document, this anthology also presents samples of Negro folklore and gospel songs. In light of its inherent propaganda potential in the East-West battle of ideologies, Hermlin's anthology carried an extraliterary bonus for the GDR; in fact, more than a decade would pass before African-American poetry received due recognition in West Germany.

Signs of new directions in West German reception of American poetry in the early postwar period were limited to small, independent presses and their publication of relative unknowns, among them two Illinois poets, Edgar Lee Masters and Carl Sandburg.[18] The 1948 publication of Sandburg's *Guten Morgen, Amerika* illustrates how the re-education program affected postwar publishing practices, as American military officials found the preface to the original 1928 American edition too negative in its portrayal of Chicago and therefore had it deleted from the German edition.[19] Although Sandburg sustained little interest in the Federal Republic, in the GDR he was judged the most important American poet of the century, a distinction that saw him assuming Whitman's role as poet both of and for the common people.[20] A translation of Robert Frost's "Stopping by Woods on a Snowy Evening" by Joachim Maass[21] marked the New Englander's first postwar appearance in Germany; another small press subsequently issued his collected po-

---

the poem "I, Too" by Langston Hughes; see *Selected Poems of Langston Hughes* (1959; New York: Vintage, 1990), 275.

[18] See Edgar Lee Masters, *Die Toten von Spoon River*, trans. Hans Rudolf Rieder (Bad Wörishofen: Drei Säulen, 1947); and the bilingual edition of Carl Sandburg, *Guten Morgen, Amerika: Ausgewählte Gedichte*, trans. Alfred Czach (Berlin: Herbig, 1948).

[19] See Hansjörg Gehring, "Literatur im Dienst der Politik. Zum Re-education-Programm der amerikanischen Militärregierung in Deutschland," in *Literaturmagazin 7* (1977): 252–70, especially 264; see also Lothar Jordan, *Europäische und nordamerikanische Gegenwartslyrik im deutschen Sprachraum 1920–1970: Studien zu ihrer Vermittlung und Wirkung* (Tübingen: Niemeyer, 1994), 76–77.

[20] See the bilingual East German edition of Sandburg's *The People, Yes / Das Volk, jawohl*, trans. Helmut Heinrich (Berlin: Aufbau, 1964).

[21] See *Die Neue Rundschau* 57.3 (1946): 340–41.

ems.[22] Two American poets renowned for their social consciousness also made inroads in the early 1950s: Archibald MacLeish, who was presented to German readers by means of a book title commensurate with his reputation,[23] and Edna St. Vincent Millay, whose main proponent in German letters was the writer Rudolf Borchardt.[24] Not until the mid-1950s collections edited by Kurt Heinrich Hansen[25] and John O. McCormick[26] appeared did German anthologies provide an up-to-date grouping of American poets. Hansen's compilation features not only a host of established names, primarily poets born in the last quarter of the nineteenth century (Pound, William Carlos Williams, Wallace Stevens, Robert Frost, Conrad Aiken, E. E. Cummings, Archibald MacLeish, and Marianne Moore[27]), but also those of the next generation including Kenneth Patchen, Muriel Rukeyser, Kenneth Rexroth, and Delmore Schwartz. In fact, Hansen brings reception into the heart of the

[22] Frost, *Gesammelte Gedichte*, trans. Alexander von Bernus (Mannheim: Kessler, 1952).

[23] Archibald MacLeish, *Groß und tragisch ist unsere Geschichte: Gedichte*, trans. Kurt Heinrich Hansen (Düsseldorf: Schwann, 1950).

[24] Borchardt's posthumously published translations of three poems ("April," "Zu S.M.," and "Das fröhliche Mädchen") in *Die Neue Rundschau* 62.1 (1951): 80–81 introduced Millay and were followed by another translation ("Kindheit ist das Reich") plus excerpts from his lengthy monograph "Die Entdeckung Amerikas: Die Poesie von Edna St. Vincent Millay" in *Die Neue Rundschau* 62.4 (1951): 80–104. The complete essay, based on a handwritten manuscript from February 1935, is printed in Rudolf Borchardt, *Gesammelte Werke in Einzelbänden: Prosa III*, eds. Marie Luise Borchardt and Ernst Zinn (Stuttgart: Klett, 1960), 429–72. Borchardt, who was not prone to praise modern trends in literature, found in Edna St. Vincent Millay a poetic voice following in the tradition of Sappho and Catullus. His enthusiasm for her work is comparable in tone to the admiration he expressed as a young man for Hofmannsthal. See Ernst Zinn's "Nachwort," 529.

[25] Kurt Heinrich Hansen, ed. and trans., *Gedichte aus der neuen Welt: amerikanische Lyrik seit 1910* (Munich: Piper, 1956).

[26] John O. McCormick, ed., *Amerikanische Lyrik der letzten fünfzig Jahre*, trans. Herta Elizabeth Killy and Walter Killy (Göttingen: Vandenhoeck & Ruprecht, 1957).

[27] See also Marianne Moore, *Gedichte: Eine Auswahl*, trans. Eva Hesse and Werner Riemerschmid with an introduction by T. S. Eliot (Wiesbaden: Limes, 1954).

1950s with the inclusion of a young W. S. Merwin, who was chosen by W. H. Auden for the Yale Younger Poets award in 1952.

These contemporary poets were, however, of marginal significance when compared to the two major American voices of the postwar period, T. S. Eliot and Ezra Pound. Eliot first reached German readers in 1927, and following the Second World War his poetry appeared in a multitude of translations.[28] In addition, he was recognized as a critic, and his essays on literature, politics, culture, and society served to enhance an already strong reputation. With a status based on his dual role of poet and critic, Eliot fit the mold of a European man of letters. Moreover, owing to this dual status Eliot possessed an authority unrivaled in English-speaking countries, a position not challenged even by those who differed with his political and religious convictions.[29] In 1954 Eliot received the Hanseatic Goethe Prize, and his acceptance speech, "Goethe as the Sage,"[30] is at times a less than flattering assessment of the German master. Yet, in spite of a plethora of publications and prestigious awards, we should not assume Eliot exercised substan-

---

[28] T. S. Eliot, *Das wüste Land*, trans. Ernst Robert Curtius, *Die Neue Schweizer Rundschau* 20.4 (1927): 348–77. Book-length editions of Eliot's poetry in translation include: *Vier Quartette*, trans. Nora Wydenbruck (Vienna: Amandus, 1948); *Ausgewählte Gedichte: englisch und deutsch*, trans. Klaus Günther Just (Frankfurt am Main: Suhrkamp, 1951); and the bilingual *Old Possums Katzenbuch*, trans. Werner Peterich, Erich Kästner, et al. (Frankfurt am Main: Suhrkamp, 1952). The Curtius translation of *The Waste Land* was reprinted in *Die Neue Rundschau* 61.3 (1950): 327–45, and then later appeared in a bilingual edition (Wiesbaden: Insel, 1957), number 660 in the series *Insel-Bücherei*.

[29] See Ernst Robert Curtius, "T. S. Eliot," *Merkur* 3.1 (1949): 1–23, here 1.

[30] See Eliot, *On Poetry and Poets* (New York: Farrar, 1957), 240–64. Wolfgang Clemen's translation "Goethe der Weise" appeared in *Merkur* 9.8 (1955): 701–23. Eliot's speech recalls his essay on "Shelley and Keats" in which he discussed differences between the poet and the philosopher and wrote: "Of Goethe perhaps it is truer to say he dabbled in both philosophy and poetry and made no great success of either; his true rôle was that of the man of the world and sage — a La Rochefoucauld, a La Bruyère, a Vauvenargues." See Eliot, *The Use of Poetry and the Use of Criticism* (1933; Cambridge: Harvard UP, 1986), 78–94, here 90–91. In "Goethe as the Sage," 256, Eliot notes in retrospect, "It is an interesting sentence: interesting because it enunciates so many errors in so few words together with one truth: that Goethe was a sage."

tial influence on German poetry. To gain perspective on Eliot's standing in Germany of the 1950s, let us turn to Hugo Friedrich who
helped to establish the parameters for West German poetry and poetics
of the decade.[31] Friedrich's analysis of modern poetry is based on a
European model, specifically the French tradition and poets such as
Baudelaire, Mallarmé, and Rimbaud. Within this context, Eliot's major
poems are noteworthy for that fragmentary quality prevalent in modern poetry since Mallarmé. According to Friedrich, Eliot's earmark is
his ability to incorporate a multiplicity of tones and voices corresponding to the montage of disjointed elements in his verse.[32] Eliot's
status is that of a learned poet, and his work reflects the characteristic
mark of modernity as summarized in Friedrich's assertion that modern
poetry is rich in texts echoing strains of the mythic and archaic traditions. A notable feature of *The Waste Land*, for instance, is the use of
quotations from a wide variety of sources, a technique likewise adopted
by Ezra Pound. Although Pound is accorded only occasional mention
in *Die Struktur der modernen Lyrik*, Friedrich does acknowledge his
significance for the twentieth century especially with regard to his concept of the metaphorical image,[33] a reference made nonetheless without citing Pound's imagist principles. Friedrich's major areas of
concern lie elsewhere; thus further treatment of Pound's place in the
tradition is limited to viewing him as a contemporary model of the
poet as chameleon, that feature of modern poetry primarily associated
with Rimbaud, who initiated the abnormal separation of the poetic
subject from the empirical self.[34]

Friedrich's recognition of Pound comes at a time when he was
first gaining fame in Germany. Unlike Eliot, with whom he shared

---

[31] Hugo Friedrich, *Die Struktur der modernen Lyrik: Von Baudelaire bis zur Gegenwart* (Hamburg: Rowohlt, 1956). Although Friedrich champions an exclusive
poetic tradition, the fact that this book sold 70,000 copies between 1956 and
1960 belies its alleged exclusivity. See Hans Dieter Schäfer, "Zusammenhänge
der deutschen Gegenwartslyrik," *Lyrik — Von allen Seiten: Gedichte und Aufsätze
des ersten Lyrikertreffens in Münster*, eds. Lothar Jordan, Axel Marquardt, and
Winfried Woesler (Frankfurt am Main: Fischer, 1981), 32–78, here 35.

[32] Friedrich, 145; see also 121.

[33] Friedrich, 152.

[34] Friedrich, 52; see also 121 where Friedrich speaks of how Pound assumes dis-
guises as part of a role-playing means to make the poetic subject a collective subject.

the highest repute within Anglo-American literary circles, Pound was slow to gain German readership. The initial appearance of Pound in postwar Germany came in *fragmente*, Rainer M. Gerhardt's international revue of modern poetry. The first issue of this short-lived journal opened with Pound's essay on Guido Cavalcanti[35] and closed with the poet's ironical epitaph for himself, "E. P. Ode pour L'Election de Son Sepulchre," the opening section of *Hugh Selwyn Mauberley*. In addition, Gerhardt published translations of Pound's version of *The Testament of Confucius* as well as *How To Read*.[36] Had he not taken his own life in 1954 at the early age of twenty-seven, Gerhardt might have gone on to provide more of Pound's work in translation. Instead, Eva Hesse became the translator most responsible for introducing Ezra Pound to German readers.[37]

Reception of both Pound and Hesse's translations was generally positive.[38] We have already noted Hennecke's failure to mention Pound in his 1946 essay on American poetry, an omission not to be misconstrued as a snub. In a 1954 essay Hennecke presents a detailed study based on the thesis that Pound is to modern poetry as Picasso to modern painting; that is, both are worthy of distinction

---

[35] From Ezra Pound, *Make It New* (New Haven: Yale UP, 1935). "Mediaevalismus" is the title of Gerhardt's translation; see *fragmente* 1 (1951): 1–7.

[36] Ezra Pound, *Das Testament des Confucius: Die grosse Unterweisung, oder das Erwachsenenstudium*, trans. Rainer M. Gerhardt (Karlsruhe: fragmente, 1953); and Ezra Pound, *Wie lesen*, trans. Rainer M. Gerhardt (Karlsruhe: fragmente, 1953).

[37] Hesse's first publication of Pound in translation featured selected poetry and prose, *Dichtung und Prosa* (Zürich: Arche, 1953) with an introduction by T. S. Eliot and her own afterword drawing heavily from Hugh Kenner, *The Poetry of Ezra Pound* (Norfolk, CT: New Directions, 1951). This was followed by *Fisch und Schatten und andere Dichtungen* (Zürich: Arche, 1954) and selections from *The Pisan Cantos, LXXI to LXXXV* entitled *Die Pisaner Gesänge* (Zürich: Arche, 1956). Later Hesse published Pound's *ABC des Lesens* (Frankfurt am Main: Suhrkamp, 1963), in actuality a partial translation of his definitive critical work *ABC of Reading*, as section two, "Exhibits," is omitted.

[38] See Peter Demetz, "Ezra Pounds Pisaner Gesänge," *Merkur* 12.1 (1958): 97–100. Reception of Pound's literary criticism, however, was not as enthusiastic; see K. G. Just, "Zur amerikanischen Literaturkritik: Ezra Pound und R. P. Blackmur," *Merkur* 10.12 (1956): 1230–33.

as innovative leaders of new movements.[39] Holthusen, who in 1955 bemoaned the fact that Pound was little known in Germany, attempts to right this wrong by examining the longevity of Pound's reputation as the leading theorist and practitioner of a new literary style.[40] In a similar show of respect Hagelstange punctuates the account of his meeting with Ezra and Dorothy Pound at St. Elizabeth's Hospital with the assessment that Pound is possibly the most linguistically talented poet of this half century.[41]

Hennecke and Holthusen concur on Pound's major contributions to modern English and American poetry. For example, the principles of Imagism, a movement founded in 1912 by Pound, Richard Aldington, Hilda Doolittle, and F. S. Flint, are given requisite attention, because this school of poetry has no pronounced corollary in German verse of the twentieth century. Likewise, both reviewers discuss Pound's ties to Provence and the language of the troubadours, his fascination with Greek and Roman antiquity, as well as his translations from the Chinese and Japanese. Most significantly, however, Hennecke and Holthusen focus on Eliot's designation of Pound as the greatest student of Robert Browning. And finally, both agree in identifying a German contemporary comparable to Pound, namely Rudolf Borchardt who also translated Provençal poets.

Neither Hennecke nor Holthusen shy away from the controversial aspects of Pound's career. Holthusen considers the expatriate's broadcasts in support of Mussolini's fascist regime within the framework of ideas proposed in such texts as *ABC of Economics* (1933) and *What Is Money For?* (1939). Moreover, he sees Pound reneging on earlier critical work, in particular, the admonition for writers not to be philosophical. Hennecke views Pound's political activities in Italy as a case of the poet in a quixotic daze, especially in light of his earlier reputation as an unwavering proponent of common sense. Additionally, Hennecke attempts to refute charges of anti-Semitism by comparing

---

[39] Hans Hennecke, "Dichtung als inspirierte Mathematik," in Hennecke, *Kritik*, 79–86.

[40] Hans Egon Holthusen, "Der Dichter im eisernen Käfig" in *Merkur* 9.1 (1955): 77–94.

[41] Rudolf Hagelstange, "Ein exemplarischer Fall von Irrsinn: Ezra Pound und die Fallstricke der Politik," in Hagelstange, *How do you like America?*, 16–30, here 16.

Pound to Karl Kraus and underscoring his admiration for Heinrich Heine. In recognition of how Pound's literary status in America remained relatively intact in spite of his dubious politics, both Hennecke and Holthusen point out that *The Pisan Cantos* earned the prestigious Bollingen Prize in 1949 on the recommendation of such writers as Hemingway, MacLeish, and Graham Greene, all of whom can be counted among Pound's political opposites.

To conclude our discussion of American influences on German poetry of the early postwar period, let us turn to Gottfried Benn's lecture "Probleme der Lyrik."[42] Speaking at the University of Marburg on 21 August 1951, Benn voiced a theory of modern poetry based on the thesis that a poem does not come into being through inspiration, but is carefully fashioned according to principles of art. "Probleme der Lyrik" draws on a variety of sources, primarily Mallarmé and the concept of the absolute poem as well as Nietzsche and his theories on art and the artist. Benn charts the course of modern poetry by concentrating on that which distinguishes modern poets from those of bygone eras. Although his primary focus is European poets, American practitioners of the art, in particular Eliot and Pound, are not ignored. Likewise of interest to this study is a passage at the beginning of the speech where Benn reports on a great poetry movement then underway in the United States. He goes on to mention a questionnaire circulated among American poets with queries regarding language, form, rhyme, the length of a poem, and the matter of to whom the poem is addressed. In answer to the latter, Benn alludes to the American poet Richard Wilbur, who claimed that a poem is addressed to the Muse as a means of covering up the fact that poems are not addressed to anyone in particular. Benn finds reassurance in this statement, noting that also in America one recognizes the poem as a monologue.[43]

In spite of the Eurocentric thrust of Benn's Marburg address, the American undercurrents here are stronger than might first appear. In

---

[42] See Benn, *Sämtliche Werke*, vol. 6: 9–44. As to the significance of this lecture, see the preface to *Mein Gedicht ist mein Messer*, where editor Hans Bender names Benn's Marburg address the *ars poetica* for West German poetry of the 1950s, a contention echoed by Friedrich, 117, and reaffirmed by Otto Knörrich, *Die deutsche Lyrik seit 1945* (Stuttgart: Kröner, 1978), 21, who calls "Probleme der Lyrik" the German catechism of modern poetry.

[43] Benn, vol. 6: 16.

fact, Eliot's essay "From Poe to Valéry" and John Ciardi's anthology *Mid-Century American Poets* provide the conceptual point of departure for a number of Benn's remarks.[44] In 1950 Eliot's essay had appeared in German translation,[45] and Benn borrows quite freely from his remarks on the introspective nature of modern poets. Similarly, Benn's reference to Richard Wilbur is taken directly from the Ciardi text, specifically Wilbur's contribution to this volume and his responses to the aforementioned questionnaire.[46] In addition to Wilbur, Benn also mentions the American poet Randall Jarrell, quoting his statement on the role of rhyme in a poem.[47] However, the relative significance of this American component in "Probleme der Lyrik" should not be exaggerated. Benn is not looking to America for aesthetic inspiration or confirmation of his poetic ideals. The U.S.A. plays an ancillary role here; both the comments on the great poetry movement and the quotes from Wilbur and Jarrell are made in passing, much like an obligatory nod in the direction of the country assuming a prominent position on the world stage in the early 1950s.

All in all, the reception of American poetry and poetics in Germany through the 1950s was of marginal import. If any one country were to be singled out for establishing the prevailing mood, that would be France for the Baudelaire-Mallarmé-Rimbaud tradition. Schäfer, in his survey of international reception during this period, notes that of Anglo-American poets only Pound, Eliot, and Auden were acknowledged; the "realistic" American poem remained unrecognized.[48] Although he does not elaborate on the

---

[44] See Reinhold Grimm, "Die problematischen 'Probleme der Lyrik,'" in Heinz Otto Burger and Klaus von See, eds., *Festschrift Gottfried Weber* (Bad Homburg: Gehlen, 1967), 299–328; see also Edgar Lohner, "Gottfried Benn und T. S. Eliot," *Neue Deutsche Hefte* 3 (1956/57): 100–107.

[45] T. S. Eliot, "Von Poe zu Valéry," trans. Hans Heinrich Schaeder, *Merkur* 4.12 (1950): 1252–67.

[46] See Richard Wilbur, "The Genie in the Bottle," in *Mid-Century American Poets*, ed. John Ciardi (New York: Twayne, 1950), 1–7, especially 2–3.

[47] See Benn, vol. 6: 28, and Ciardi, 183.

[48] See Schäfer, "Zusammenhänge" in *Von allen Seiten*, 36. Auden (born in York, England in 1907 and later naturalized as a U.S. citizen in 1946) stands as a borderline figure to this study. As to the reception of his poetry after 1945: *The Age of Anxiety: A Baroque Eclogue* (1947) appeared as *Zeitalter der*

term realistic, we can assume Schäfer is alluding to the poetry of William Carlos Williams. Moreover, publications of Pound and Eliot in postwar Germany did little to promote any sense of a nascent American leverage in the realm of poetry, as both poets drew on sources, material, and legacies decidedly un-American.[49] Finally, that Eliot's poems of a spiritual quest and his socio-cultural writings did attract attention in West Germany reflects the fact that his position complemented, perhaps even served to corroborate, the conservative mood of the Adenauer restoration period.

Any chance for the successful introduction of a truly American style of contemporary poetry during this decade most likely faded with the death of Rainer M. Gerhardt in 1954. Thanks to the correspondence of Charles Olson and Robert Creeley[50] we can look back on the role of these two Americans in the birth of *fragmente*. Gerhardt had initially sought editorial guidance from Ezra Pound who, long known for supporting aspiring poets, suggested he contact Creeley. During the summer of 1950 Creeley writes to Olson about "a man from Germany" with an interest in their work for publication in a new journal.[51] At the time Olson and Creeley were not well established as poets in America; hence Gerhardt's invitation came as promising news. Creeley, having a working knowledge of German, served as go-between for Gerhardt and Olson as well as William Carlos Williams. Questions pertaining to Gerhardt's ability as translator as well as his editorial bias are documented in the Olson-Creeley correspondence. As Creeley explained, the title *fragmente* carries the suggestion of Germany having been cut off from the literary world and postwar life in Europe as "shivered" into fragments.[52] Moreover, Creeley assured

---

Angst: ein barockes Hirtengedicht, trans. Kurt Heinrich Hansen with an introduction by Gottfried Benn (Wiesbaden: Limes, 1952).

[49] As a corollary to this point, see Friedrich, 25, where Eliot, in deference to his adopted homeland and citizenship, is identified as "Der Engländer."

[50] *Charles Olson & Robert Creeley: The Complete Correspondence*, 9 vols. (Santa Barbara, CA: Black Sparrow, 1980–1990). Please note: vols. 1–8 were edited by George F. Butterick who, due to failing health, turned over editorship of vol. 9 to Richard Blevins. Subsequent references to the letters of Olson and Creeley will be identified by a Roman numeral designating volume, followed by page number.

[51] *Olson & Creeley* II, 118.

[52] *Olson & Creeley* III, 153.

Olson about Gerhardt's proficiency as translator, even though he rec-
ommended some system of maintaining control, especially as to sound
values and movement.[53] As intermediary Creeley felt it necessary to
fine-tune certain concerns, explaining to Olson that Gerhardt held a
different understanding of content, and that when he spoke of form,
the meaning is more akin to what Americans perceive as method.[54]

During the course of preparing the first issue of *fragmente*,
Gerhardt composed his "Brief an Creeley und Olson,"[55] a poem in
the form of a letter. Olson responded to Gerhardt's letter-poem
with one of his own entitled "To Gerhardt, There, Among
Europe's Things of Which He Has Written Us in His »Brief an
Creeley und Olson«."[56] Olson's poem can be understood as a
negative reaction against the influence of Eliot on Gerhardt;[57] furthermore, one can read Olson's poem as a warning to Gerhardt that
culture is not a commodity to be exchanged, and that personal experience carries greater meaning for poetry than book knowledge.[58]
In brief, Olson encouraged a more personal and less abstract style

[53] See *Olson & Creeley* III, 154. As to Gerhardt's translation skills, see also IV,
27 where Creeley praises him as a translator who "has the ear"; and IV, 39–
40, where he expresses amazement at Gerhardt's indefatigability in preparing
the first issue of *fragmente*.

[54] See *Olson & Creeley* IV, 26–27. See also IV, 109 where Creeley highlights
some of the problems in bringing Olson's poetics to a German audience, noting that Gerhardt's method of analysis tends to divide the integral components
form and content and treat them as if they had no such relation to each other.

[55] See *Olson & Creeley* IV, 125–28 where Creeley calls it a "pretty damn good"
poem and provides a translation of the opening section in order to give Olson an
idea of its contents. Olson's reply to Creeley (IV, 139–35) expresses an interest in
seeing the poem in its entirety so to better gauge Gerhardt's "compositional
power." A translation of the complete poem by Werner Heider and Joanna Ja-
lowetz appeared in *Origin* 4 (Winter 1951–1952); the full text of the original is included in Rainer M. Gerhardt, *Umkreisung* (Karlsruhe: fragmente, 1952), 25–30.

[56] See *The Collected Poems of Charles Olson*, ed. George F. Butterick (Berkeley:
U of California P, 1987), 212–22.

[57] See Fleischmann, 72.

[58] See the translator's afterword to Charles Olson, *Gedichte*, trans. Klaus Reichert (Frankfurt am Main: Suhrkamp, 1965), 129.

of verse from Gerhardt.[59] Creeley reported that Gerhardt seemed "crushed" by Olson's reaction; nevertheless, Gerhardt's later poems suggest that he took the criticism as sound advice.[60]

Bracketed by the prose and poetry of Pound, the contents of the inaugural issue of *fragmente* presented German translations of Basil Bunting, Olson ("The Praises"), Williams ("The RR Bums"), Saint-John Perse, as well as the poetry of primitive peoples from throughout the world. Issue two of *fragmente* continued with a strong American flavor featuring German translations of Pound's "Pisan Canto LXXXIV," Olson's "Projective Verse," a prose poem by Creeley, and Williams's poem "Choral: The Pink Church." Although Gerhardt had plans for fifteen issues of *fragmente*, including a special American issue,[61] these hopes never materialized. The journal was under constant financial strain and, even when money was available, suffered from the paper shortages afflicting postwar Germany well into the 1950s. Gerhardt's suicide in 1954 thus eliminated a meaningful international revue of literature, cut short the promising career of a poet and translator, and ended his valuable role as a mediator of poetry between Germany and the United States. "The Death of Europe,"[62] Olson's funeral poem for Gerhardt, reads then as the final word on the dreams shared by aspiring poets in the early postwar era. Yet aside from mourning a premature loss, this poem celebrates the common ground, albeit fragmentary, on which their intercontinental literary exchange was based.

Gerhardt's accomplishments are considerable. First of all he launched the reception of an American style of poetry not tied to Europe. He recognized a special strain in Pound's poetics leading to a new generation of American poets.[63] The contents of the two

---

[59] See *Olson & Creeley* V, 142, where Creeley comments on Germans in general and Gerhardt in particular, noting that "once they, he, get, gets, on the 'abstract,' it's hard to pull them back."

[60] See *Olson & Creeley* V, 141; see also Gerhardt's far less abstract poem "fragmente" in *fragmente* 2 (1952): 50.

[61] See *Olson & Creeley* IX, 17 and VIII, 139 where Olson encourages Creeley "to hammer" two lines into the proposed special American issue: (1) the William Carlos Williams admonition of "no ideas but in things" in order to offset the German affinity for the abstract; and (2) the concept that form is never more than an extension of content.

[62] See *Collected Poems of Olson*, 308–16.

issues of *fragmente* opened a new epoch for German poetry and show how far ahead in time Gerhardt stood in relation to his literary compatriots. His translations of Creeley, Olson, and Williams[64] are noteworthy for bringing German readers a blend of American verse devoid of the expatriate élan of Eliot. Like a miner, Gerhardt struck a claim in an unexplored field, but his untimely death caused the rich deposits to remain largely ignored. In fact, the groundbreaking efforts of *fragmente* were not renewed until nearly a decade later. This loss in time was crucial, for when the poetry of Williams, Olson, and Creeley finally gained widespread recognition in Germany, much of its relevance was obscured by the latest rage — the American poets of the Beat Generation.

[63] See Fleischmann, 70.

[64] See *Olson & Creeley* VI, 213, where Olson calls Gerhardt's translation of his poem "terrific." A similar appreciation of Gerhardt's translations of William Carlos Williams can be found in Olson's "The Death of Europe" (309) where he proclaims his thrill at seeing "Bill's RR BUMS in futura!" As a sign of the trust Williams had in Gerhardt he sent him a manuscript copy of Book 4 of *Paterson* before it had appeared in print; see *Olson & Creeley* IV, 57

3: The 1960s: Jazz Beats
Rhythms of Change

IF PREJUDICES AGAINST American poetry had existed in the early postwar years, then signs of change came in 1959 with the publication of Allen Ginsberg's *Howl* in German translation.[1] However, since the 1950s had done little to promote contemporary American poets in Germany, Ginsberg appeared virtually out of nowhere. To fully appreciate this radical new voice as well as Ginsberg's place in the American tradition, German readers required a more comprehensive picture of prevailing standards in American poetry, one extending beyond the realm of Eliot and Pound. The subsequent publication of three anthologies in the early 1960s fulfilled this need and paved the way for the reception of a new breed of American poet in the German-speaking world. The first to be considered here is Hans Magnus Enzensberger's *Museum der modernen Poesie* (1960). Conceived as an international gallery housing the work of ninety-six poets, this text contains poems mostly written during the years 1910 to 1945. These thirty-five years, as the editor claims, are notable for the development of a world language of modern poetry.[2] Reflecting the editor's interest in America's literary heritage,[3] the United States is proportionately well represented in this who's who of twentieth-century verse. In addition to selections by Pound and Eliot, the reader will find the poems of E. E. Cummings, Langston Hughes, Robinson Jeffers, Archibald MacLeish, Marianne Moore, Kenneth Patchen, Wallace Stevens, and William Carlos Williams — all in the original along with German

[1] Allen Ginsberg, *Das Geheul und andere Gedichte*, trans. Wolfgang Fleischmann and Rudolf Wittkopf (Wiesbaden: Limes, 1959).

[2] See Hans Magnus Enzensberger, ed., preface, *Museum der modernen Poesie* (Frankfurt am Main: Suhrkamp, 1960), 13.

[3] Enzensberger's travels in America in 1957, "Dunkle Erbschaft, tiefer Bayou," are recounted in Alfred Gong, ed., *Interview mit Amerika* (Munich: Nymphenburger, 1962), 256–87.

translations by Enzensberger, Erich Fried, Eva Hesse, Kurt Heinrich Hansen, and Paul Celan. Of these ten American poets, a representative if not complete list,[4] several are worthy of consideration here.

Cummings, world-renowned for his clever play with syntax and typography, gains special stature for Enzensberger as literary *enfant terrible* of the United States.[5] Politically an anarchist, he refused to align himself with any party or political persuasion; thus for Enzensberger his poetry retains an air of purity. Langston Hughes, with his "The Negro Speaks of Rivers," brings not merely a minority voice but the very constituents of this non-elitist world language of modern poetry the editor is promoting. The appearance of Hughes in Enzensberger's *Museum* is by no means token as this African American's writings generated more than just passing interest among German readers of the 1960s. A collection of his poems appeared in the same year as this anthology, followed later by a translation of *The First Book of Jazz*, in essence a handbook for the uninitiated, thus serving as a companion piece to his distinctive brand of poetry written in the spirit of an American musical art form.[6]

As shown by the inclusion of Hughes and Cummings, Enzensberger's editorial choices exhibit a tendency to celebrate both the underdog and the rebel voice. Other such examples are Kenneth Patchen, a role model for younger poets due to his nonconformist life style, and Archibald MacLeish[7] who, owing perhaps more to the

---

[4] Most notably absent are Robert Frost, Carl Sandburg, Allen Tate, Conrad Aiken, and Hart Crane; cf. Hans Egon Holthusen's review "Anmerkungen zu einem 'Museum der Modern Poesie'" in *Merkur* 15.11 (1961): 1073–84, especially 1077. Hart Crane's *White Buildings*, however, did appear in German as *Weisse Bauten: Gedichte*, trans. Joachim Uhlmann (Berlin: Henssel, 1960).

[5] See also the bilingual edition of Cummings, *Gedichte*, trans. Eva Hesse (Ebenhausen bei München [Munich]: Langewiesche-Brandt, 1958).

[6] See Langston Hughes, *Gedichte*, trans. Eva Hesse and Paridam von dem Knesebeck (Ebenhausen bei München [Munich]: Langewiesche-Brandt, 1960); and Hughes, *Das Buch vom Jazz*, trans. Paridam von dem Knesebeck (Munich: Domino, 1965).

[7] Although MacLeish failed to generate lasting interest in Germany, his lectures published as *Poetry and Experience* (1961) did reach German readers as *Elemente der Lyrik*, trans. Bazon Brock and Reinhold Grimm, ed. Reinhold Grimm (Göttingen: Sachse & Pohl, 1963).

public offices he held than to the poetry he wrote, represents the poet as political activist. Enzensberger, on the other hand, does not shy away from American writers of decidedly different backgrounds, including both the poet-insurance company executive Wallace Stevens and Robinson Jeffers, the descendant of a family of rich bankers and industrialists. Finally, there is William Carlos Williams, the one writer who most clearly embodies the antipode of the Pound-Eliot tradition in twentieth-century American letters with his glimpses of everyday life rendered in a distinctive American idiom. *Museum der modernen Poesie* is, in the end, a celebration of one hundred years of modern verse. Its 352 poems in sixteen languages document the contributions of a generation of poets born in the last quarter of the nineteenth century. Moreover, Enzensberger recognizes poets of the Americas on a par with European standard bearers; thus, with respect to foreign influence on contemporary German poets, the U.S.A. is beginning to assume a leading role at the start of a new decade. If there is but one criticism to be directed at the anthology, it is that women are poorly represented. Marianne Moore is one of only five women in the entire collection.

William Carlos Williams is worthy of a more detailed examination at this point since Enzensberger would expand this introductory sample in the *Museum* by bringing out a bilingual text of his poems.[8] In his lengthy afterword on Williams, Enzensberger begins by asking if there is a distinctively American style of poetry unique to North America and not Great Britain. He responds in the affirmative and names Williams the founding father of a poetry liberated from the European legacy and spreading across the entire continent from New York to San Francisco. The essay goes on to document the career of a man termed a rarity in the annals of literature by reason of Williams's lifelong refusal to play the role of a literary pontifex. Enzensberger's style is anecdotal as he draws on numerous personal incidents in order to highlight the poet's distinguishing traits.[9] Of primary interest is how Williams pursued

---

[8] Williams, *Gedichte*, ed. and trans. Hans Magnus Enzensberger (Frankfurt am Main: Suhrkamp, 1962), from *The Collected Earlier Poems* and *The Collected Later Poems*.

[9] Enzensberger's main source is *The Autobiography of William Carlos Williams* (New York: Random House, 1951).

both a writing career and a medical practice in his birthplace, Rutherford, New Jersey — a hometown allegiance unique in an age when many American writers sought inspiration as expatriates in Paris and London or in the bohemian quarters of New York City. Noting how Williams's early writing failed to attract the attention of his more cosmopolitan contemporaries, Enzensberger addresses Williams's standing amongst his better-known peers, especially Eliot and Pound, the latter a friend since Williams's days as a medical student at the University of Pennsylvania, as well as Gertrude Stein. In still another reference to a contemporary poet, Enzensberger alludes to Wallace Stevens and the notion of the antipoetic in Williams's work, a quality understood as the power to make poetry out of rubble and ashes. From this point of departure, Enzensberger embarks on a detailed examination of Williams's verse, focusing primarily on the poet's visual sharpness and his unerring ear for the spoken language of everyday life.

There remain two matters for discussion, both marginal in nature, relating to Enzensberger's contributions to the reception of American poetry in Germany of the early 1960s. The first involves Allen Ginsberg, the opening lines of whose poem "Howl" Enzensberger quotes near the conclusion of his essay on Williams. The mention of Ginsberg in the afterword is no doubt legitimate; Williams did, as Enzensberger indicates, write the introduction to *Howl* with which Ginsberg burst upon the American literary scene in 1956. By 1962, however, Ginsberg and his Beat cohorts held such sway over the reception of American poetry in Germany that the impact of Williams's poetry was decidedly lessened. If the purpose of the afterword is to promote the poet under consideration, then Enzensberger's mention of this link between the two poets was almost obligatory, perhaps as important for Williams in Germany as it originally had been for Ginsberg in America.

The second matter deals with Enzensberger's reference to a review of Williams's long poem *Paterson* written, as he notes, by the "Kritiker" Robert Lowell. Although Lowell did write critical reviews and occasional essays, he is first and foremost known as a poet. This oversight is minor and by no means crucial as concerns the content of the afterword; it does, however, convey a skewed message regarding American poetry of the early 1960s. Enzensberger's essay on Williams is most informative, for the average German reader an ideal introduction to a pivotal figure in twentieth-century American letters. But the lack of recognition for a poet such as Robert Lowell — coupled with a ringing endorsement of Ginsberg — suggests a tunnel vision taking in only the literary headline makers.

To better understand how Williams was overshadowed by a younger generation of poets, let us consider two additional anthologies focusing exclusively on America.[10] *Junge amerikanische Lyrik* is the result of a project begun in 1958, the same year Höllerer published a contribution by Gregory Corso to an international symposium addressing the topic of the relationship between the writer and society.[11] Corso's essay is geared to a foreign audience and presents the Beat movement as an alternative to mainstream, academically oriented American literature of the 1950s. What Corso initiated, Höllerer continued with his own essay on contemporary American literature.[12] Before the publication of *Junge amerikanische Lyrik* Corso visited Berlin in the summer of 1960 for a reading promoting its upcoming release. During his Berlin stay Corso also provided input on final editorial decisions regarding the anthology and added a postscript to the introduction he had written two years earlier.

Whereas Corso's *Akzente* essay maintains, for the most part, an air of conventionality, his introduction to *Junge amerikanische Lyrik* adopts a more roguish tone. Although he shows no lack of enthusiasm in promoting the Beat movement, Corso is self-deprecating in his role as editor and middleman for his fellow American poets and their new-found German audience. As a result there develops not just a complementary function but also a distinct polarity in style between the two co-editors. If, for instance, Corso's introduction questions its own seriousness as well as the very contents of the anthology, then it is Höllerer's task in the afterword to lo-

---

[10] Gregory Corso and Walter Höllerer, eds., *Junge amerikanische Lyrik* (Munich: Hanser, 1961); and Karl O. Paetel, ed., *Beat: Eine Anthologie* (Reinbek bei Hamburg: Rowohlt, 1962).

[11] Gregory Corso, "Dichter und Gesellschaft in Amerika," trans. Erika Gilbert, *Akzente* 5.2 (1958): 101–12.

[12] Höllerer, "Junge amerikanische Literatur," *Akzente* 6.1 (1959): 29–43, an essay opening a new series entitled "Akzente stellen vor" introducing foreign writers to German readers. Höllerer's afterword to *Junge amerikanische Lyrik* is an abridged version of this essay.

cate the Beat poets in the literary tradition. He does so by drawing lines to forerunners such as E. E. Cummings, Gertrude Stein, and European Dadaists.

Likewise Paetel's *Beat: Eine Anthologie* seeks to highlight the features of what was commonly known as the Beat Generation. His informative preface probes beyond the image of vagabond rebels in order to elucidate the essential trademarks of this movement. He discusses the term Beat, identifying its biblical origins in the word *beatific* as well as its ties to jazz music. Even though he does not deny the role of alcohol, drugs, and sexual promiscuity in this youth-oriented culture, Paetel recognizes the undeniable religious undertones of Beat poetry and, in specific cases, a fascination with Zen Buddhism.

Taken together, *Junge amerikanische Lyrik* and *Beat: Eine Anthologie* form a complementary pair. The most important poets of a new generation — names such as Charles Olson, Robert Creeley, John Ashbery, Frank O'Hara, Kenneth Koch, Lawrence Ferlinghetti, LeRoi Jones, Gary Snyder, plus Ginsberg and Corso — appear in both books with only a minimal overlapping of material. Literary ties between the United States and Germany are also celebrated, most notably in the poem that opens the Corso/Höllerer anthology, Olson's eulogy for Rainer M. Gerhardt, "The Death of Europe." *Beat: Eine Anthologie* has a broader scope than its counterpart. In addition to an ample selection of poetry, one finds prose fiction by Jack Kerouac, William S. Burroughs, Neal Cassady, and others, plus essays by Norman Mailer, Henry Miller, and Ginsberg. Besides its varied contents and Paetel's conscientious preface, this text is perhaps most valuable for its thorough documentation. In an appendix filled with the most pertinent details, the editor provides not just the usual biographical notes and bibliographical sources. Paetel goes beyond this with a five-page "BEAT Diktionär" to explain the unique vocabulary of these literary hipsters. The bibliography thoroughly covers the subject matter with twenty-seven pages enumerating authors, original texts, anthologies, translations, and secondary literature (both in English and German) on the Beat Generation. Finally, the editor provides a directory of American literary journals regularly or even occasionally featuring Beat writers. As a result, *Beat: Eine Anthologie* served as an indispensable tool for the German reader wishing to investigate these new directions in American writing.[13]

Of the many Beat Generation poets relatively few published individual volumes of poetry in Germany. The first to do so, as we have seen, was Ginsberg, whose bilingual edition of *Howl* reached a German audience three years after its original publication in America.[14] In addition to Ginsberg, Lawrence Ferlinghetti and Gregory Corso[15] also found readers in Germany. However, other poets who appeared in *Junge amerikanische Lyrik* and *Beat: Eine Anthologie*, especially the non-Beat writers, were slower to publish book-length collections in German translation. Not until 1965 did Charles Olson[16] achieve a solo breakthrough, with Robert Creeley[17] following in 1967. American poets of the New York school, most notably Frank O'Hara, would not attract increased attention in Germany until even later in the decade.

Throughout the 1950s and 1960s anthologies played a critical role in shaping developments in German poetry. The texts discussed earlier in this chapter brought greater recognition to American poets. Enzensberger's efforts in promoting the dean of

---

[13] In a personal interview on 14 June 1988 Jürgen Theobaldy cited Paetel's anthology as the single most important American influence on his poetry. He also acknowledged the influence of Gregory Corso, especially his book of poems *Gasoline* (San Francisco: City Lights, 1958); Theobaldy himself edited a small magazine in the early 1970s with the title *Benzin*, the German word for gasoline. As to Beat influences on German poetry, see also Hans-Jürgen Heise, "Beat, Pop, Underground: Einflüsse aus den USA" in Heise, *Einen Galgen für den Dichter: Stichworte zur Lyrik* (Weingarten: Drumlin, 1986), 115–41.

[14] As a sign of his popularity in Germany, *Das Geheul und andere Gedichte* enjoyed five reprints between 1959 and 1970. Following *Howl* was a second bilingual collection of Ginsberg's poetry, *Kaddisch: Gedichte*, trans. Anselm Hollo (Wiesbaden: Limes, 1962).

[15] Ferlinghetti, *Ein Coney Island des inneren Karussells*, trans. Erika Güttermann (Wiesbaden: Limes, 1962); Corso, *In der flüchtigen Hand der Zeit*, trans. Anselm Hollo (Wiesbaden: Limes, 1963).

[16] See Olson, *Gedichte*, trans. and afterword by Klaus Reichert (Frankfurt am Main: Suhrkamp, 1965); and Olson, *West*, trans. Klaus Reichert (Berlin: LCB, 1969).

[17] Creeley, *Gedichte: amerikanisch und deutsch*, trans. and afterword by Klaus Reichert (Frankfurt am Main: Suhrkamp, 1967).

contemporary American poetry led to signs of the influence of William Carlos Williams on German poets. One example is Harald Hartung, whose poem "Zechenkolonie"[18] employs a distinctively Williamsesque antipoetic style:

> Im engen Hofe
> stanken Hühnerställe.
> Im Garten wuchs
> Spinat, Tomaten, Dill.
> Im Sommerglast
> kam mit der Hitzewelle
> das Mittagspausenpfeifen
> dünn und schrill.
>
> Im Krüppelwald
> in Laub, Abfall und Asche
> spielten die Kinder
> Räuber und Schandit.
> Ein schwarzer Mann
> verrußt, mit Kaffeeflasche
> nahm mich
> zum Reibekuchenessen mit.

The distinguishing features of this poem are decidedly non-lyrical, especially in the associative powers of the verb *stanken*, the adverb *schrill*, and the predicate adjective *verrußt*. Much in the Williams mode, both the subject matter and places named in this poem (chicken coops, garden, dwarf-timber forest) are simple and non-majestic, just as is the manner of depicting children at play in deadwood and ashes. Moreover, the language is free from affectation and ornament. Hartung's guiding principle is one of economy, a trait underscored by the poet's resistance to commentary, as evident in the passing allusion to the humane gesture on the part of the soot-blackened man with which the poem concludes. Hartung refrains from attempting to communicate a message beyond that which is portrayed, as the overall scene must speak for itself.

---

[18] In Peter Hamm, ed., *Aussichten: Junge Lyriker des deutschen Sprachraums* (Munich: Biederstein, 1966), 59; rpt. in Harald Hartung, *Traum im Deutschen Museum: Gedichte 1965–1985* (Munich: Piper, 1986), 10.

The poetry of Hans Magnus Enzensberger likewise exhibits certain affinities with Williams, for instance, in the use of language in the title poem of his second book of verse, *landessprache*.[19] Yet, one could also make a case for comparing him to Ginsberg in that both share a radical approach of using poetry to criticize the government and society of their respective countries. Enzensberger, however, is far more programmatic in his political stance than the anarchic Ginsberg; in fact, a more fitting comparison would be of his early work to that of Great Britain's "Angry Young Men."[20] Moreover, and especially as pertains to this study, it is important to note that Enzensberger does not restrict his poetic attacks to Germany. In "manhattan island"[21] he lodges a protest against the American way of life by directing attention to the dubious practices carried out in New York's financial district. Here deception and artificiality dominate, as one encounters flowers made of newspaper and a populace held in check by falsehoods. The effect on the citizenry is, Enzensberger suggests, one of acrid discomfiture, for each of the poem's three stanzas closes with a substantive preceded by the adjective *bitter*.

A second Enzensberger poem, "middle class blues,"[22] shows a less definitive link to United States. Here the poet takes his title from an American form of music, but there is nothing in the poem itself to imply that the American middle class is the target. (Assuming the text addresses the middle class of the poet's homeland

---

[19] Enzensberger, *landessprache: Gedichte* (Frankfurt am Main: Suhrkamp, 1960), 5–12; see also "Gedicht für die Gedichte nicht lesen," *landessprache*, 31–32.

[20] See Patrick Bridgwater, "Hans Magnus Enzensberger," *Essays on Contemporary German Literature*, vol. 4 of *German Men of Letters*, ed. Brian Keith-Smith (London: Wolff, 1966), 239–58, here 241; also 250 where the author cites two other poems from *landessprache*, "Schaum" (33–34) and "Gewimmer und Firmament" (83–95) as failed imitations of Ginsberg's "Howl"; and 253 on Enzensberger's indebtedness to Williams for his "precise colloquialism and concentration on particulars." See also W. S. Sewell, "Hans Magnus Enzensberger and William Carlos Williams: Economy, Detail and Suspicion of Doctrine," *German Life and Letters* 32.2 (1979): 153–65; Krolow, *Aspekte zeitgenössischer Lyrik*, 114; and Theobaldy, "Begrenzte Weiten," 408.

[21] Enzensberger, *landessprache*, 52–53.

[22] Enzensberger, *blindenschrift: Gedichte* (Frankfurt Main: Suhrkamp, 1964), 32–33.

and reads as a parody of the West German economic miracle, we can read the title as an insinuation of American values permeating West German society.) Furthermore, the title must be regarded as ironic, indeed oxymoronic, since the blues in the original form have no association whatsoever with the middle class; within this context, Enzensberger's poem bears a connection to the Leadbelly song "Bourgeois Blues." In the true sense of the word, the blues imply a lamentation. Enzensberger, however, replaces melancholy with resignation. Likewise there is an absence of any underlying social protest, another key feature of the blues. In the end, the middle class as presented here co-opts the black man's lament, diminishing its power and denying grounds for grievance by turning the impetus to document one's plight into the acquiescent conclusion "wir können nicht klagen."

Other poets take a less political stance toward America. Dieter Leisegang, for instance, celebrates American agriculture in "Selbstportrait mit Zigarette,"[23] where the import commodity of note is tobacco:

> Im Grase am Fluß
> Unter der Eisenbahnbrücke
> Sitz' ich
>
> Inhalierend Virginias
> Riesige Felder

The first two words, "Im Grase," borrow the title of a poem by Annette von Droste-Hülshoff,[24] thus evoking a nineteenth-century mood of romantic reverie in an aristocratic setting. Leisegang indeed strikes a romantic pose, but the cigarette does not trigger contemplation, and the epigrammatic style denies any chance for reflection, personal or otherwise. Furthermore, the content is far from aristocratic, even if an American cigarette could be considered a luxury item. In short, this self-portrait depicts not a life of leisure but a brief moment of pleasure.

---

[23] First published in Dieter Leisegang, *Überschreitungen* (Darmstadt: Bläschke, 1965); rpt. in Leisegang, *Lauter letzte Worte*, ed. Karl Corino (Frankfurt am Main: Suhrkamp, 1980), 29.

[24] See Annette von Droste-Hülshoff, *Sämtliche Werke in zwei Bänden*, ed. Günther Weydt and Winfried Woesler, 3rd ed. (1973; Munich: Winkler, 1989), vol. 1, 436–37.

Besides celebrating American tobacco, Leisegang rejoices in American literary influences, in particular the imagistic tenets of Pound, H. D., and Amy Lowell. The designation self-portrait is but an ironic tag as the text focuses not on the self, but on the environs surrounding the human subject. Consistent with a painting, the poem has the static quality of a still-life, yet the mode of composition is dynamic as the portrait grows into an ever-widening panorama — a technique suggesting big-screen cinematic cigarette commercials. Moreover, the stanza break is a transatlantic leap facilitated by the present participle *inhalierend,* a polysyllabic loan word with a prolonged sound quality complementing the very act it depicts. Finally, the allusion to Virginia's vast tobacco fields employs reverse order synecdoche, with this expansive image having been reduced in minimalist fashion to the single cigarette of the title.

Portrayals of the American Beat Generation also surface in German poetry of the 1960s. For example, Yaak Karsunke's "Frag mich nach Geno"[25] tells the story of a new breed of American antihero:

> Geno im hemd
> im pyjama und barfuß
> in stiefeln mit perlen bestickt
> in zerfallenden jeans
> nackt in der sonne
> an deck eines seelenverkäufers
> in der karibischen see
> in tanger in brooklyn in rom
> lieber im kittchen als im
> ehrenkleid seiner nation

In accordance with the hint of flight as a draft dodger, Geno's grand tour suggests nothing of an organized, paid-in-advance tourist excursion:

> Geno allein ohne alles
> ohne zahnpasta travellerschecks
> ohne farbfilm und schmalfilm
> ohne abgangszeugnis auch ohne

---

[25] See Hamm, ed., *Aussichten,* 94–96.

> nur die mittlere reife
> Geno ohne manieren
> ohne schlips ohne kragen
> ohne einen gedanken
> ohne geld ohne schnaps
> nie sehr lange

Aside from an ability to do without, this wayward Beatnik displays a brand of counterculture cultivation distinguished by a list of select possessions:

> Geno mit einem seesack
> voller pläne und platten
> Vivaldi und orgelsonaten
> entwürfe für ein ganz spezielles
> schlachthaus für heilige kühe
> dicht neben dem ganges
> Geno mit diesem sack
> voller socken marihuana
> schuhen gedichten adressen
> telefonnummern und noten

Perhaps the most revealing aspect of Karsunke's portrait of Geno, however, is that characteristic of the Beat Generation which understands status in terms of an outsider's underdog role:

> Geno mit seiner guitarre
> und seinem banjo
> einem kopf voller schwarzer musik
> einem mund voller ganz schwarzer zähne
> aber leider kein neger
> verdammt nochmal Yaak warum bin ich
> nicht wenigstens jude
> oder marxist
> armer ami armer ami
> so weiß so weiß so unrasiert

This stanza is reminiscent of a passage from Kerouac's *On the Road* where the narrator confesses his disillusionment with the "white world" and identification with oppressed minorities, distinctions serving to explain why Beat adherents so willingly cast themselves as outcasts to mainstream society.[26] Nonetheless, "Frag mich nach Geno" is not an all-out celebration of nonconformity, in that the final stanza tears away Geno's fun-loving exterior pose to reveal a contradiction-laden personality with an inherent death wish.

As we have seen, the 1960s are marked by increased recognition for American culture in Germany, and one of the leading cultural imports from the U.S.A. during this decade is jazz music. Its status as an exotic art form no doubt helps explain the European fascination with jazz; the influx of Beat culture and writers such as Langston Hughes likewise contributed to its growing acceptance. Furthermore, German poets played a crucial role in spreading the word about this uniquely American style of music, and one reason for the popularity of jazz music throughout Europe can be gleaned from the following poem by Ernst Jandl:[27]

jazz
jazz
jazz
jazz
neinzz

ojazz
jazz
jazz
jazz
jazz

Once again, Jandl's deft wordplay defies any long-winded analysis. Here jazz is synonymous with optimism, and the poet wastes neither letter nor word in celebrating jazz music as an inherently affirmative art form triumphantly rejecting all nay-sayers.

---

[26] See Jack Kerouac, *On the Road* (1957; New York: Viking, 1971), 180. As to what it means to be "hip," see Norman Mailer, *The White Negro* (San Francisco: City Lights, 1957). An abridged version of this essay appeared in translation in Paetel, *Beat*, 226–30.

[27] Jandl, *poetische werke*, vol. 6, *übung mit buben & serienfuss & wischen möchten*, 67.

With its ties to the Black American experience, jazz music functions as a transcendent force in the face of overwhelming odds. In terms of performance, it emphasizes improvisation and freedom of expression, aspects gaining increased import to German poets. For East German poets of the 1960s jazz music took on special significance. In a project paying tribute to American masters, Jens Gerlach wrote a series of jazz portraits examining the artistic temperament of jazz and blues musicians.[28] In terms of content, the majority of the poems are biographical accounts relying on anecdotal references to highlight the individual personalities. Gerlach frequently takes a Brechtian approach, accentuating the heroic struggles of the underclass by showing how the victims of a racist system achieve success through a resilient artistic spirit. The style of individual poems invariably conforms to the musician under consideration; hence, Gerlach relies heavily on formal structure and rhyme. For instance, in his tribute to the blues singer Billie Holiday, he employs a quatrain stanza form and *abab cdcd* rhyme scheme, that is, a form corresponding to ballads sung by Lady Day. Among the more sophisticated compositions are those poems dedicated to more progressive jazz musicians. In "Charlie Parker" the man and the music become one as Gerlach takes on a dramatic role in adopting the voice of his subject. Instead of a biographical sketch, this poem employs fleeting images, glimpses into the world of a jazz artist, to recreate the life and music of Charlie Parker. In addition to pronounced aural and visual qualities, the language is highly sensual with recurrent allusions to smell, touch, and taste. The content works on various levels: on one hand everyday things — nameless people and places — on the other a mysterious if not threatening undercurrent characterized by the wonders of music and the dangers of drugs. Gerlach succeeds in capturing not only the essence of the man but also the atmosphere of a jazz club, and does so by incorporating internal rhyme into an otherwise free verse style much like a jazz artist employing rhythmic riffs within wandering melodic journeys.

Equally innovative is Gerlach's "Miles Davis,"[29] quoted here in its entirety:

[28] See Jens Gerlach, *Jazz: Gedichte*, 2nd ed. (1966, Berlin: Aufbau, 1967).

[29] Gerlach, 49.

O Phönix, sing dein Lied vom warmen Wald!
Naht jäh die Nacht, wird sich dein Traum verwirren:
Die tauben Elektronenhirne girren,
Und nur die Jerichoposaune schallt . . .
O Wildnis Welt, du vertikales Land:
Gestirne zittern drüber hin und irren,
Zersplittern lautlos, blitzen auf und schwirren
Wie Projektile von brillantner Wand . . .

    Die starren Fenster, leerer Glanz vor Gas,
    Erkennen nichts mehr wie gebrochne Augen:
    Rubin, Azur — die Hoffnung unter Glas . . .

    O Phönix, zeig, daß deine Schwingen taugen!
    Die Hoffnung steigt aus weißgeglühtem Haß. —
    O Phönix, zeig, daß deine Schwingen taugen!

    Azur, Rubin — die Hoffnung unter Glas,
    Und nichts erkennend wie gebrochne Augen:
    Die starren Fenster, leerer Glanz vor Gas . . .

Wie Projektile von brillantner Wand
Zersplittern lautlos, blitzen auf und schwirren
Gestirne, zittern drüber hin und irren:
O Wildnis Welt, du vertikales Land . . .
Nun, da die Jerichoposaune schallt
Und nur die Elektronenhirne girren,
Naht jäh die Nacht, mein Traum will sich verwirren:
O Phönix, sing dein Lied im warmen Wald!

Once again, Gerlach chooses to create a mood rather than to follow a narrative line. Here the focus is more on the music than the man. The regenerative powers of the phoenix, the convoluted world of dreams, a biblical reference, an apostrophe to a wilderness landscape turned on its side, stars exploding in the nighttime sky — all serve as analogs to the ingenious trumpet style of Miles Davis. Most effective is the manner in which Gerlach blends sight and sound. By means of exotic colors and brilliant flashes of light, this poem helps the reader *see* the music of Miles Davis. Gerlach relies on a variety of literary techniques: a blend of masculine and feminine rhymes, the reversal of lines (as well as subtle changes) in the first and last stanzas, and the variation on terza rima in the middle three stanzas. The overall effect is to suggest that the improvisational nature of jazz is far from haphazard.

For another East German poet of the 1960s, Rainer Kirsch, jazz music carries meaning as an expression of iconoclastic vitality, especially in poems such as "Jazz Me Blues" and "Tanzsaal."[30] Along similar but more sophisticated lines, Volker Braun explores the theme of improvisation and individual creativity in a poem simply titled "Jazz."[31]

> Das ist das Geheimnis des Jazz:
> Der Baß bricht dem erstarrten Orchester aus.
> Das Schlagzeug zertrommelt die geistlosen Lieder.
> Das Klavier seziert den Kadaver Gehorsam.
> Das Saxofon zersprengt die Fessel Partitur:
> Bebt, Gelenke: wir spielen ein neues Thema aus
> Wozu ich fähig bin und wessen ich bedarf: ich selbst zu
>   sein —
> Hier will ich es sein: ich singe mich selbst.
> Und aus den Trümmern des dunklen Bombasts Akkord
> Aus dem kahlen Notenstrauch reckt sich was her über uns
> Herzschlag Banjo, Mundton der Saxofone:
> Reckt sich unsere Harmonie auf: bewegliche Einheit —
> Jeder spielt sein Bestes aus zum gemeinsamen Thema.
> Das ist die Musik der Zukunft: jeder ist ein Schöpfer!
> Du hast das Recht, du zu sein, und ich bin ich:
> Und mit keinem verbünden wir uns, der nicht er selber ist
> Unverwechselbar er im Haß, im Lieben, im Kampf.

Although carefully controlled, this poem is, in a word, bold. Not only does Braun claim to be able to reveal the secret of jazz, he does so by incorporating the teamwork and improvisation of a jazz band into Marxist ideology. In this sense, the secret revealed is what jazz can mean for the East German populace. According to Braun, individual creativity, as exemplified by jazz ensemble solos,

---

[30] See Sarah und Rainer Kirsch, *Gespräch mit dem Saurier: Gedichte* (Berlin: Neues Leben, 1965), 48 and 85–88, respectively.

[31] Braun, *Provokation für mich* (Halle an der Saale: Mitteldeutscher, 1965), 18.

serves the common goal of not only a jazz orchestra but also society as a whole. The overall tone, however, is far from that of a jazz-induced utopia. Nouns such as *Kadaver* and *Trümmer*, adjectives like *erstarrt*, *geistlos*, and *kahl*, plus the verbs *sezieren*, *zertrommeln*, and *zersprengen* all point to destructive elements undermining the powers that be. More telling is that this jazz orchestra performs without the guidance of a conductor. The results, nevertheless, are anything but anarchic as "Jeder spielt sein Bestes aus zum gemeinsamen Thema." Although "Jazz" touched a nerve in orthodox Marxists,[32] its American influences follow prescribed East German doctrine. Aside from paying tribute to an African-American art form, thus expressing solidarity with an oppressed minority, Braun also celebrates the American poet most highly regarded in East Germany by singing a Whitmanesque song of the self.

In addition to jazz, other forms of American music traditionally associated with African Americans have provided both subject matter and formal structure for German-language poets. Such is evident in the work of Alfred Gong, a Jewish writer who was particularly interested in the black experience. Born Arthur Liquornik in Czernowitz of the Bukovina in 1920, he survived both the Stalinist and National-Socialist purges of his homeland before settling as a refugee in postwar Vienna and then emigrating to the United States in 1951. A generation younger, Gong arrived in New York with a literary reputation far less established than Ernst Waldinger, yet their careers as emigrant poets followed a similar course. Gong's poetry reveals a strong identification with immigrants and minorities, and individual poem titles show a fascination with musical forms, as in "Grünhorn Blues" and "Manhattan Spiritual,"[33] the opening two stanzas of which convey the scope of Gong's voice and vision:

---

[32] See Christine Cosentino and Wolfgang Ertl, *Zur Lyrik Volker Brauns* (Hanstein: Forum Academicum, 1984), 55–56; as to the orthodox Marxist reaction, see Hans Koch, "Unsere soziale Wirklichkeit im Spiegel der Literatur," *Neues Deutschland*, 26–27 July and 2–3 August 1966.

[33] See Gong, *Israels letzter Psalm*, ed. Joachim Herrmann (Aachen: Rimbaud, 1995), 43, 46, and 48, respectively; see also Gong, *Early Poems: A Selection from the Years 1941–1945*, ed. Jerry Glenn, Joachim Herrmann, and Rebecca S. Rodgers (Columbia, SC: Camden House, 1987) and Gong, *Gras und Omega*, ed. Joachim Herrmann (Aachen: Rimbaud, 1997).

> Männlein und Weiblein Manhattans,
> helfen Couch und Pillen euch nicht,
> schlagt dann in der Bibel nach,
> sie weist euch den Weg ins Licht.
>
> Adam, verbleu deine Rippe
> samt Apfel und Feigenblatt.
> Noah, mix den Martini:
> wir haben das Wasser satt.
> Josua, blas die Trompete,
> Stahl und Glas, sie stürzen nicht ein.
> Jonas, kriech aus dem U-Boot
> und kehr «Zum Walfisch» ein.

Though drawing on ancient traditions, Gong is unmistakably post-1945 in his mode of expression. A comparable range of tone can be found in his poems on the African-American experience, in particular "Interview mit Harlem" and "Harlem-Improvisation."[34] While the former adopts a parody of the children's song "Zehn kleine Negerlein," the latter is a bombastic apostrophe to the sun voiced in an improvisatory jazz style. Moreover, these poems highlight how Gong, in sharp contrast to Waldinger, embraced novel postwar trends in the world language of poetry. A German-language poet writing in America as a naturalized U.S. citizen, Gong features a unique viewpoint in his America poems. Unlike, say, Hagelstange, who addresses similar topics in his American travel poems, Gong shares neither an objective distance to subject matter nor the privileged status of visiting writer on tour. Thus, although he may carry the title of emigrant poet in terms of language, Gong writes from an immigrant perspective in terms of his firsthand ties to the American experience.

Gong also invites comparison with Rose Ausländer, who was born in Czernowitz in 1901, but lived in America first from 1921 to 1931 and then again between 1946 and 1965. The majority of her time in America was spent in New York, the city serving as the

---

[34] Gong, *Israels letzter Psalm*, 52–53. and 54, respectively. For a close reading of the latter, see Divers, "Noch ein 'Geheimnis des Jazz': Saying 'oja' to Afro-German Studies," *Die Unterrichtspraxis* 28.2 (1995): 127.

primary topic for her America poems. In "New York fasziniert,"[35] for instance, she captures the quiet beauty of New York on an early Sunday morning. Like Gong, Ausländer shows a fascination with American minorities, and in conjunction with the Black American experience, let us consider her poem "Harlem."[36]

> Melancholischer
> Mond
> über Slums
>
> Blues schluchzen
> in Bars
>
> Canyons verschlucken
> die Sterne
>
> Rock-and-roll
> Neonnacht
> bis der Tagtraum
> erwacht
>
> Laß leuchten
> deine
> Schneezähne
> Harlem
>
> wenn der Nachtwandler
> Mond
> in die Schlucht
> fällt

As with Bachmann in her poem of the same title, Ausländer creates a mood rather than a story line. Personification also plays a key role with a melancholy moon presiding over the slum scene and ghetto canyons swallowing up stars dotting the night sky. Music adds to

---

[35] Rose Ausländer, *Gesammelte Werke in sieben Bänden*, ed. Helmut Braun (Frankfurt am Main: Fischer, 1984), vol. 2, *Die Sichel mäht die Zeit zu Heu: Gedichte 1957–1965*, 32.

[36] Ausländer, vol. 3, *Hügel aus Äther unwiderruflich: Gedichte und Prosa 1966–1975*, 50. See also Ausländer's "Harlem bei Nacht" in vol. 2, *Gedichte 1957–1965*, 250.

the atmosphere, and the wailing sound of the blues is reinforced by the repetition of the *u* sound in *schluchzen, verschlucken,* and *Schlucht.* A literal sign of the times, neon illuminates the urban setting, and in parallel fashion Ausländer adds some rhythm to the blues by means of rock 'n' roll. Throughout the world Harlem is synonymous with Black America, and the command voiced in the penultimate stanza plays off this notion while encouraging Harlem's residents to brighten the night with a smile. Noteworthy here is how economy of language and sharpness of image eliminate any sentimentality or hint of racial stereotyping. The final stanza returns to the personified moon — now, however, a sleepwalker exiting along with melancholy. Thus, Ausländer not only brings the poem full circle, but also transcends the very mood established at the outset.

The poems discussed above highlight new developments in German poetry of the early 1960s. The traditional European fascination with the exotic takes on a new twist in this decade with attention directed not only to North American settings, import products, and art forms, but also to the unique life-style of the Beat Generation. This interest in the American counterculture likewise engendered influences in literary expression. As a case in point, both the form and content of Karsunke's "Frag mich nach Geno" are clearly nontraditional. In addition to its Cummings-style orthography, this free verse portrait of an American antihero is related in a prosaic, storyteller style with a higher premium placed on cataloguing pertinent details than employing traditional literary techniques. In short, the poem is as randomly packed as the duffel bag Geno carries on his travels. A similar blend of subject matter and poetics can be found in Leisegang's "Selbstportrait mit Zigarette" as the principles of imagism enhance a specific image of America. In other examples, the American literary influences are more subtle, as in Hartung's "Zechenkolonie" and the poet's unassuming nod to William Carlos Williams. The interest in jazz music, especially as expressed by East German poets, conveys both the universal appeal of an American art form and the underlying sociopolitical tensions when America surfaces in postwar German verse. Moreover, the poetic portraits of Black America by Gong and Ausländer draw upon a transcendent spirit within the African-American community echoing the belief that we *shall* overcome.

The poems discussed in this chapter show a growing awareness and appreciation of America's literary tradition. More importantly, the early-1960s reception of American poetry in Germany moves this awareness and appreciation out of the nineteenth and early-twentieth century and clearly into the postwar era. In short, the 1960s bring the reception of American poetry more up-to-date, thus laying the groundwork for significant developments circa 1965 that would thrust America into a prominent role shaping the future of German poetry and poetics.[37]

---

[37] Jürgen Theobaldy and Gustav Zürcher, *Veränderung der Lyrik: Über westdeutsche Gedichte seit 1965* (Munich: Text + Kritik, 1976), 26-27.

4: O Taste and See the Projective Verse: Höllerer's "Thesen zum langen Gedicht"

W E HAVE ALREADY seen evidence of the part played by Walter Höllerer in introducing contemporary American poetry to German readers. After establishing himself as a poet in the early 1950s, he along with Hans Bender co-founded the literary magazine *Akzente* in 1954.[1] His interests in contemporary American poetry followed from several trips to the United States in the late 1950s, both on lecture tours and as guest professor at Harvard and at the University of Wisconsin. Postwar German poets, as has been documented, were forced to relearn the world language of poetry after the isolation of the Hitler years, and Höllerer played a central role in achieving this end. *Akzente* actively advanced new literary trends, and as the 1960s progressed the journal became more international in focus. For example, a 1964 special issue featured Höllerer's title-essay "Veränderung" along with a multinational grouping of authors whose work highlighted changes taking place in world literature. American writers stood at the forefront of these literary innovators, and the tone for this double issue was established on its opening page by Denise Levertov's poem "O Taste and See."[2] Levertov's poem served as a model of the New Realism Höllerer was promoting and by which he sought to encourage a

---

[1] See Walter Höllerer, *Der andere Gast: Gedichte* (Munich: Hanser, 1952), a collection including the frequently anthologized poem "Der lag besonders mühelos am Rand."

[2] See *Akzente* 11.5–6 (1964): 385, trans. Christa Langenscheidt. Although born in Ilford in Essex, England, Levertov lived in the U.S.A. from 1948 until her death in 1998. As a result, her poetry has closer ties to the American tradition than to that of her native land. In fact, Levertov herself admits a certain affinity with the Americans Robert Duncan and Robert Creeley, naming them "the chief poets among my contemporaries." See Donald Allen, ed., *The New American Poetry: 1945–1960* (New York: Grove, 1960), 412.

movement away from the intellectual poetry of the 1950s. The poem, he argued, should operate on a level less cerebral and more sensual. "O Taste and See" is particularly effective in advancing these poetic ideals, as the imperative verb forms in the title carry an undeniable sense of urgency. The poet's task, then, becomes not one of speculation but rather a conscientious attention to detail in the here and now.

Höllerer presents a second representative example of change in literature with William S. Burroughs's essay on the literary techniques of Lady Sutton-Smith.[3] Burroughs's contribution to this special issue is a synopsis of an eccentric method of composition, best described by the term "cut-ups." The principles advanced here are easily recognizable, namely a collage technique with the arbitrary whims of the author guiding both selection and arrangement of the material comprising the resultant text. Taken together, Levertov's poem and Burroughs's essay mark the bounds of specific changes taking place in contemporary literature circa 1964. While the former represents the new poetic norm with its emphasis on the concrete world of sensory awareness, the latter displays brazen reliance on chance as a constituent part of the act of composition. As Höllerer takes care to point out, however, Levertov's precept is not to be understood as an updated version of nineteenth-century Naturalism. Likewise, the radical suggestions for change put forth in the Burroughs essay are not to be linked with avant-garde writers of the 1920s. Höllerer's purpose with this special issue was to present selected texts to support his claim that developments in the literature of the 1960s were truly new. His role was that of a promoter of change in German letters, and his goal was to point the way for further cultivation of fresh modes of thought and expression.

This special issue of *Akzente* was merely a prelude to more a pivotal development, the publication of Höllerer's "Thesen zum langen Gedicht."[4] The relative importance of these sixteen theses

---

[3] "Die literarischen Techniken der Lady Sutton-Smith," *Akzente* 11.5–6 (1964): 420–424, trans. Peter Behrens and Katharina Behrens.

[4] First published in *Akzente* 12.2 (1965): 128–30; rpt. in Hans Bender and Michael Krüger, ed., *Was alles hat Platz in einem Gedicht?* (Munich: Hanser, 1977), 7–9.

can be measured in terms of the resulting discussion. As Höllerer recalls, his original intention was to employ a series of theses in order to provoke a reaction and set a discussion in motion.[5] A discussion did indeed follow with pros and cons vigorously voiced by H. C. Artmann, Horst Bienek, Johannes Bobrowski, Günter Eich, Hans Magnus Enzensberger, Erich Fried, Peter Rühmkorf, and Helmut Heißenbüttel.[6] In addition to these names, Karl Krolow bears separate mention for "Das Problem des langen und kurzen Gedichts — heute," an essay earning a response from Höllerer himself.[7] The strength of Krolow's essay lies in his recognition of both the American models standing behind Höllerer's postulates and the inherent notion of the democratization of poetry.

Höllerer subsequently summarized the upshot of his American experience in co-editing *Junge amerikanische Lyrik* and how this endeavor led to the formation of his own poetics in the theses.[8] In brief, he sought a blend of voice and breath in the poem. His aim was to capture the expansive, dynamic rhythms of Whitman as well as the rebellious strains of Ginsberg and the Beats. The recognition of these literary traits in praxis was step one; the formulation thereof as theory became, then, the task at hand. To Höllerer's aid came another American, Charles Olson, whose role can be determined by reading his essay on "Projective Verse" side-by-side with the "Thesen zum langen Gedicht."

Höllerer's first three theses are distinctly axiomatic;[9] thesis 1, for instance, reads:

---

[5] See Höllerer, "Anmerkungen zur Autorenpoetik," in Jordan, Marquardt, and Woesler, ed., *Lyrik — Von allen Seiten*, 27.

[6] As to American influences on Heißenbüttel, in particular Gertrude Stein, see Harald Hartung, *Experimentelle Literatur und konkrete Poesie* (Göttingen: Vandenhoeck & Ruprecht, 1975), 24–25 and 30–32.

[7] See *Akzente* 13.3 (1966): 271–87; Höllerer's "Gedichte in den sechziger Jahren," followed in *Akzente* 13.4 (1966): 375–83; rpt. in *Was alles hat Platz?*, 10–28 and 29–38, respectively.

[8] See Höllerer, "Autorenpoetik," 21.

[9] Lothar Jordan, Axel Marquardt, and Winfried Woesler, eds., *Lyrik — Blick über die Grenzen* (Frankfurt am Main: Fischer, 1981), 144.

> Das lange Gedicht, so wie es hier verstanden wird, unterscheidet sich nicht nur durch seine Ausdehnung von den übrigen lyrischen Gebilden, sondern durch seine Art sich zu bewegen und da zu sein, durch seinen Umgang mit der Realität.

Theses 2 and 3 declare that the long poem is, according to its form, political, and procures for those who write "die Perspektive, die Welt freizügiger zu sehen." In theses 4 and 5 Höllerer moves into the realm of perception, and here the echoes of Olson ring clear. To summarize briefly: Olson's "Projective Verse" examines the kinetics of the poem in its "Field Composition" according to the principle: "Form is never more than the extension of content." Moreover, the poem shapes and transfers energies through a process regulated by a second principle: "One perception must immediately and directly lead to a further perception."[10] Höllerer's variation on this maxim, though somewhat camouflaged by the verbiage, finds expression in thesis 4:

> Die Auseinandersetzung mit den Augenblickselementen, mit den Überbleibseln aus der Summe der Wahrnehmungen in der geringfügigsten räumlichen und zeitlichen Ausdehnung wird im langen Gedicht eher noch verstärkt als vernachlässigt.

Less obvious are the strains of Olson in thesis 5, which explains how the appropriate "sum of perceptions" is to be achieved. For Höllerer, this involves a denial of the most strenuous sort requiring poets "von uns selber . . . abzusehen."[11] The long poem, he goes on to postulate, enables us to construct "eine mögliche Welt um uns." But how, in turn, is this to be accomplished? Höllerer's more pragmatic side surfaces in thesis 6 with the answer: "mit freierem Atem, der im Versbau, im Schriftbild Gestalt annimmt." And here we have the key word in the theses, *Atem*, employed in a manner

---

[10] This synopsis is from the editor's introduction to *Selected Writings of Charles Olson*, ed. Robert Creeley (New York: New Directions, 1966), 16–17. We should also note that Olson borrowed the two principles cited here from Creeley and Edward Dahlberg, respectively.

[11] Much the same sense is expressed in Olson's "Mayan Letters" where he contrasts Pound and Williams with regard to the poet's ego. Pound's work, says Olson, is "ego-dominated," hence it exhibits "no flow." See *Selected Writings*, 81–83. See also Olson's pamphlet *Proprioception* (San Francisco: Four Seasons, 1964), 1, where he urges, "Wash the ego out."

clearly finding its conceptual basis in the writings of Olson.[12] Of the three major components of Olson's poetic theory — syllable, line, field — the notion of the poetic line is given the most attention by Höllerer.[13] Additionally, the length of the poetic line, as Olson claimed in "Projective Verse," is directly dependent on breath and breathing.

Other theses adopt a similar practical approach. Number 14, for example, recognizes entire sentences and longer lines for their potential momentum, an observation evoking not only Olson's theory, but also Whitman's style and the tradition — so admired by Höllerer — carried on by Ginsberg and the Beat poets. Moving from form to content, thesis 9 proclaims a preference for "Banalitäten" in long poems over "die erzwungene Preziosität und Chinoiserie des kurzen Gedichts." In related fashion thesis 13 begins: "Subtile und triviale, literarische und alltägliche Ausdrücke finden somit notgedrungen im langen Gedicht zusammen." Here the American influx extends beyond Olson as one recalls Ezra Pound's *Cantos* as well as William Carlos Williams's *Paterson*. Therein, however, lies a crucial sticking point in Höllerer's theses, as number 13 is simply too all-encompassing. As a case in point, if Pound's *Cantos* are exemplary of the art of literary allusion, then why do so many passages read like enciphered poems against which Höllerer warns in thesis 14? Viewed in their entirety, the most vexing element in Höllerer's theses is that such suggestions can neither control nor guarantee results. Furthermore, the final thesis declaring "Das lange Gedicht als Vorbedingung für kurze Gedichte" rings hollow in light of Williams's career. In fact, one could argue that only after years of writing short, precise poems was he prepared to write the long poem *Paterson*.[14]

All criticism notwithstanding, the importance of the "Thesen zum langen Gedicht" for German poetry after 1965 is undeniable. With these sixteen proclamations Höllerer sought to establish a new theo-

---

[12] Höllerer's debt to Olson is evident in that the German word for breath or breathing *Atem* (or a variation thereof, e.g. *Kurzatmigkeit*) appears four times in the sixteen theses.

[13] See Jordan, "Dichtung unter Einfluß," 145.

[14] See *The Autobiography of William Carlos Williams*, 60–61.

retical foundation supplanting the European elitist and hermetic tradition with a democratic, more accessible American approach. Olson's writings provided an impetus for this treatise on modern poetics, and following publication of the theses he remained a central figure for Höllerer. In the winter of 1966/67 the *Literarische Colloquium Berlin*,[15] under Höllerer's directorship, invited twenty-one writers from eleven countries to participate in a special literary program. The United States was represented by Olson, Creeley, and Lawrence Ferlinghetti.[16] Yet, even if Olson is the single most important figure shaping the formation of Höllerer's poetics, there still exist major differences between Olson's "Projective Verse" and the theses. First and foremost, poetic theory is not an article to be packaged for export and import; there are more than cultural and language boundaries to be crossed. Additionally, the matter of historical time is crucial: let us not forget that Olson's essay begins "Verse now, 1950" — and what might have held true then in America does not necessarily remain so fifteen years later in Germany. Furthermore, it is misleading to suggest that Olson's "Projective Verse" was the authoritative text of an era as Höllerer led many to believe.[17] Granted, William Carlos Williams offered high praise to this essay and quoted from it at length in his autobiography. And even though Olson exercised a marked influence on fellow Black Mountain poets, other schools of American poetry reflect little of either his own style of verse or what he promulgated as theory. "Projective Verse" represents an age in American letters when poetic theory

[15] The LCB was beneficiary of financial support from the Ford Foundation; as to the literary-political ramifications of this connection to corporate America, see Klaus Schumann's preface to *Denkzettel: Politische Lyrik aus den sechziger Jahren der BRD und Westberlins*, eds. Annie Voigtländer and Hubert Witt (Frankfurt am Main: Röderburg, 1977), 6 — the West German edition © by Verlag Philipp Recalm jun. Leipzig 1976.

[16] See *Ein Gedicht und sein Autor: Lyrik und Essay*, ed. Walter Höllerer (Berlin: LCB, 1967). The program was also filmed, and Höllerer enthusiastically recalls Olson communicating his poetics more through body language than conceptual terminology; see Höllerer, "Autorenpoetik," 21. Not everyone, however, shared Höllerer's fervor for his performance; see Dieter E. Zimmer, "Weltausstellung der Lyriker," *Die Zeit*, 10 Feb. 1967.

[17] See the bio note on Olson in *Junge amerikanische Lyrik*, 268; and Walter Höllerer, *Theorie der modernen Lyrik* (Reinbek bei Hamburg: Rowohlt, 1965), 395.

was held in comparatively high regard. In the 1960s, however, American poets (especially the Beats and members of the New York School) distanced themselves from theoretical discourse. Thus, Höllerer's championing of Olson in mid-1960s Germany says less about the then current state of poetry in the U.S.A. than about the tastes and good fortune of a theorist in search of a theory.

Another difference between Olson's "Projective Verse" and Höllerer's theses involves voice. Regardless of the attributive adjective — colloquial, pompous, vulgar, erudite, long-winded — Olson's essay style exhibits voice, a quality not unlike that of a poem as dramatic monologue with an implied listener. Above all, Olson writes in a manner that posits a reader listening in and taking part in the thought process. The thesis-style of Höllerer's tract, on the other hand, restricts both range of voice and degree of reader participation. With Olson the reader experiences the to-and-fro exchange of a dialogue; with Höllerer, however, the reader is faced more with a choice of accepting or rejecting the given set of propositions.

Höllerer's "Thesen zum langen Gedicht" did more than generate a lively debate in German literary circles. Both the theses and his editorial efforts influenced writers of the mid-1960s. Nonetheless, not all reactions were positive. For example, Dieter Leisegang took umbrage at the sardonic insinuation in thesis 9, responding to Höllerer in "Coca-Cola."[18]

> Gerade weil
> heute alles nach außen geht, das Private verfemt ist
> als Chinoiserie, und die Lösung unsrer Probleme
> abhängen soll nicht von »Kunst und nochmals Kunst«
> sondern von Politik, Haltung, Gewissen, haben
> wir unseren Frieden innen errichtet.

Ironically Leisegang's rebuttal takes the form of a long poem, not one of his distinctive epigrams.[19] Furthermore, in "Coca-Cola" and other

---

[18] Dieter Leisegang, *Hoffmann am Fenster* (Frankfurt am Main: Heiderhoff, 1968), 11–12; rpt. *Lauter letzte Worte*, 39–41.

[19] See Hans Dieter Schäfer, "Dieter Leisegang" in *Die deutsche Lyrik 1945– 1975: Zwischen Botschaft und Spiel*, ed. Klaus Weissenberger (Düsseldorf: Bagel, 1981), 404–14, here 407; see also 474 (Note 12) where Schäfer explains the

long poems Leisegang refuses to adopt Höllerer's fundamental premise as expressed in thesis 10: "Im langen Gedicht will nicht jedes Wort besonders beladen sein." And in this regard, Leisegang steadfastly follows the poetics of Ezra Pound by charging each word with meaning.

Others were more receptive to these innovative trends in literature, following Höllerer's path to American role models. Nicolas Born, for example, reveals American influences in a programmatic statement seeking to displace the old with a new system of poetics. German poetry, he argues, must move away from symbol, metaphor, and decorative language. Poems should be raw, devoid of artificiality, and directly confront the world in which we live. Quoting Olson on the relationship between form and content, Born calls for a poetry without the predetermined restrictions of a metrical mechanism. Höllerer also shows his influence, especially in Born's frequently quoted assertion: "Es gibt keine Banalität außer der Banalität des Ausdrucks."[20]

Unlike Höllerer, who looked to Olson for his theory of the poetic line, Born turns to Olson for his concept of the poem as field, that notion pertaining to the interplay of form and content within a selected field of perception. In addition to Born, Jürgen Becker also adopted this aspect of Olson's "Projective Verse."[21] Becker warrants attention not only for signs of Olson's "open-field" form, but also as a practitioner of the long poem as encouraged by Höllerer. His "Momente · Ränder · Erzähltes · Zitate"[22] is composed of the elements listed in the title and epitomizes the open, free-form writing style for which he is known.[23] Here is the opening stanza:

---

genesis of the poem "Coca-Cola" and why Leisegang distanced himself from both pop culture and pop art.

[20] For this quote and the synopsis above, see the book jacket of Nicolas Born, *Marktlage: Gedichte* (Cologne and Berlin: Kiepenheuer & Witsch, 1967).

[21] See Jordan, "Dichtung unter Einfluß," 145; and Harald Hartung, "Die eindimensionale Poesie. Subjektivität und Oberflächigkeit in der neuen Lyrik," in *Neue Rundschau* 89.2 (1978): 222–41.

[22] First published in *Kursbuch* 10 (1967): 164–77; rpt. with the subtitle "Fragment aus Rom, 1966" in Becker's first book of poems, *Schnee* (Berlin: LCB, 1971), 7–20; and as "Fragment aus Rom" in Becker, *Gedichte: 1965–1980* (Frankfurt am Main: Suhrkamp, 1981), 9–21.

[23] See Walter Hinck, "Die »offene Schreibweise« Jürgen Beckers," in *Über Jürgen Becker*, ed. Leo Kreutzer (Frankfurt am Main: Suhrkamp, 1972), 119–39.

hier,
    wo immer das ist: das ist jetzt die Frage
(jetzt immer): was ist und was drankommt,
                hier
ist jetzt . . . /
    neuerdings wieder nachts,
in diesen Träumen, diesige weiße Pisten
und plötzlich die heiße Last der Luft,
            Miami
wirklich, wie
    zehn, täglich, Zypressen vor Augen,
Quadrat-Himmel drüber. Luft.
Brauchbarer Blick zum Ausruhn, wie jetzt,
in der heißen Stille
        von hier
fortgehen
           kommt
der ganze Sommer noch (?)

Becker's free and open style does not completely defy understanding. As the revised subtitle makes all the more clear, the contents of this poem draw upon Becker's stay in Rome as a scholarship holder in residence at the Villa Massimo during 1965. Within this setting, the poet reflects not only upon his host country but also upon telling aspects of his native land's past and present:

    . . . *und in dieser Stille* . . . kann man (Ehrengast)
nur sagen von einer gewissen Schwerhörigkeit an;
ELEZIONI COMMUNALI:
        im Dröhnen, wochenlang,
der Lautsprecherkämpfe schläfts sich schlecht
in unserer Lorbeer-Kolonie;
Hammer & Sichel
sah ich erst wieder, ganz legal,
auf der
    Piazza Bologna
        kreisen
mit Horst-Wessel-Lied die Fiats 500 des MSI.

In these two excerpts we find Höllerer's theory put into practice, as the long poem distinguishes itself through political content, flow, and how it deals with reality. Moreover, both the language and formal techniques employed reveal a subtle control at work within this — as appears on first reading — free and open writing style. For instance, the sound quality of the lines "im Dröhnen, wochenlang,/ der Lautsprecherkämpfe schläfts sich schlecht" corresponds to the message conveyed, that is the vowel sounds *ö*, *o*, and *a* in the first line enhance the sense of an extended period of time, and the repetition of the *ch* and *sch* consonant clusters in the second line reinforces the annoying attributes of electronically amplified speech. In similar fashion, the three typographically stepped lines "auf der/ Piazza Bologna/ kreisen" add to the visual image of communist party banners waving above the square.

Becker's long, fragmentary poem tells of more than just the poet's stay at the Villa Massimo. Other sections reveal his unique take on American pop culture, in particular Andy Warhol.

> aber
> es war immer einunddasselbe Gesicht
> NICO
> es war immer einunddasselbe Gesicht
> NICO
> (from Cologne)
> es war immer ein Lidschlag
> drei Stunden
> ein Lidschlag: nach dem andern
> und
> es war immer
> NICO
> einunddasselbe Gesicht
> bis
> drei Stunden
> ein Lidschlag: nach dem andern
> Andy Warhol
> aber
> es war immer einunddasselbe Gesicht
> dunkel
> macht

This excerpt warrants a background sketch on several particulars. Nico, a striking beauty and pop-culture icon herself, was born in Germany and came to America with a reputation as an international star. A fashion model and aspiring actress, she had a minor role in Fellini's *La Dolce Vita* (1960) and later appeared in a number of Warhol's underground film productions. In addition, for a time she was lead singer of The Velvet Underground, the group serving, so to speak, as the house band at Warhol's Factory. Becker's use of the phrase "einunddasselbe Gesicht" suggests several possible readings. One, it became common practice at Velvet Underground concerts to project a giant film image of Nico's face onto a screen behind the group as they performed on stage; and two, this repeated allusion recalls the trademark feature of Warhol's films and his minimalist treatment of cinematic duration. Whether with human subjects as in the film *Sleep* or inanimate objects such as the Empire State Building in *Empire*, Warhol appropriated the moving picture medium for static portraits and thus advocated the camp component of cinéma vérité.[24] Becker's Warholian interlude gains depth when viewed in conjunction with the ensuing section. This segment, reminiscent of Höllerer's call for a mix of the subtle and trivial, literary and everyday expressions in the long poem, relates details of an encounter with an inconsiderate patron at a New York City hotel:

> und noch in der selben Nacht, in der wir,
> ich weiß nicht woher, spät und erschossen heimgeschlingert
> kamen, ins MARTINIQUE,
>   begriff ich,
> morgens erst so gegen sechs, nachdem ich ein paar Mal

---

[24] See Peter Wollen, "Raiding the Icebox" in Michael O'Pray, ed., *Andy Warhol: Film Factory* (London: British Film Institute, 1989), 14–27, especially 16–17.; see also Stephen Koch, *Stargazer: The Life, World and Films of Andy Warhol*, 3rd ed. (1973; New York and London: Boyars, 1991). As to further aspects of the role of Warhol in Becker's writings, see his radio play *Bilder* in Becker, *Bilder Häuser Hausfreunde: Drei Hörspiele* (Frankfurt am Main: Suhrkamp, 1969), 7–46, and the repeated allusions (10, 19, 28, and 39) to Warhol's film *Empire*; cf. Peter W. Jansen, "Dann und wann das Empire State Building," in Kreutzer, 86–90. See also "Gedicht über Schnee im April," Becker, *Gedichte*, 29, in which Becker metaphorically examines the Warholian notion of fifteen minutes of fame, and Jürgen Becker and Wolf Vostell, eds., *Happenings, Fluxus, Pop Art, Nouveau Réalisme: Eine Dokumentation* (Reinbek bei Hamburg: Rowohlt, 1965).

gegen die Wand gedonnert hatte, vergeblich, und
hinübergerannt war und da Ruhe verlangt hatte,
vergeblich,
        warum der Beknackte mit seiner Sonnenbrille
nachts in seinem schwarzen Zimmer, dieser Bekokste, das
war er, immer
           einunddieselbe
             Single laufen ließ:
PERCY SLEDGE —
          ohne Stop, bis ich wie gesagt
mit den Nerven an den Rand geriet, immer
dieselbe Scheibe, bis ich, morgens als die Negermädchen
in den Gängen draußen anfingen, endlich selber hinein
geriet und mitdrehte und
            begriff —
ich weiß nicht warum;
           aber das wars ja immer,
die Art von amerikanischem *Zustand*, in dem ich immer
(einunddasselbe)
        begriff und nicht wußte warum
und nur wußte:
          ohne Stop, immer höher, weiter,
bis es dunkel oder hell wird.

This account (an example of "Erzähltes" in the original title) of a trivial incident reveals both personal particulars and insight into the "American condition."[25] In the process, Becker revives the "einunddasselbe" leitmotiv initiated in the Warhol excerpt; what was formerly a visual component (Nico's face) now turns acoustic through mention of the non-stop, repeated playing of the hymn-like hit song "When a Man Loves a Woman" by Percy Sledge. With these two passages Becker not only highlights Warhol's pop aesthetics but also hints at techniques utilized to assure that pop music becomes popular. The marketing ploys of the music industry are furthered by the programming methods of radio stations; that

---

[25] See also "Aus der Geschichte einer Trennung" from the prose volume Becker, *Erzählen bis Ostende* (Frankfurt am Main: Suhrkamp, 1981); rpt. in *Dimension* (1983): 54–65.

is, listeners become buyers through repeated hearing of songs played over the airwaves. The hotel scene as captured by Becker, however, employs a minimalist reduction of this practice to the point where the song plays on the listener's nerve endings.

Throughout the poem Becker depends on particulars of name and place. References to Nico, Warhol, and Percy Sledge can be listed under the heading of Anglo-American influences in pop art, culture, and music. In various sections of the poem Becker mentions The Beatles, Carnaby shops, and The Rolling Stones. These allusions, however, do not indicate a full-fledged endorsement of the 1960s cultural revolution. For example, whereas the lyric persona eventually joins in on the fun at the Hotel Martinique, a more resolute demeanor is conveyed in the following:

> Dagegen . . . ; nein,
> die Fünfzehntausend in Nervis Palasport waren ja
> schon ziemlich alle *in delirio*, als
> > endlich
> die STONES in die Arena hüpften —
> > na schön,
> Mick Jagger riß uns ganz schön auf, aber
> ich blieb dann doch wieder ganz kalt und sah
> dem Rauch in den Scheinwerfern der Kuppel zu (ich
> setzte ja noch immer einen mehr auf
> John Lennon und die anderen)
> > und natürlich, ja,
> kam dann auch das obligate Erinnern an
> SPORTPALAST
> > und sagte nicht auch einer: das
> ist ja *faschistoid* . . . ?

Here the lyric persona maintains a critical distance to pop culture mania. The hotel episode, in comparison, was but a private affair; a rock concert, on the other hand, is a public event with ramifications extending beyond the realm of entertainment. Becker draws parallels between a rock concert and a political rally — particularly in a nighttime setting — and calls into question the mass hysteria of an audience in the hands of the figure behind the microphone. Furthermore, this concert-goer is obliged to recall how an earlier Rolling Stones performance in Berlin had turned flagrantly fascist.

"Momente · Ränder · Erzähltes · Zitate" is indicative of how trivial aspects of popular culture find expression in a serious literary text. Becker's presentation of Anglo-American pop heroes bespeaks a 1960s attitude in which cultural innovations carry political import. In this post-Beat era, outsider status means taking an active role in addressing issues of the day; hence, the parenthetical aside declaring a preference for John Lennon and others over Mick Jagger. In other words, a respect for rebels *with* a cause. Both Becker and Born can be counted among the poets who followed up on proposals for new directions in German poetry initiated by Höllerer. Although America played a positive role in shaping these new trends, its image became increasingly more negative from 1965 through the remainder of the decade. The one factor contributing most to this change in status was the war in Vietnam. The following two chapters will examine various aspects of the Vietnam protest poem with recognition of how American military intervention in Southeast Asia revitalized the political poem in Germany.

5: Vietnam and Erich Fried: America and the German Political Poem of the 1960s

A NY DISCUSSION OF the Vietnam War in German poetry must begin with Erich Fried. Born in Vienna in 1921, Fried fled to England in 1938 and later became a naturalized British citizen and London resident. Nevertheless, he continued to write in German and established the reputation as a pivotal, as well as highly controversial figure in German literary circles until his death in 1988. In 1962 Fried began writing the poems that first appeared in the political-literary magazine *Konkret* and then later in *und Vietnam und,*[1] the book credited with revitalizing the political poem in the Federal Republic of Germany.[2] With the single thematic focal point of the war in Vietnam, this volume of poems generated a heated debate in which Fried's detractors initially far outnumbered his supporters. Whereas Martin Walser praised the book as one of the most significant of the decade, the near unanimous opinion dismissed the poems as unliterary, agitprop poetry. Most telling, however, was the refusal of most major West German newspapers to pre-print individual poems or to review Fried's book. Their feigned disinterest hinged on the argument that the poems were aesthetically unsatisfying.[3] Crucial to this study is how Fried's Viet-

---

[1] Erich Fried, *und Vietnam und: 41 Gedichte mit einer Chronik* (Berlin: Wagenbach, 1966). Subsequent references to poems from this book will be cited in the text with the page number in parentheses following the poem title.

[2] See Harald Weinreich, "Gegen die Musterschüler, Schönfärber und Falschspieler," *Frankfurter Allgemeine Zeitung,* 26 March 1977.

[3] This summary of the initial reception of *und Vietnam und* from the afterword by Fried's publisher, Klaus Wagenbach, to Erich Fried, *100 Gedichte ohne Vaterland* (Berlin: Wagenbach, 1978), 121. See also Peter Demetz, *Postwar German Literature: A Critical Introduction* (New York: Pegasus, 1970), 64–65, who considers the poems too Brechtian.

nam poems remind us that the war in Southeast Asia was viewed as an American war, and how this war affected the image of America both at home and abroad.

Fried's Vietnam poems follow a method first practiced in his *Warngedichte*, poems imparting information by means of a coded message.[4] The forty-one poems of *und Vietnam und* are appended by a "Vietnam-Chronik," a historical documentation of foreign military intervention in Indo-China. The poems and chronicle work in unison, forming a complementary pair and enabling — indeed requiring — the reader to participate in the process of deciphering Fried's intended message. The poems highlight both the military and the political side of the war as in the oft-cited "17.–22. Mai 1966" (23):

> Aus Da Nang
> wurde fünf Tage hindurch
> täglich berichtet:
> Gelegentlich einzelne Schüsse
>
> Am sechsten Tag wurde berichtet:
> In den Kämpfen der letzten fünf Tage
> in Da Nang
> bisher etwa tausend Opfer

This poem is characteristic of Fried's epigrammatic style and his use of factual material. Particulars of time and place are authentic, as are the two quotations closing each stanza. Commentary is minimal — "it was reported" — and free of bias or opinion. Nevertheless, the blatant discrepancy between the two sets of reported facts precludes the need for editorial remarks. Thus, the reader must take the judgmental step, first by recognizing the inherent contradiction in the accounts, and then by drawing the obvious conclusions on the integrity of the American military's press releases. Fried's methodology here is Brechtian in that the reader is faced with a specific gap or contradiction to be bridged or re-

---

[4] Erich Fried, *Warngedichte* (Munich: Hanser, 1964); see also Harald Hartung, "Lyrik als Warnung und Erkenntnis: Zur Zeitlyrik Erich Frieds," *kürbiskern* 3 (1966): 182–87; rpt. in *Geschichte der deutschen Literatur aus Methoden: Westdeutsche Literatur von 1945–1971*, 3 vols., ed. Heinz Ludwig Arnold (Frankfurt am Main: Athenäum, 1972), 3: 71–77.

solved. The participatory nature of the reader's role is decisive, for without it the poem can neither expose lies nor reveal the truth.

Other examples of Fried shedding light on the questionable nature of the American military's press policy are "Beim Zeitunglesen in London" (21), "Presseklub" (31), and "Pressekonferenz LBJ, Frühjahr 1966" (48). These poems illustrate Fried's perceptive awareness of the politics of carrying on an undeclared war in a far-off land. His insight recognizes the importance of chicanery in how the hostilities are reported in the press and that military concerns often become subjugated to the public relations task of selling the war to both the American public and U.S. allies. As for laying blame, Fried's criticism extends from the ordinary foot soldier to political leaders, including those who sit "Im Pentagon" (51), a poem that captures the detached, coldly objective attitude of the chiefs of staff who, safe within the confines of their Washington offices, calculate the destructive firepower necessary to maintain the status quo of the military-industrial complex. At the opposite end of the spectrum are the soldiers whose duty is to carry out the policies established by Pentagon leaders. Fried addresses the mind-set of the common infantryman in his "Preislied für einen Freiheitskrieger" (59–60), based on an interview with an American soldier broadcast by BBC television on 13 June 1966. The poem fosters the image of a non-thinking automaton acting strictly according to training procedures. Thus, this freedom fighter lacks nothing of that required to make him the ideal combatant: he is "frei/ von weibischen Skrupeln" and so hardened that killing becomes matter of fact. Not even the death rattle gurgling in the throats of his own comrades evokes a response.

While such poems consider the role of the media in reporting the war, another group of Fried's Vietnam poems looks back in time and draws historical parallels. Examples include "Einleuchtend" (57), "Falls es vorübergeht" (24), and "42 Schulkinder" (16–17), the last a poem reading, on the surface, like a lesson in world geography:

> Wie weit ist es
> von Guernica nach Man Quang
> von Washington nach Berchtesgaden
> von München nach Prag
> von Berlin und Moskau
> nach Warschau?

This poem, however, is concerned with more than just geography. Fried's mention of Warsaw in relationship to Berlin and Moscow suggests Poland's history of suffering through a series of invasions from both east and west. Moreover, stanza three sharpens distinctions and leaves no doubt as to the comparisons being made:

> Von Saigon nach Hanoi so weit
> wie von Berlin nach Kiew
> oder von Münster hinunter nach Guernica
> Ich habe Guernica gesucht auf der Karte
> weil ich mir Man Quang
> anders nicht vorstellen kann

With this reference the poem changes its focus from geography to history, reminding the reader that the military tactic of long-range flight and aerial bombardment began with Hitler's *Luftwaffe* ravishing Guernica in support of Franco's fascist regime. Fried places the American bombing of Man Quang in a historical context reduced to the lowest common denominator of victims — here forty-two school children. As such, the poem censures that stratagem of refusing to distinguish military targets from civilian centers, hence the references to Coventry, Dresden, and Nagasaki in stanza four.

A third category borrows from the world of fairy tales and fables. One example is "Greuelmärchen" (45–47), a poem with a fairy tale quality apparent both in its language and in its simplistic depiction of good and evil.

> Der Menschenfresser
> kein Auge auf seiner Stirn
> nur Sorgenfalten
> wie ein Dackel der leidet an Tollwut
>
> Er haßt alles Rohe
> und läßt flüssiges Feuer verspritzen
> daß weit und breit
> alles gebraten wird

The simile employed in the first stanza is likewise typical of a fairy tale: the image of a mad dog conveys a message clear even to a child. Equally comprehensible is the distinction between raw and cooked in the second stanza which, in turn, serves to explain the

cannibal's penchant for "flüssiges Feuer," Fried's working defini-
tion of napalm. However, even though the allegorical "Greuelmärchen" convincingly adopts the fairy tale mode, other poems
such as "Tiefer Trunk" (52) and "Vom Gleichgewicht durch Be-
friedung" (54) are less successful in their appropriation of the fable form.[5] These two poems fail to convince due to the
incompatibility of the war in Vietnam and an animal fable, in that
the bestiality of U.S. war policy in Southeast Asia finds no counterpart in the animal kingdom.

Fried employs a variety of stylistic approaches in addressing the
topic of Vietnam. Unfortunately, his poetry is frequently clouded
by controversy or dismissed for lacking sophistication. For example, while one reviewer notes the comparative simplicity of his poetry and its relative accessibility to the average reader,[6] another
thinks his prolific output suggests an almost mechanical production
of verse.[7] An exception to the general trend in Erich Fried studies
is the approach taken by Alexander von Bormann,[8] who strives to
rebut Fried's critics by analyzing the poems according to form and
method of composition. Bormann's attempt to reconcile rhetoric
and poetry acknowledges a contempt for the principles of rhetoric
prevalent since the days of German classicism. Hermann Schlüter
identifies the force behind this attitude as Goethe, who maintained
that the natural powers are to be valued more highly than those
acquired artificially or by means of applied principles.[9] Bormann
opposes this precept and begins his examination by identifying literalism as central to Fried's poetry, particularly as it relates to his
concept of humanity. One example of Fried's literalism is "Was alles heißt" (14–15), a poem reading as a lexicon of the specialized

---

[5] See Ulla Hahn, *Literatur in der Aktion* (Wiesbaden: Athenaion, 1978), 42.

[6] See Marcel Reich-Ranicki, "Die Leiden des Dichters Erich Fried," *Frankfurter Allgemeine Zeitung*, 23 January 1982.

[7] See Walter Hinck, "Erich Fried, der rasende Verworter," *Frankfurter Allgemeine Zeitung*, 14 January 1984.

[8] See Alexander von Bormann, "Ein Dichter, den Worte zusammenfügen:
Versöhnung von Rhetorik und Poesie bei Erich Fried," *Text + Kritik* 91
(1986): 5–23.

[9] See Hermann Schlüter, *Grundkurs der Rhetorik* (1974; Munich: dtv, 1985), 9.

vocabulary growing out of the war in Vietnam. Part one opens with a question followed, in turn, by a footnote-like explication of the simile employed in the first line:

> Warum warst du nicht wie der Baum Trung Quan?
> sagt ein Mädchen
>
> Das heißt
> ihr Geliebter ist einer von den Verbrannten
>
> Die Blätter des Baumes Trung Quan fangen nicht Feuer
> wie Bambusstäbe oder wie Menschenhaut

Other sections of this poem focus on the language of the perpetrators and feature a metonymic method reminiscent of Adam's role as the first poet and giver of names. Once again, the explanation for the given name accentuates the plight of the victim:

> Sicherheitszünder
> heißt ein Bauer den man vorantreibt
> an einem Strick über ein Minenfeld

Although "Was alles heißt" is not a found poem, the procedural method is similar in that the poet appropriates that which had circulated among military personnel by way of mouth and finally made its way into the civilian press. Fried makes use of those English expressions, readily finding German equivalents, highlighting not only the cavalier attitude of those who coin such phrases but also how the clever use of language serves as a diversionary tactic to cover up a total disregard for humanity.

Fried is not averse to showing how the grotesque provides shock value, as evident in the poem "Die Drahtzieher."[10] The title, in and of itself, suggests a marionette theater with puppeteers actuating wires in order to effect the desired movements in attached puppets. Yet in this poem, Fried's metonymic twist adroitly depicts a gruesome puppet show as staged in the Southeast Asian theater of war:

---

[10] Erich Fried, *Unter Nebenfeinden: Fünfzig Gedichte* (Berlin: Wagenbach, 1970), 59.

Einen Draht
kann man durch alles ziehen

durch Ohren
durch Hoden und Glied
durch Brüste
durch beide Wangen

Ein kleiner Ruck an dem Draht
macht Gefangene fügsam
und bringt sie zum Reden

Consistent with Bormann's contention about Fried's poetry, this poem demonstrates how literalism can most effectively illustrate man's inhumanity to man.

One of the longer and more formally structured poems in *und Vietnam und* is "Der Freiwillige" (40–41). The poem consists of a series of interlocking, rhyming couplets in which the principal word in the final line of one distich is repeated in the first line of the next. This method, a form of anadiplosis, creates a self-perpetuating poem with its own built-in rhythmic momentum. In addition, "Der Freiwillige" reads as a soliloquy with the poet assuming a dramatic role mirroring the spiraling chain of events into which the volunteer soldier admits himself. Fried's sense of irony is well suited to the role he adopts, especially with regard to those alluring qualities that draw the young man into military service:

Als ich die Reden hörte von Pflicht
wars wie ein Buch das man liest ohne Licht
Als ich im Buch las von Freiheit und Helden
wars als müßte ich gehn und mich melden

Once inducted, however, the volunteer is pulled along by forces far beyond his control:

Als sie die Meldung entgegennahmen
wars als wüßten sie schon meinen Namen
Als ich den Namen unterschrieben
wars als wär das Blatt leergeblieben
Als ich sie fragte warum bleibt es leer
wars als hörte mich keiner mehr
Als ich fragte ob keiner mich hört
wars als hätt ich sie alle gestört

The cumulative effect of the form, to say nothing of Fried's use of anaphora, adds to both the dramatic intensity and the narrative tempo. Compared to other poems in this volume, particularly those epigrammatic in nature, "Der Freiwillige" reads as a tour de force speeding along to its prescribed end. And, need the reader be reminded, the closing couplet leaves no doubt that this is an antiwar poem:

> Als ich sah daß mein Wille gut war
> wußte ich warum ich voll Blut war

This final distich is especially effective in that the harshness of its content is counterbalanced by the delicacy of its composition: a feminine rhyme incorporating two monosyllabic words with the unstressed, intransitive verb meekly dropping off as in a dying breath.

Taken as a whole, the poem is successful primarily due to the manner in which Fried handles dramatic irony. The content of the entire poem — save the final two lines — carries a meaning unperceived by the speaker himself. The irony lies in the contrast between that message as intended by the dramatic hero and the added significance of the words as understood by the reader. This disparity is first recognized in the final couplet when the volunteer realizes the truth of his predicament. Appropriately, the two principal words in the final distich are *Wille* and *Blut*. These two nouns, one abstract, the other concrete, sum up the essence of the full circle the poem travels. It is, at the poem's beginning, of his own free *will* that the young man enlists. But at the end, fully cognizant of his own *blood*-soaked self, this volunteer finds little consolation in affirming that his intentions were good.

"Letzter Brief nach Boston" (38–39) reinforces the notion of Vietnam as an overseas setting for an American war. Though not utilizing a poetic form per se, Fried borrows the formal structure of the Socratic method for this poem as a letter. In accordance with this structure, the poem employs a series of conditional clauses in which presumed ignorance of the matter under discussion serves as the starting point:

> Wenn ich weiß
> daß ich nicht mehr weiß
> wofür ich hier kämpfe
> ist mein Weiterkämpfen
> vielleicht nicht sinnlos

As in "Der Freiwillige" this poem grows in a cumulative fashion. Its effectiveness depends not so much on the conceptual terminology employed but rather in the textual entanglement reflecting the conscience-stricken young man's state of mind. Traditionally the Socratic method, with its inherent irony, makes use of the initial pretense of ignorance to gain a step up on the opponent. But this Platonic youth has no adversary other than himself. Thus, any momentary advantage gained necessarily becomes the detriment of the dramatic persona. Unlike "Der Freiwillige" this poem does not come full circle. Whereas the initial dilemma, as expressed in the doubts about fighting on, is directly linked to the concrete world of military service, the applied method of argumentation leads into a realm of conflicting abstract terms:

> und mein Unglaube
> an das Wissenkönnen des Sinns
> wird zum Glauben
> an das Wissen
> des Unsinns

Despair is heightened as logic provides no rational escape from an evermore perplexing situation. Eventually a loss of will prevails, and the letter concludes "ohne Glauben/ und Können und Wissen und Willen." Bormann views the conclusion as the deconstruction of the foregoing text into individual words, a trademark of postmodern poetry.[11] Although accurate, this interpretation requires elaboration in order to better illuminate Fried's stylistic method and thematic intent.

The final stanza begins: "Wenn ich nicht weiter will/ und nicht wollen kann" — two lines emphasizing both the strain exacted on one grappling with ethical concerns and the importance of human will. Volition is a crucial element in "Letzter Brief nach Boston," functioning much like a source of energy fueling the dramatic persona's sense of self-direction. In postmodern literature energy is understood in terms of its counterpart, entropy, a word originally coined for thermodynamics that can be defined as follows: the entropy of a system is the measure of the unavailability of its energy for

---

[11] See Bormann, 22.

conversion into mechanical work.[12] Whereas the first three stanzas of the poem are energetically winding upwards in a syllogistic frenzy, the final stanza finds the poem and its Socratic method lacking the energy required to sustain itself. The thermodynamic analogy applies in that the universe of the dramatic hero winds down due to a preponderance of entropy resulting from the absence of systemic sustenance in the form of will power. The reasoning process indeed deconstructs by breaking down into its constituent elements — words, and moreover, abstract concepts. Nevertheless, this is less attributable to a destructive force than to loss of cohesion heretofore provided by the subject's propensity to persevere. Therefore, any postmodernist reading of "Letzter Brief nach Boston" must focus on the dissipation of will resulting from an overly conscientious application of the Socratic method. Without the ability to convert the by-product of applied logic into a steadfast willingness to continue, the reasoning process must perforce self-deconstruct.

Although "Letzter Brief nach Boston" and "Der Freiwillige" incorporate sophisticated rhetorical techniques, Fried's poetry is generally known for his wordplays with the language. One example is "Logik" (25), the title of which must be understood on two levels, first formally and second in the more colloquial, here sarcastic, sense of the word.

Wenn es
gestattet ist
daß man
die Kinder
bestattet
dann
ist es
auch
erlaubt
daß man
die Bäume
entlaubt

---

[12] See *The Compact Edition of the OED*, vol. 1, A-O (1971; Oxford: Oxford UP, 1984), 879. See also Rudolf Arnheim, *Entropy and Art* (Berkeley: U of California P, 1971); and Thomas Pynchon's "Entropy" in Pynchon, *Slow Learner: Early Stories* (Boston: Little, 1984), 79–98.

Fried makes adroit use of interchanging verb prefixes. He posits phonetic likeness as a conditional basis for semantic identity. From the linguistic standpoint, the logic is sound; the human and ecological ramifications, however, make the reasoning process absurd. Fried's "Logik" demands a literal reading; its message, however, depends on an intrinsic effect of alienation entreating the reader to step back, apply common-sense logic, and then deny the propriety of both premise and conclusion.

Fried calls for another sort of reader participation in "Einbürgerung" (36), a poem noteworthy for its reduction to the bare minimum:

> Weiße Hände
> rotes Haar
> blaue Augen
>
> Weiße Steine
> rotes Blut
> blaue Lippen
>
> Weiße Knochen
> roter Sand
> blauer Himmel

Most noticeably absent here are the verbs. The text of the poem is reduced to a repeating series of three adjectives paired respectively with a varying sequence of substantives. Thus, each stanza presents a miniature still life, and the poem as a whole is analogous to a triptych with its three imagistic panels forming an implicit narrative line. Fried's mastery, then, lies in the economy of telling a story without the use of verbs.

From the first stanza — hands, hair, and eyes — one can imagine a human being. The blood of stanza two suggests a wound, blue lips its severity, and the stones a seriously wounded human lying prostrate. Stanza three implies a jump in time. The sand has turned red from the blood of the wound, and all that remains of the human being are white bones. The closing reference to blue sky is reminiscent of the cinematic technique of pulling focus, that is, lifting up and away from a ground-level, tight shot to an ever-widening, bird's-eye view of the scene. This technique often signals an impending conclusion; yet here no credits follow, nor does Fried append an explanatory footnote. There are no consequences to consider, no aftereffects to resolve. There is not even a proper burial. The landscape loses its human element as nature takes its unimpeded course.

The title "Einbürgerung" — with its political connotations — casts a revealing light on the contents of the three stanzas. As with many of Fried's poems, the title is to be read ironically. The text has nothing to do with conferring citizenship to an alien. The naturalization process as depicted here is quite literal, and therefore devoid of irony, in that the dead soldier simply becomes one with nature. (In this regard the German word *Einbürgerung* bears only a figurative link to the process of naturalization, whereas its English equivalent is directly tied to nature via its Latin derivation: *naturalis* from *natura* < *natus*.) The political allusions in the poem follow from the three colors used as adjectives: white, red, and blue. These colors clearly intimate the American Stars and Stripes, yet the French *tricolore* of Vietnam's colonial era cannot be overlooked. Due to the minimalist style, any political message must be deduced from the formal structure of the three stanzas. The reduction to adjectives and substantives forms three symmetrical constellations or modifier-noun clusters. The constancy of the color modifiers as juxtaposed with the variation in nouns creates a certain tension, thus adding to the political content. That the colors remain the same parallels the steadfast — if not obstinate — policy of the U.S. government in Vietnam.[13] Moreover, the color constancy is a reminder of the ongoing presence — whether French or American — of a foreign military power in Indo-China.

In the end, this poem focuses on a special category of soldier. If the ironic title depicts the verbatim return to nature, then its irony can only be understood by inverting its literal meaning: denaturalization. The content of the three sparse stanzas is, after all, decidedly dehumanizing in that a human body decomposes. And with such a loss of life comes, in effect, a figurative loss of citizenship in that this soldier's service to the homeland led to a fate never to be determined with certainty. Thus, Fried's "Einbürgerung" can be read as homage to all soldiers assumed dead and listed as missing in action.

Much of the controversy stirred up by Fried's *und Vietnam und* was fueled by Peter Härtling and Günter Grass. Härtling's review-essay "Gegen rhetorische Ohnmacht: Kann man über Vietnam Gedichte

---

[13] See Theobaldy/Zürcher, 100.

schreiben?"[14] answers the question of its subtitle with an emphatic no. The primary objections raised by Härtling can be summarized as follows: Fried relies on secondhand material to voice his protest, and the dependency on news reports negates his legitimacy as an antiwar poet. Härtling's criticism of Fried is not to be misunderstood as support of U.S. aggression in Indo-China. In fact, his essay contains an obligatory paragraph outlining the atavistic tendencies and horrific nature of the American war machine. Härtling's point: he shares Fried's moral outrage; his problem: how to give it literary expression? The answer is that it cannot be done. Any attempt to do so is doomed to failure since, according to his criteria, Da Nang and Hanoi defy metrics and the geography is not poetic. Härtling adopts a similar posture in his discussion of the overall antiwar movement of the late 1960s, essentially a diatribe against the younger generation, questioning the forms of dissent, and ridiculing the frivolities of the "Vietniks." His put-down, however, ignores one simple fact: that these allegedly frivolous adolescents react politically should, in itself, give pause for thought.[15]

Günter Grass raised objections by citing the political impotence of Vietnam protest poems. Unlike Härtling, his rebuttal takes a specific literary form as an essay in verse. The section "ZORN ÄRGER WUT" of *Ausgefragt* features four poems in which Grass speaks out against the protest poem.[16] The first poem, "In Ohnmacht gefallen" begins:

> Wir lesen Napalm und stellen Napalm uns vor.
> Da wir uns Napalm nicht vorstellen können,
> lesen wir über Napalm, bis wir uns mehr
> unter Napalm vorstellen können.
> Jetzt protestieren wir gegen Napalm.

---

[14] Originally published in *Der Monat* 19.5 (1967): 57–61; rpt. in Rudolf Wolff, ed., *Erich Fried: Gespräche und Kritiken* (Bonn: Bouvier, 1986), 151–59.

[15] See Harald Hartung, "Poesie und Vietnam: Eine Entgegnung," *Der Monat* 19.7 (1967): 76–79, here 77.

[16] Günter Grass, *Ausgefragt* (Neuwied and Berlin: Luchterhand, 1967), 57–69, Grass's contribution to the 1967 international program of *Lyrik und Essay* organized by Walter Höllerer and sponsored by the LCB. See also Höllerer, *Ein Gedicht und sein Autor*, 180–91. Rpt. in Günter Grass, *Gedichte und Kurzprosa*, ed. Volker Neuhaus and Daniela Hermes (Göttingen: Steidl, 1997) vol. 1 of *Werkausgabe*, 174-82.

Here napalm is used as a figure of speech carrying meaning beyond the real and concrete. The intent is to test, if not tease, the powers of imagination, and the mode of argument leads human reason *ad absurdum*:

> Aber es gibt, so lesen wir,
> Schlimmeres als Napalm.
> Schnell protestieren wir gegen Schlimmeres.

Peter Rühmkorf replied to such charges by defining the political function of Fried's Vietnam poems. The primary purpose of the protest poem, he maintains, is education, and with this comes the duty to sow seeds of doubt.[17] If Grass attacks the "Vietnam Complex" of German writers, adding that Vietnam is too easy a target for the antiwar poet, Rühmkorf counters by concentrating on the practical aspect of Vietnam poems and how each functions as a decoding device following in the Brechtian tradition of didactic poetry. Moreover, Rühmkorf recognizes the participatory nature of such poetry in that the reader discovers truth by means of a subtle disclosure strategy.[18] Hartung argues in parallel fashion, calling Fried's Vietnam poems demonstrations in the dual sense of the word: explanation by example and protest.[19]

The debate over Fried's Vietnam poems led to misconceptions about his image of America. His poem "Amerika" (61) reveals an attitude often overlooked. The title is significant for its simplicity. There is no suggestion of the "other" America as a gesture in deference to those Americans not in agreement with official policy; nevertheless, Fried draws a clear line between two segments of 1960s American society. First and foremost, "Amerika" is an expression of solidarity signifying that international protest against the U.S. government is justified by the same dissent within the American populace. Thus, this poem is both about and for a special class of American citizens:

---

[17] See Peter Rühmkorf, "Die Mord- und Brandsache," *Der Spiegel* 24 April 1967: 166–67; and Rühmkorf, "Haben wir zu viele Vietnam Gedichte?" *Konkret* 5 (1967): 36.

[18] See Rühmkorf, "Das Gedicht als Lügendetektor," in *Die Jahre die Ihr kennt*, 214–42.

[19] Hartung, "Poesie und Vietnam," 78–79.

> Die Hungerstreiker
> die Studenten die auf dem Protestmarsch
> niedergeschlagen werden
> mit Hickoryknüppeln
> und einer der sich verbrannte
> in Washington

The second stanza assesses the import of these protesters by means of a not so subtle distinction:

> Die werden wichtiger für Amerika sein
> als der sich die Galle hält
> mit der Hand
> die nie mehr vor Zeugen
> seinen Hund
> an den Ohren hochheben wird

This sense of long-term confidence in the face of present-day setbacks is carried over into the final stanza where Fried offers a modicum of American self-esteem:

> Wenn es später irgendwo heißt:
> Sie sind alle wie der mit der Galle
> kann Amerika zeigen auf die
> die der mit der Galle nicht mochte
> Hungerstreiker Geschlagene Verbrannte
> und kann sagen: Woher waren denn die?

"Amerika" is, then, a corrective to brusque judgments and *en masse* characterizations of a country. To accomplish his aim, Fried adopts an unsophisticated approach, concentrating on the polarity of American society resulting from Vietnam. In democratic fashion, both sides are left nameless. Since Fried does not specify any one protester as representative of the opposition,[20] the president of the

---

[20] This is not to overlook the motto *in memoriam Norman Morrison*, for the protestor "who burned himself to death." See George Starbuck's poem "Of Late" in Walter Lowenfels, ed., *Where is Vietnam? American Poets Respond* (New York: Doubleday, 1967), 129, an anthology taking its title from a poem by Lawrence Ferlinghetti also appearing in *Kursbuch* 6 (1966): 1–2.

United States remains "der mit der Galle." Dissenters are described in terms of what they do or is done to them: "Hungerstreiker Geschlagene Verbrannte." Lyndon B. Johnson, on the other hand, is identified through allusions to media coverage of private matters shaping his image in the eyes of the American public.

Among Fried's most provocative poems is "Gleichheit Brüderlichkeit" (55–56), where he renders Germany and Vietnam identical. Here are the first four stanzas:

Vietnam ist Deutschland
sein Schicksal ist unser Schicksal
Die Bomben für seine Freiheit
sind Bomben für unsere Freiheit

Unser Bundeskanzler Erhard
ist Marschall Ky
General Nguyen Van Thieu
ist Präsident Lübke

Die Amerikaner
sind auch dort die Amerikaner
Katholiken und Protestanten
sind dort Katholiken

doch die Sozialdemokraten
sind die Buddhisten
die Gewerkschaften sind die Vietcong
Hanoi ist Pankow

The basis for the likeness expressed in line one is that both countries are divided, but Fried's approach transcends the basics and casts this premise in a more controversial light. Stanza two contains the most confrontational lines in that West German politicians are equated with the leaders of South Vietnam. Yet, these alleged identities warrant deliberation in conjunction with assertions made in stanza three. Fried creates, as it were, a political triangle with America as the common partner to respective halves of both countries. Within this arrangement, South Vietnam and West Germany demonstrate their similarity in

---

See also the German edition of this anthology, *Wo ist Vietnam? 89 amerikanische Dichter gegen den Krieg in Vietnam* (Darmstadt: Melzer, 1968).

terms of shared ties with the United States, the one undeniable factor lending legitimacy to Fried's daring comparisons. Moreover, stanza four suggests that West German-American ties are based on shared cold war attitudes and instances of red-baiting tactics.[21] Typical of Fried's style, this poem does more to create a context for its title than vice versa. On first impression, the heading "Gleichheit Brüderlichkeit" reads as a truncated version of the slogan of the French Revolution. The sense here, however, differs from its original usage. In fact, one may conclude that in the absence of *Liberté*, the meaning of the remaining two components is altered radically. Thus, *Gleichheit* conveys less a meaning of equality as an unalienable right of humankind and more a sense of identity as in a mathematical equation. Similarly, *Brüderlichkeit* loses its connotation of fraternity as a quality of being brotherly, and instead comes to insinuate a brotherhood of rogues.

Erich Fried's effect on the German political poem since 1966 can be explained, in part, by the unique blend of influences on his poetry. Although German critics invariably point to Bertolt Brecht, other influential voices are left unmentioned. Having been uprooted from his Austrian homeland at the age of seventeen, Fried represents a second generation of German poetry on foreign soil. Unlike the first generation of writers in exile, he did not arrive in London with an established voice and style. As a result, Fried developed and maintained his own artistic autonomy by successfully merging two divergent cultures. He was able to draw on his own native tradition and the works of German expressionism, then add the by-products of his work as translator. Ever wary of exclusive tags, Fried was quick to point out the broader picture when others chose a more limiting view of his poetic techniques. If critics suggest Fried's translations of Dylan Thomas explain certain nuances in his poetry, then Fried will clarify the correlation by alluding to common influences and interests, for example, mutual admiration for writers such as Hopkins, Joyce, Owen, and Cummings — names highlighting the Anglo-American forces at work in his poetry.[22] Even if his epigrams lack the bravura of Dylan Thomas, Fried displays more than a touch of the Welshman's verve. From James

---

[21] See Hahn, 39.

[22] See Fried, afterword, *Befreiung von der Flucht*, 142.

Joyce and E. E. Cummings come both an eye and ear for the precise, innovative use of language, to say nothing of the former's literary life in exile and the latter's "bad boy" image. If Fried fails to reflect the religious, indeed Christ-centered poetry of Gerard Manley Hopkins, he does share the Jesuit's steadfast moral stance and support for the underdog. And without a doubt, Fried's penchant for the gruesome detail can be traced directly to Wilfred Owen who, in spite of a promising future cut short by the First World War, remains a paragon of twentieth-century antiwar poets, due to his depiction of the technological horrors of modern warfare.

With this background and the single-issue focus of *und Vietnam und*, Fried initiated a new course in German poetry. The attempts of Grass, Härtling, and others to deny the viability of the Vietnam protest poem did little to stem the resultant trend. If anything, their efforts — representative of the conservative literary establishment — simply incited a younger, emerging generation of poets to prove them wrong. Fried's significance is that he first provided an impetus and then demonstrated the manifold stylistic possibilities for approaching the subject matter. Furthermore, his overt partisanship fostered an aggressive brand of protest and gave new meaning to the concept of a poem's intrinsic value.[23] Like the war itself, Fried's Vietnam poems forced both readers and writers to take sides, and the resulting divisions within literary circles laid the groundwork for subsequent developments in German poetry. Accordingly, the following chapter will examine select protest poems from 1967 onward with an eye for how politically engaged poets followed the course established by Erich Fried.

---

[23] Criticism of the United States for its military intervention in Indo-China also gave rise to growing support for North Vietnam in its struggle against an imperialist power. In conjunction with the February 1968 *Internationale Vietnam Kongreß* convened in West Berlin, an anthology of poems and speeches was published entitled *gegen den krieg in vietnam* in which thirty-nine authors voiced their protest. According to the copyright page, net proceeds from this anthology went for medical aid to North Vietnam and the FNL. See riewert qu. tode, ed., *gegen den krieg in vietnam* (Berlin: amBEATion, 1968).

6: Kilroy Was Here:
Vietnam and the Image of America

HÄRTLING'S PRIMARY CRITICISM of Fried's Vietnam poems is the poet's dependence on secondhand information. One category of protest poems is exempt from such charges, those where any mention of the war is indirect — where focus is on the media and the misuse of language in reporting the facts. An example is Uwe Timm's "Bundesdeutsche Kriegsberichterstattung,"[1] a poem based entirely on quotations taken from the West German press:

> Heimtückisch überfiel der Vietkong das Dorf
> das von den Amerikanern tapfer verteidigt wurde
>
> Mit Hubschraubern griffen die Amerikaner ein Dorf an
> das von dem Vietkong fanatisch verteidigt wurde
>
> Hinterrücks griffen Vietkong-Einheiten
> die amerikanischen Stellungen an
>
> Frontal griffen amerikanische Panzereinheiten
> die Stellungen des Vietkong an

Related material is paired in order to highlight differences in vocabulary. Adverbs are the key in reporting how the war is waged: Americans fight bravely and engage in frontal attacks, while the Vietcong battle fanatically and employ underhanded practices. Thus, the press conveys a sense of fair play on the part of the Americans and a lack thereof by the Vietcong:

> Rücksichtslos metzelte der Vietkong
> eine amerikanische Militärpatrouille nieder
>
> Überraschend stellten die Amerikaner
> eine Patrouille des Vietkong

---

[1] Uwe Timm, *Widersprüche* (Hamburg: Neue Presse, 1971), 21.

In einer Woche
wurden knapp 4000 tote Vietkong gezählt

244 Amerikaner fielen
gegenüber nur 90 in der Vorwoche

The final two couplets say a great deal about the value of human life. The purely quantitative aspect of the reports suggests that notably fewer — although growing — losses translate into victories for the Americans. More telling is how the Vietcong dead are tallied up and rounded off, while the number of Americans who honorably fell is given in precise figures.

All information here is presented without commentary or judgment. Timm questions neither the implied honor of the Americans nor the insinuated guile of the Vietcong. Any conclusions to be drawn are made by the reader, and the methodology of the poem directs attention away from the war so that the verdict necessarily falls against the West German press for collusion. Arnfrid Astel's poem "Neue Waffe"[2] bears likeness to Timm's war report through its appropriation of previously printed material. Like Timm, Astel voices no explicit criticism, either of the media or military personnel, and refrains from poetic embellishment to heighten the effect of his message. Unlike Timm, however, Astel's purpose is not to expose the dubious methods of the press. His approach is more direct and goal more fundamental — to shock the reader:

Im «Stern» vom 16. Mai lese ich,
daß die Amerikaner in Vietnam
neben Gas und dergleichen
auch ein neues Gewehr erproben.
Jeder Treffer mit der Waffe
ist tödlich. Das Geschoß
benimmt sich im Körper
des Opfers wie ein Kreisel,
wodurch ein hydrodynamischer
Choc ausgelöst wird, der

---

[2] Arnfrid Astel, *Notstand* (Wuppertal: Hammer, 1968); see also Jürgen Theobaldy, ed., *Und ich bewege mich doch: Gedichte vor und nach 1968* (Munich: Beck, 1977), 60–61.

das gesamte Nervensystem lähmt.
Ein amerikanischer Soldat schreibt:
Ich sah, wie ein Vietcong
in die Hand getroffen wurde.
Er war sofort tot.

Besides identifying his source, the poet's only contribution is to highlight pertinent information and to provide line breaks in accordance with the syntax and impartial tone of the cited material. Unlike poems by Fried and Timm, "Neue Waffe" does not require a reader who participates in a reasoning process leading to a desired conclusion. Here the reader, like the victim in the poem, plays a passive role undergoing an experience that "numbs the entire nervous system." The overall effect is one-dimensional; nonetheless, the poem is significant for its portrayal of the U.S. war effort in Vietnam. Astel introduces a new weapon by means of a quasi-scientific description comprehensible to the lay public. And despite its objective tone, the poem imparts a thoroughly negative image of the United States by suggesting that American know-how has perfected the science of killing.

"Ein Foto"[3] by F. C. Delius is equally shocking, but uses quotations to create a most original poem out of a scant amount of original material:

1
1966 sehen wir unter anderen Fotos aus Vietnam dies:
Vier Soldaten der US-Army
(Gesichter wie auch sonst in Fotoalben)
warten auf den Auslöser.
Zwei halten Köpfe an den Haaren,
die an zwei Leichen,
die weiter vorne liegen, fehlen.

2
1967 lesen wir:
Im Unterschied zu früheren Geschlechtern haben die heute
Herrschenden nicht nur gelernt, ihre Untaten zu verbergen,

---

[3] F. C. Delius, *Wenn wir, bei Rot: Achtunddreißig Gedichte* (Berlin: Wagenbach, 1969), 60–61.

sondern auch, das Verbergen ihrer Untaten zu verbergen. Das verbergen sie z.B. dadurch, daß sie scheinbar, in gewissem Sinne sogar wirklich, ihre blutigen Aktionen präsentieren. Da sie diese aber nicht anders präsentieren als jene »fiction«, nicht anders als jene Greuelszenen, die sie in ihren Filmen und Fernsehthrillers täglich präsentieren, können sie damit rechnen, daß das an Filmmord und Filmblut und Filmgrausamkeit gewohnte Publikum die Abbildungen der wirklichen Greuel genauso konsumieren wird wie die tägliche Greuelkost, daß es gar nicht in der Lage sein wird, sich selbst zuzurufen: »Dies geschieht *wirklich*!«

3

1968 hören wir:
Wir, die wir wahrlich nichts zu verlieren haben, sind in ein hübsches Spiel sozialen Protestes verwickelt und versuchen, einen moralischen Einfluß auf Menschen auszuüben, die kein moralisches Bewußtsein haben.
Protestieren ist ein intellektueller Akt, so als würde man sagen: »Mein Herr, ich protestiere!«, wenn man geohrfeigt wird. Widerstand leisten heißt, nicht nur sagen: »Ich will nicht«, es heißt: »Ich werde dafür kämpfen, daß jeder andere auch nicht will.«
Widerstand leisten heißt: Ich werde nicht nur nicht dulden, was die Kapitalisten tun, sondern ich werde sie hindern zu tun, was sie wollen.

4

1969 sehen wir das Foto
anders als drei Jahre vorher.
Wir drucken es hier noch einmal nach:
Vier Soldaten der US-Army
(Gesichter wie auch sonst in Fotoalben)
warten auf den Auslöser.
Zwei halten Köpfe an den Haaren,
die an zwei Leichen,
die weiter vorne liegen, fehlen.

As explained in notes appended to *Wenn wir, bei Rot*, parts two and three are direct quotations from an essay by the philosopher Günther Anders and a speech given by the American political scientist Dale A. Smith at the 1968 *Internationale Vietnam Kongreß* in West Berlin. The description of the photo in part one and then repeated in part four builds a framework enclosing the two quotations. However, the poem *in toto* reverses the effect of the structural relationship captured in print.[4] As a result, the two quotations frame the 1966 photo with new meaning in 1969. Delius is not attempting to document the daily atrocities in Vietnam;[5] his purpose is to provide evidence of a learning process associated with the protest movement over the course of three years. Thus, the four-part poem functions like an information packet providing educational material on how to build support for the opposition. If the collective *we* is numbed by the exploits of American headhunters in 1966, then the essay by Anders will serve to reveal the devious machinations of political leaders behind the scenes while Smith's speech outlines what action can be taken. By returning to the photo in part four Delius not only provides a sense of symmetry to the poem but also reaffirms the sense of moral outrage that set the learning process in motion.

One step removed from direct quotation is the presentation of facts as if lifted from a source-book. Such a poem gives the impression of relaying information that is, or at least should be, common knowledge. In effect, the magnitude of the message outweighs any need to document whence it came. Arnold Leifert's "weißer Riese"[6] is an example of this practice:

> zehn von hundert
> der Jungen

---

[4] See Klaus Schuhmann, *Weltbild und Poetik* (Berlin and Weimar: Aufbau, 1979), 437–38.

[5] As to atrocities committed in Vietnam, see the "Einzelfälle" section in Erich Fried, *Unter Nebenfeinden: Fünfzig Gedichte* (Berlin: Wagenbach, 1970), in particular the poem "Aufzählung" (61) that begins: "Fünfhundertsiebenundsechzig alte Männer Kinder und Frauen/ erschossen in einem Dorf das My Lai heißt oder Song My." In this defiantly anti-epigrammatic poem Fried lists a number of incidents of civilian slaughter to underscore the fact that My Lai was not an "individual case." Most effective is the choice to write out the number 567 in order to intensify the quantitative impact.

[6] In Frank Brunner, Arnim Juhre, and Heinz Kulas, ed., *Wir Kinder von Marx und Coca-Cola* (Wuppertal: Hammer, 1971), 54.

der Staaten
sind schwarz
vierzig von hundert
der US-Toten
in Vietnam
sind schwarz

Statistics supersede commentary, and the discrepancy in the figures says less about the cost of American aggression abroad than the fabric of America's Great Society at home. The only authorial intrusion occurs in the title — "white giant" — thus suggesting that the Vietnam War is another of the iniquitous means by which the white race maintains its domination.

Joachim Fuhrmann's "Guam"[7] takes a similar approach in sharing specific information with the aim of teaching a lesson. Yet where Leifert relies on understatement, Fuhrmann opts for a more pointed attack:

Guam ist eine Insel im Pazifik
B-52 bezeichnet amerikanische Bomber
die starten von der Insel Guam
im Pazifik und fliegen westwärts
bis sie das Meer des Friedens
hinter sich verschwinden sehen
bringen ihren Gruß und klinken
und übersetzen den Menschen unten was
Frieden heißt auf Amerikanisch.

Just as the crews of the B-52s watch the Pacific Ocean disappearing behind them, the objective tone of the poem fades with line six. In its place comes Fuhrmann's cynicism, first manifested in the word *Gruß* and then topped off by the crowning metaphorical touch of the final line. "Guam" makes the most of its didactic attributes by holding its firepower — like the B-52 bombers — until the final third of the poem. Thus, the poem itself is on a bombing run: a retaliatory mission to avenge the Vietnamese recipients of American greetings. In light of its partisan potential, it is fitting that a variation

---

[7] In *Wir Kinder von Marx und Coca-Cola*, 15.

of the final line — "Frieden auf amerikanisch" — serves as a title for a section of the East German anthology *Denkzettel*.[8] Furthermore, "Guam" reveals an attitude typical of the German view of the Vietnam War. Whereas the American perception, as influenced by media coverage during the war and Hollywood films, sees Vietnam in terms of a foot soldier engaged in jungle warfare, German protest accentuated the air war and the tonnage dropped from the relative safety of high-flying B-52s.[9]

Other Vietnam poems instruct by means of historical references, a method we have seen employed by Fried, underscoring the fact of how history is often shamelessly repeated. Harry Oberländer's "orte"[10] is another study in comparative geography:

> als wir hörten
> es sei abermals
> ein dorf in vietnam
> samt bewohnern
> hausrat
> vieh
> endgültig
> von allen landkarten verschwunden
> brannten wir einen fleck in den atlas
> und nannten ihn
> lidice

The power of Oberländer's poem extends beyond its symbolic gesture in alluding to the Czech village with the name signifying the ruthless destruction of an entire community. The *abermals* of line two emphasizes how this practice became commonplace during phases of the Vietnam war.

In order to present a subjective impression without the overt intrusion of personal opinion, another category of Vietnam poems

---

[8] See *Denkzettel*, 393 and 401 where Fuhrmann's "Guam" appears.

[9] See, e.g., "Infamer als Rambo? Ein Gespräch mit Günther Giesenfeld über Oliver Stones Vietnam-Film *Platoon*," *die tageszeitung*, 14 May 1987, belittling the notion of heroic man-to-man combat in light of the daily carpet-bombing missions carried out by the USAF.

[10] In *Wir Kinder von Marx und Coca-Cola*, 14.

achieves its aim by blending objective reports on the war with scenes from the outside world. These protest poems rely on contrasts that cannot be ignored and a reader who will draw the appropriate conclusions. One example is Günther Weisenborn's "Mekong-Ballade,"[11] a poem that presents, true to its ballad form, a dramatic episode by means of a simple narrative. Weisenborn focuses on one brief moment — a span of three seconds — and what happens on opposite sides of the globe:

> Im Dschungel ein Dorf. Es zwitschern drei Schüsse,
> nicht länger als drei Sekunden lang.
> In der ersten wird ein Bambushaus durchschlagen,
> In der zweiten wird die Kugel in ein Kind geschickt,
> In der dritten eine Pflanze, nein, eine Frau geknickt.
>
> Nie wird sie ihr Kind mehr nach Hause tragen.
> Zur selben Zeit sitzt in Ohio ein Mann,
> der am Tisch mit seiner Familie frühstücken kann.
> In der ersten Sekunde hebt er die Tasse ans Kinn,
> in der zweiten stellt er sie wieder hin,
> in der dritten Sekunde hört er noch keinen Schuß,
> weil er rasch in die Stahlfabrik fahren muß.

While "Mekong-Ballade" can claim no absolute authenticity, plausibility is on its side. Even if the depicted simultaneity is but a literary device, its service to the poem — like rhyme and meter — is to heighten the impact of the political message. The poet creates, in a word, urgency, and he does so by means of more than the obvious contrast in settings. The verb *zwitschern* in line one, for instance, prepares the reader for the chirping sound of birds in a jungle village. Instead, three shots (a direct reference to how American soldiers were trained to fire their M-16 rifles) replace the expected with a cadence accenting the description of what follows in the remainder of the stanza. The corrective *nein* in line five, besides providing a clever rhythmical caesura, indicates the rapidity with which all this happens. That is to say, the human eye cannot focus quickly enough to identify all particulars within the scene. Furthermore,

---

[11] Quoted here from *Denkzettel*, 401–2.

the mistake acts as a hidden simile suggesting how the woman —
like a plant — bends and falls. And finally, the intrusive *nein* is just
as much recognition of visual error as an exclamatory refusal to believe what has transpired.

Stanza two shows a similar adroit use of language, especially
the modal verb *kann* in line three. Doubtless, the choice is attributable as much to rhyme as to any intrinsic meaning, but here is an
example of how the demands of form enhance the capacity of
content. That this man in Ohio *can* sit down to breakfast with his
family emphasizes those basic privileges he enjoys as compared to
the Vietnamese family in stanza one. Although the poem draws
upon strong pacifist-humanist principles, its ultimate purpose is to
take a firm stand against capitalism and the American military-
industrial complex. As seen in the following couplet from stanza
three, Weisenborn's objectivity begins to fade once he has communicated the details of the three-second interlude:

> Die einen verdienen Dollars an jedem Schuß
> die anderen sterben, weil man sich wehren muß.

Thus, the focus is not on the soldier who fired the shots, but on
the one man, as everyman, representing those who live off the mu-
nitions industry.

Other poems move one step further into the subjective realm
by combining Vietnam with experiences from everyday life. In such
poems Vietnam triggers reflection, and the lyric persona contrasts
personal matters with events in a war-torn land. Fried provides an
example with "Gespräch über Bäume,"[12] the opening lines of
which read:

> Seit der Gärtner die Zweige gestutzt hat
> sind meine Äpfel größer
> Aber die Blätter des Birnbaums
> sind krank. Sie rollen sich ein
>
> In Vietnam sind die Bäume entlaubt

---

[12] Fried, *Anfechtungen: Fünfzig Gedichte* (Berlin: Wagenbach, 1967), 60.

Meine Kinder sind alle gesund
Doch mein jüngerer Sohn macht mir Sorgen
er hat sich nicht eingelebt
in der neuen Schule

In Vietnam sind die Kinder tot

The title is a direct reference to Brecht's poem "An die Nachgeborenen," and the first stanza suggests that a conversation about trees remains a crime.[13] Fried's use of irony diminishes the mundane concerns of the lyric persona through a series of intrusive references to Vietnam. Thus, the refrain line "In Vietnam. . . . " echoes like an inner voice of conscience lending a sense of proportion to personal affairs.

Whereas Fried's "Gespräch über Bäume" employs ironic counterpoint, Nicolas Born applies a different mode of irony in "Fünfzehnte Reihe,"[14] a poem depicting the emotional detachment of moviegoers seated in the fifteenth row watching a newsreel about Vietnam before the start of the feature film. This theme of emotional distance is also found in Roman Ritter's "Der Krieg ist anderswo."[15] Comparable to Weisenborn's "Mekong-Ballade," this poem describes a restaurant meal in Germany concurrently with an aerial attack in Vietnam. Instead of separate stanzas for two spheres of action, Ritter combines both in a series of couplets.

während der ober das gedeck auflegt
gehen die bomber auf angriffshöhe

während wir allerseits guten appetit wünschen
fliegen die bomber das ziel an

während ich das besteckmesser ergreife
klinken die bomben aus

---

[13] See Brecht, vol. 9, *Gedichte 2*, 722–25. See also Hiltrud Gnüg, "Die Aufhebung des Naturgedichts in der Lyrik der Gegenwart," in *Lyrik — von allen Seiten*, 267–68.

[14] Nicolas Born, *Wo mir der Kopf steht* (Cologne and Berlin: Kiepenheuer & Witsch, 1970); rpt. in Born, *Gedichte 1967–1978* (Reinbek bei Hamburg: Rowohlt, 1978), 75.

[15] Quoted here from *kürbiskern* 3 (1967): 112.

The craft of this poem lies in pairing disparate activities according to analogous procedural stages. Present-tense verbs create a sense of immediacy, and the couplets work best when enhanced by diction as in the third distich where *ergreife* suggests another verb with the same root but different prefix: *angreife*. In similar fashion, stanza four effectively links the two story lines, adding to the inherent tension created by the repetitious form and deliberate, step-by-step narrative style:

> während ich mich unauffällig nach der serviette bücke
> sucht man im zielgebiet deckung auf

The form used in "Der Krieg ist anderswo" contributes to a degree of impatience in the reader. If we assume a greater sense of urgency in the Vietnam half of the poem, then each step forward in telling this tale is followed by one step backward with the intrusion of the restaurant scene. Creating a sense of restlessness in the reader is, however, crucial. Ritter resorts to a self-deprecating lyric persona in order to address the general public. The purpose is agitation, for the casual demeanor displayed in these routine occurrences becomes incongruous when set side-by-side with everyday life in Vietnam. Thus, when Ritter writes

> während ich mir die lippen abtupfe
> wird die zahl der verletzten unübersehbar

the reader recoils in disgust at such pretentious politesse. The war may be elsewhere, but reader identification with the depicted scene will make its presence felt.

Perhaps the classic example of a poem combining introspective reflection, an autobiographical style, and Vietnam is Günter Herburger's "soso Vietnam aha."[16] This poem is best understood when read alongside Herburger's essay "Dogmatisches über Gedichte,"[17] an engaging polemic against traditional poetry and the hermetic poem. Herburger calls for poetry without restrictions as to lan-

---

[16] In *Kursbuch* 10 (1967): 162–63, later appearing in Herburger, *Training* (Neuwied and Berlin: Luchterhand, 1969) with the title "Vietnam" and its stanza sequence altered.

[17] The essay preceding "soso Vietnam aha" in *Kursbuch* 10 (1967): 150–61.

guage, form, or content. The more refined these conventions, the more confined the poet's possibilities for expression. For Herburger any subject matter is appropriate, and the lyric persona must reign supreme. Furthermore, Herburger — like Höllerer — takes a stand against the aphoristic tendency in poetry that promotes the pithy observation at the expense of more lengthy, associative thought processes. The poem "soso Vietnam aha" is, then, Herburger's theory put into practice. If, however, "Dogmatisches über Gedichte" heralds a grand new style of poetry, "soso Vietnam aha" initially makes no great claim for itself. In fact, the opening lines build little sense of expectation or promise:

> Was weiß ich, was wißt ihr, was möchten wir gern wissen,
> jetzt wenn ich schreibe, ein großes Thema suche wie damals,
> als ich nachts auf dem Fensterbrett saß und nichts mehr half,
> Glühwürmchen, Flötenspiel, die dicken Weiber, die ich
>   haben wollte,
> beinahe wäre ich gesprungen, mir tat das Kreuz weh.

Herburger approaches the topic indirectly, introducing selected personal particulars as a starting point for the ensuing chain of subjective impressions in which Vietnam surfaces. Memory plays a decisive role as reflection on the past enhances perspective on the present:

> Mein Vater in Uniform, ein Brustbild, das mich rührt,
>   wenn ich
> an geschätzte Belichtungszeiten denke,
>   Entfernungsmesserschritte
> zwischen Opfer und Selbstauslöser, da wurden neulich
>   am selben Tag
> Ein Lagerdenkmal geweiht, ein Soldatenfriedhof
> und ein Arzt, der Juden geholfen hat.

These recollections serve to establish a number of thematic features at work in the poem: a military motif, the indelible ties of a father-son relationship, and the delicate matter of victims and their persecutors. For example, in the account of a daily breakfast routine, the lyric persona targets the subject matter as if through a range finder:

> Mein Jagdstand ist der Frühstückstisch, wo ich ein weiches Ei
> Bissen für Bissen auf Nachrichten verteile, die nacheinander
> gekaut werden, ich brösle Toast, überschlage Kalorien,
> spüle mit Tee nach, schmecke wie üblich genau

The impression conveyed is that of tedious forethought and vigilance, of concentration bordering on meditation. Yet this selfsame persona is prone to trivial personal distractions and vanity at the most inappropriate times:

> und wenn ich meinen Sohn, der hinter mir sitzt,
> in den Kindergarten fahre, sehe ich im Rückspiegel
> meine Zunge, die Goldkronen abtastet,
> kippt, vibriert, in der feuchten Höhle steht und vorschießt,
> draußen herrscht starker Verkehr, ich werde aufpassen
>   müssen.

Then in the one stanza with sustained attention to Vietnam, the lyric persona reassumes a circumspect pose, triggered by the broadcast media:

> Oder vor dem Fernsehkasten auf der Lauer liegen,
> denn jetzt könnte ich schreien, wenn endlich wieder
>   geschossen wird,
> sie sollen Gefangene köpfen, pfählen, auf dem Boden
>   gespreizt
> lebendigen Leibes, wie es heißt, ausweiden, man sieht es
>   nicht,
> hört nur davon, fliegt über dem Dschungel mit,
> auf dem der Flugzeugschatten, dann ein Feuerball liegt,
> geliertes Benzin klebt fest, frißt brennend durch die Haut,
> Großvater sang, das Gewehr sei des Soldaten Braut.

This stanza illustrates the principles of Herburger's "Dogmatisches über Gedichte" in action. The details and images shown here are more than the poet's projections as the lyric persona is literally projected into the scene. Here we find no coldly detached viewer as in Born's "Fünfzehnte Reihe." Senses keen, the lyric persona lies in wait before the television set absorbing the suspense of the moment. Totally engrossed, this viewer becomes part of the spectacle flying along with the camera crew relaying the action. Yet Herburger does not exploit the event for the sake of a vicarious thrill. If anything, the lyric persona succumbs to the tension with the need to scream when the stillness is broken by gunshots. Likewise, he voices no disappointment when told of but not shown atrocities. Hearing will suffice when a fertile imagination is at work.

The language in this stanza warrants closer attention. Herburger's use of *auf der Lauer* is another example of his appropriation of combat terminology to describe the lyric persona. In addition to its intrinsic meaning, to lie in ambush, the sound quality rings of *auf die Dauer* and suggests a considerable amount of time spent in front of the television. The compound noun *Flugzeugschatten* establishes point of view, creating a multilevel perspective with the treetops of the jungle dividing the victims on the ground below from the assailants in the airplane above. By directing attention to the airplane-shadow, Herburger makes the presence of the fighter plane all the more threatening, and with minimal delay this dark image atop the jungle explodes into a fireball. Herburger identifies the cause of the fireball as *geliertes Benzin*, infusing the language with a tactile quality and forcing the reader to perceive of napalm in terms of its glutinous nature, not the chemical compounds — *na*phthene + *palm*itate — used in its manufacture. Moreover, the consonantal repetition in the words *fest* and *frißt* adds a sizzling auditory coefficient to the visual component, thus sharpening the image of both foliage and human skin being consumed by flames. The final line of the stanza brings a sudden shift in perspective. The rhyme of *Haut* with *Braut* not only eases the transition from Vietnam to a German military song two generations removed but also heightens the irony in this commentary on twentieth-century weaponry. Technological advancements, as well as jungle warfare, have relegated the rifle to a subordinate status. Thus, the song sounds more than old-fashioned when accompanying the Vietnam footage: as difficult as it may be to imagine a soldier's intimate relationship with his rifle, the thought is utterly absurd when that weapon becomes an incendiary bomb.

If this combat stanza illuminates the *aha* of the title, then the opening lines of the following stanza reverberate of *soso*:

Sitzend auf meinem Balkon in der windgeschützten Ecke,
prüfe ich die Aussicht, sehe Häuser, Straßen, Nachbarn,
auf die ich je nach Laune hinunterfluchen kann,
mit dem Klappmesser fuchtle ich, wenn mir nichts mehr
    einfällt,
wie ich es im Kino gelernt habe, am Schreibtisch, Dreck
wächst unter den Fingernägeln, wird täglich entfernt.

The poem has already reached its dramatic climax, and this, the penultimate stanza, ushers in the corresponding elements of peripeteia and falling action. Having retreated to a sheltered vantage point overlooking the comparative calm of a residential district, the lyric persona is no longer caught in the crossfire. Vietnam now seems like dirt under the fingernails for it, too, can be removed simply by turning off the television set. Herburger's persona, ever upbeat, retakes his position center stage:

Heilige Mutter Gottes von Portugal, Spanien, Griechenland,
wo ich in der Sonne gegammelt habe auf Freitreppen,
als ich photographiert wurde im Hagel von Zigarettenkippen,
immer laut ein fröhlich hüpfendes Beispiel, solange ich
für die nächste Nacht eine Platzkarte der vielsprachig
gerammelt vollen Jugendherberge in der Tasche hatte,
Mama schickt Geld, hat den Schein in Kohlepapier gewickelt,
damit er bei der Briefkontrolle unterm Röntgenschirm
nicht sichtbar wird, notfalls auf dem Domplatz
im Schlamassel jedem den Paß zeigen,
wenn Arbeiter mit Steinen werfen, das schützt,
wer Angst bekommt, fährt gesund nach Haus.

Nevertheless, the prevailing air of optimism begins to erode in the second half of this stanza. The self-assurance displayed in the clever, anti-authoritarian tip on how to send money through the mail — wrapped in carbon paper to escape X-ray detection — is undermined by mention of parental support: mama sends money. Likewise, that spirit of rebellion flaunted by protestors is revealed as fleeting, especially when personal welfare takes precedence over the cause: whoever gets scared, drives home.

Like an interlude, these factors ease passage into the final stanza where judgment is passed by means of the images that remain:

Das weiß ich, kann von jedem wiederholt werden,
der noch ein bißchen Bewegung will nach den Indianerspielen,
als wir unter Wasser saßen und aus Schilfstengeln Luft lutschten,
Bambus hängt in der Blumenecke, Reis esse ich gern,
Diskus, Weitsprung, Schmetterlingsstil, was haben wir gelernt,
verdammte Scheiße, da gehen wir hintereinander
auf abgesperrten Fahrbahnen
mit Plakaten und Kinderwagen als Sturmgepäck,
einige haben Sandalen aus Autoreifen an.

The *Das weiß ich* here balances the *Was weiß ich* opening stanza one. However, the question — what have we learned? — demands an answer addressing more than technique in athletic events. What Herburger has learned, and henceforth bemoans, is that the protest movement has style but lacks substance. Bamboo and rice imply solidarity with the Third World, yet the reference — in context — is ostentatious. The expletive outburst *verdammte Scheiße* resounds of the frustration brought on by viewing the collective *we* marching in single file along the prescribed demonstration course as cordoned-off by the authorities. The image is all the more distressing for the way it clashes with the very sense of independence and spontaneity on which the poem — until now — has thrived.

The feeling of retrospective malaise expressed in the final stanza mirrors the poem's date of composition, in that Herburger's criticism is directed at the early protest movement with its Easter Sunday marches and peace rallies. His uneasiness surfaces during a turning point shortly before the days of greater unrest and turmoil from mid-1967 through 1968. Hence, the portrayal of protesters outfitted with banners and baby carriages as assault gear shows Herburger playing out the military motif to ludicrous extremes. Once again, point of view is critical in specifying Herburger's message. In the concluding lines of the poem the lyric persona is part of a protest march. Even though the objects named in the final two lines — banners, baby carriages, and sandals — all carry meaning in and of themselves, more significant is the order in which they are mentioned. By first naming the banners carried by the protest marchers, the angle of view is directed upward. However, the subsequent points of reference (baby carriages and sandals) move in a steady downward arc. Lest one forget the poet's dogmatic claim

"Ich bin die Hauptperson,"[18] the final, and therefore lasting impression left by Herburger's "soso Vietnam aha" is clearly not a commentary on counter-culture footwear, but rather the head-bowed image and pavement-searching gaze of the lyric persona confronting an ever-growing sense of shame.[19]

As seen in the poems discussed thus far, the dominant images created by the war in Vietnam can be listed as follows: American soldiers are depicted as barbarous headhunters and emotionless automatons, military and political leaders as ruthless and scheming manipulators with a callous disregard for the lessons of history, and press reports on the war as untrustworthy. The image of America is thoroughly negative; in fact, one of the few positive views of the country is provided by Erich Fried's poem "Amerika" and its expression of solidarity with the American protest movement.[20] As tensions mounted in the late 1960s, the target of protest grew beyond the United States to include the Federal Republic of Germany. This trend can be attributed to two factors: a common political-economic system and joint actions carried out under auspices of the NATO alliance. Like Fried in "Gleichheit Brüderlichkeit" Martin Walser attacks the complicity of the West German government in "Osterpflicht '68"[21] and stages a call to action with direct appeal to the reader's sense of duty to humanity. A more subtle approach is taken by Volker Braun in "Der ferne Krieg."[22]

---

[18] See Herburger, "Dogmatisches über Gedichte," *Kursbuch* 10 (1967): 154.

[19] As to this head-bowed image and its association with a sense of personal shame, see Kleist's "Über das Marionettentheater" in Heinrich von Kleist, *Werke und Briefe*, ed. Siegfried Streller, 2nd ed., 4 vols. (Berlin: Aufbau, 1984) 3: 473–80, especially 475–77 and the passages regarding mankind's fall from grace.

[20] See also Yaak Karsunke's "Rede zum Internationalen Vietnam-Tag," a speech given in Munich on 20 October 1967 and then printed as the preface to the anthology *gegen den krieg in vietnam*, 6–10.

[21] In *elan* 4 (1968): 26; also quoted in Hahn, 50–51.

[22] Volker Braun, *Wir und nicht sie: Gedichte* (Halle an der Saale: Mitteldeutscher, 1970), 29.

Sechs Kilometer von meinem Zimmer
Hinter einem Kanal, einem Grenzverhau
Wenigen kurzen Straßen, dünnem
Gesträuch die stille Fabrik in Britz
Deutlich der Rauch.
Fern
Nicht auszumachen am Himmel
Mit bloßen Händen, man sagt:
Ein Regen trüber Abkunft, fast
Unaufhaltbar dort, falln
Sprühstoffe leicht in das Feld
Und das Laub
Vietnams: schon
Undeutlich wie ein Gerücht.

Although the title implies combat action far removed, the poem itself counters with proof of how close at hand the war is being waged. Braun's detached tone is supported by his vantage point: a room in East Berlin some six kilometers from a chemical factory just beyond the border canal in the Britz district of West Berlin. The content is conveyed by means of paired opposites operating on various levels: two sides of a divided city, images clear and obscure, rising factory smoke and falling chemical spray. This strategy yields a political thrust to the poem without pointing fingers or naming names. Indeed, the implicit nature of its message works in a manner not unlike the potency of chemical defoliants on fields of green, that is — to borrow the simile in the final line — spreading with the unremitting speed of a rumor. If the final image leaves Vietnam's foliage an obscure, fleeting memory, then the sky over Berlin provides clear evidence of how this occurred.

Vietnam changed the image of America throughout the world. Visions and impressions centuries in the making were displaced in less than a decade by an undeclared war fought half way around the globe. The onetime colonies had become colonial aggressor. America's loss of status resulting from its military intervention in Indo-China is succinctly captured in the following concrete poem[23] by Hansjörg Mayer:

[23] In Eugen Gomringer, ed., *konkrete poesie: deutschsprachige autoren* (Stuttgart: Reclam, 1972), 96.

s a u

a u s

u s a

The clever orthographic derivation of the German word for *sow* from the letters *USA* serves as an expeditious résumé of America's late-1960s image. Consistent with the principles of concrete poetry, this poem operates on a visual level and offers a swift, near instantaneous assessment of America's standing in the eyes of select members of the German-speaking world.

The war in Vietnam not only altered America's image, for many throughout the world it led to a sense of disillusionment and betrayal. Unique among protest poems owing to its documentation of the change in America's image is Yaak Karsunke's "Kilroy war hier."[24]

als ich 11 war stand
›Kilroy is here‹
auf den geborstenen mauern
auf gestürzten säulen
auf kneipentischen in klos
die amis schrieben
es überall hin

als ich 11 war trugen
meine schwestern rote röcke
den weißen kreis mit dem vierfach
gebrochenen kreuz
hatte meine mutter selber
abgetrennt & verbrannt
jetzt war Kilroy hier

als ich 11 war war
der krieg aus & ›Hitler kaputt‹
wie die häuser die fenster die juden
& deutschland (was war das?)
dafür war Kilroy gekommen
brachte uns basketball bei
& kaugummi & cocacola

---

[24] Yaak Karsunke, *Kilroy & andere: Gedichte* (Berlin: Wagenbach, 1967), 65–66. As to how this poem documents one generation's disillusionment with America, see Domin, afterword, *Nachkrieg und Unfrieden*, 156.

als ich 11 war lehrte
mich Kilroy worte wie fairneß
& demokratie
parolen wie nie wieder krieg
brachte mir jitterbug bei
& selbst an Shakespeare-sonetten
noch den brooklyn-akzent

als ich 11 war waren
das drei goldene worte
›Kilroy is here‹
fast so schön wie die drei
der french revolution
von der er erzählte
freiheit & gleichheit & brüderlichkeit

als ich 11 war hatten
meine eltern
mich falsch erzogen
Kilroy gab sich die mühe
erklärte mir menschenrechte
& uno-charta
erzog mich um

als ich 11 war
war Kilroy der beste
freund den ich hatte
sein haus stand mir offen
in seinem keller
hörte ich jazz & Strawinsky
& keine sirenen

:viel von dem blieb zurück
— jahre später —
als Kilroy sein flugzeug bestieg
es mit napalm belud & verschwand
jetzt steht auf pagoden
& den rauchschwarzen resten von dörfern
›Kilroy is here‹

— wir
sind geschiedene leute

Karsunke relies heavily on understatement, and the power of his message lies in the straightforward delivery of highlights from the childhood of the lyric persona. "Kilroy war hier" speaks for a generation of Germans born in the mid-1930s, but its political content addresses an audience not restricted by nationality or date of birth. The poem is similarly a history lesson for any reader of any age, and herein lies its political slant. Stanzas one through seven recall 1945 — the war over — and the immediate postwar years. The image of America and Americans is not unlike that portrayed in Günter Eich's "Pfannkuchenrezept." This is the United States as celebrated liberator and one of the allied armies of occupation that helped make "Hitler kaputt." Karsunke, however, does more than just catalogue items out of a CARE package. In addition to chewing gum and Coca-Cola Kilroy brings along basketball and jitterbug, even renditions of Shakespearean sonnets, albeit with a Brooklyn accent. Such cultural imports are not to be underestimated, nor is Karsunke's valuation of them to be overlooked. By juxtaposition of a popular dance step with Shakespeare he acknowledges a fresh attitude toward American culture that has developed since 1945. The lyric persona represents a new generation and posture quite apart from that, say, captured in Gottried Benn's poem "Der Broadway singt und tanzt." Whereas Benn ridicules America as a land of trifling musicals, Karsunke does more than merely avow the infiltration of English words like *fairneß* into the postwar German vocabulary: he even dares to place jazz and Stravinsky side by side.

"Kilroy war hier" succeeds by telescoping time. In doing so, the poem postulates an inherent sense of rectitude in the naiveté of an eleven-year-old child. Things were, no doubt, much simpler in 1945, especially in terms of right and wrong, good and bad. But what the lyric persona learned at eleven is not something one outgrows: "worte wie fairneß/ & demokratie/ parolen wie nie wieder krieg" serve as the foundation for the process of re-education, and their meanings are not subject to arbitrary application. Stanza eight, circa twenty years later, depicts Kilroy's new visage and exposes the utter hypocrisy of what the U.S.A. had propagated in West Germany since 1945. The jump in time is crucial for it serves to highlight the sharp contrast in commodities Kilroy delivers to foreign lands. Instead of chewing gum and Coca-Cola he now drops napalm on villages and pagodas in Southeast Asia.

Karsunke leaves us with a charred image of smoldering remains, a pictorial correlative to the suppressed anger aroused by America's ethical about-face. In the end, "Kilroy war hier" portrays neither loss of innocence nor loss of trust. The poem operates on a less sophisticated level, and the loss portrayed is summed up in the lines "der beste/ freund den ich hatte" where the preterit tense carries added weight. Finally, the abrupt and pathetic tone of the concluding couplet suggests the irreversible, indeed irreconcilable differences that ended the friendship.[25]

German protest poems with America as target eventually expanded the focus to address more than Vietnam. Karsunke, we recall, equates the words "Kilroy was here" with the motto of the French Revolution as a basis for human rights. In America in the 1960s human rights meant civil rights, specifically Black America's struggle to attain racial equality. In certain German poems of the late 1960s, this topic is addressed within the context of Vietnam and the machinations of the military-industrial complex. For example, "Detroit, Sommer '67"[26] by Erwin Jedamus outlines the discriminatory practices carried out against "Jimmy Craw" as a prelude to his depiction of the riots in Detroit during the summer of 1967. Jedamus likens racial unrest in Detroit to the war in Vietnam, as both are a sign of how minorities are exploited by the ruling class. Furthermore, Detroit and Vietnam point to another motif in German poetry focusing on America — violence. For instance, in the poem "Amerika"[27] Rolf Haufs depicts a race war lurking in the background of an otherwise idyllic scene:

---

[25] See Egon Schwarz, "Die sechste Schwierigkeit beim Schreiben der Wahrheit," in Paulsen, 25. See also Heinz D. Osterle, ed., *Bilder von Amerika: Gespräche mit deutschen Schriftstellern* (Münster: Englisch Amerikanische Studien, 1987), 78, where Fried speaks of the Vietnam War as a tragic disappointment.

[26] In *kürbiskern* 2 (1968): 247–48, a political song following in the tradition of Wolf Biermann's "Die Ballade von dem Briefträger William L. Moore aus Baltimore." See Wolf Biermann, *Die Drahtharfe: Balladen Gedichte Lieder* (Berlin: Wagenbach, 1965).

[27] Rolf Haufs, *Vorstadtbeichte: Gedichte* (Neuwied and Berlin: Luchterhand, 1967), 49.

Und Blumen sah ich in Amerika
Als ich die Zeitung mühsam las
Daß da von Krieg die Rede war
Von einem Mann der einen andern niederstach
Weil seine Haut aus Schokolade war

Like Karsunke, Haufs charts the change in America's image since 1945. In his "Amerika" chocolate symbolizes that transformation, initially appearing as a gift to a young boy after Nazi Germany had raised the white flag to the oncoming American tanks, then later highlighting the black-white dichotomy tearing apart the fabric of American society.

The issue of racism in America generated considerable interest in the Black Panther Party among German writers and intellectuals.[28] Black militancy complemented the aggressive anti-American stance of the German protest movement. Names of leaders such as Eldridge Cleaver, Huey Newton, Angela Davis, and Bobby Seale attained a status not unlike that of Ho Chi Minh or Che Guevara, which is to say, the Black Panthers were viewed as freedom fighters engaged in an all-out struggle against an imperialist power. Jürgen Theobaldy's poem "Die Freiheit für Bobby Seale"[29] reflects this attitude in its account of a demonstration in Heidelberg on 13 December 1969 protesting the war in Vietnam. In conjunction with the analysis of its contents, let us recall several of Walter Höllerer's "Thesen zum langen Gedicht" with an eye to how they apply to Theobaldy's long poem, for here we find another example of American influences on poetic form merging with America as subject matter. Most noticeable is the absence of any sense of the forced precision and chinoiserie Höllerer associated with the traditional short poem. Theobaldy tells the story of this demonstration in a most colloquial manner. He employs both trivial and everyday expressions to recount the day's events and refrains from any overt ceremonial observance. Even though Theobaldy's poetic line is not characterized by the rolling rhythms of those American models Höllerer promoted, the poem does gain a sense of momentum through repetition of the title's rally cry, "Freiheit für Bobby Seale."

[28] See *Kursbuch* 22 (1970), an issue focusing on North America and featuring an interview with Eldridge Cleaver.

[29] In *kürbiskern* 3 (1970): 492–94.

What Theobaldy does not embrace, however, is Höllerer's dictum of denial, that is, to look away from the self. The introspective persona is a key component of the poem, for it is through this subjective eye that the story and its implications are communicated. The focal point of the poem is, nonetheless, "Mr. Seale," and its central image

> ein Bild von ihm:
> wie er gefesselt und geknebelt
> im Gerichtssaal sitzt
> und es war eine Zeichnung
> und somit ohne Beweiskraft
> denn verboten war zu fotografieren
> während dieses Prozesses

This excerpt captures the reportorial tone of a poem documenting a news item circulated throughout the world at the end of 1969: the courtroom sketch of Bobby Seale bound and gagged during the trial of the Chicago Seven. Theobaldy does not depend on an overt display of solidarity with the accused. He neither dares to call him comrade nor does he employ the moniker Chairman Bobby. Furthermore, Theobaldy does not expound on background material surrounding the case. The trial is a point of departure and the poet's purpose is to reveal the conspiracy pertaining to the goings-on behind the scenes of this demonstration in Heidelberg. Thus, the poem is not concerned with debating the charges levied against Bobby Seale; instead the task of the poet is to make known the fact that Seale's

> Genosse von der Black Panther Partei
> — Emigrant in Algerien —
> durfte ja nicht einreisen
> in die Bundesrepublik an jenem Tag
> und es gab noch niemanden, dies zu verhindern
> und der Minister sagte später:
> es war ein Versehen
> > und wahrscheinlich hatte der Minister
> es vornehmer gesagt:
> es handelte sich um ein Versehen

Theobaldy's protest works, then, on a second level, namely revealing the complicitous dealings of the West German government in

denying an entry visa to Seale's fellow Black Panther, Eldridge
Cleaver, at the time in exile in Algeria.[30]

In retrospect, Theobaldy's poem provides a summary of developments in German political poetry of the 1960s. Starting with a
wave of Vietnam protest poems, anti-American sentiments spread to
other issues, in particular racial injustice in the United States. "Die
Freiheit für Bobby Seale" is exemplary, however, for matters beyond
its political content. As mentioned earlier, Theobaldy refuses to look
away from the self, and his introspective persona is as much center
stage in this poem as its title character. The subjective nature of this
approach is all the more significant in that it anticipates a movement
in German poetry synonymous with the 1970s, *Neue Subjektivität*.
Even though the term has come to be associated with poems of a
comparatively trivial nature in which the persona responds in a personal manner to the banal concerns of everyday life, Theobaldy's
"Die Freiheit für Bobby Seale" shows how the New Subjectivity of
the 1970s grew out of political poetry of the 1960s. This poem,
based on an event in late 1969 and published in 1970, depicts a period after the West German protest movement had reached its peak.
The lyric persona, far from being caught up in the fervor of dissent, is
marked by a circumspect manner and introversion. Moreover, the
pronounced reflection upon personal motives is a sign that the energy of the opposition movement has begun to wane.

With the close of a turbulent decade, the United States becomes less and less the focus of German protest poems. In fact,
America's image displays remarkable resilience in the early 1970s as
non-political matters start to displace the issue-oriented topics of
Vietnam and racism. The following chapters will examine the post-
1968 era with special attention to America's role in the birth of
German Pop Poetry and the emergence of the U.S.A. as a favored
travel destination for German poets.

---

[30] It is noteworthy that Theobaldy leaves Eldridge Cleaver unnamed as if to
refuse sharing Bobby Seale's spotlight with his better-known cohort. Cleaver's
Soul on Ice had appeared a year earlier in Germany: *Seele auf Eis*, trans. Céline
and Heiner Bastian with an afterword by Kai Hermann (Munich: Hanser,
1969). Two years later Seale's *Seize the Time: The Story of the Black Panther
Party and Huey Newton* (New York: Random House, 1970) was published in a
German edition: Bobby Seale, *Wir fordern Freiheit: Der Kampf der Black Panther*, trans. Regine Wolf (Frankfurt am Main: Fischer, 1971).

7: Fiedler Crosses the Border, Brinkmann Closes the Gap: German Pop Poetry

IN JUNE 1968 at the University of Freiburg im Breisgau, as part of a symposium on contemporary literature in Europe and America, Leslie Fiedler delivered his lecture "Cross the Border, Close the Gap: The Case for Post Modernism."[1] The text was then translated and published in two parts as "Das Zeitalter der neuen Literatur" in the weekly newspaper *Christ und Welt* on 13 and 20 September 1968 with the respective subtitles "Die Wiedergeburt der Kritik" and "Indianer, Science Fiction und Pornographie: die Zukunft des Romans hat schon begonnen." In part one, on the re-birth of literary criticism, Fiedler envisions a new style for the critical essay, namely that it "must be aesthetic, poetic in form as well as substance," plus "comical, irreverent, and vulgar." The topics discussed in part two of his essay — westerns, comics, science fiction, and pornography — reflect the fundamental principles of his concept of a new literature devoid of an elitist notion of art and distinguished by its popularity among the masses. Fiedler's self-proclaimed role is that of an agitator whose purpose is to challenge the accepted ideas of art, in particular the notion of art as the domain of a cultured elite. His push for change emphasizes the subversive nature of pop art, and the goal is the formation of a classless society for literature bridging the gap between author and reader by dispensing with categories of serious and trivial reading material.

After the publication of "Das Zeitalter der neuen Literatur," *Christ und Welt* featured a series entitled "Fiedler-Diskussion" in which German writers and critics responded to the American pro-

---

[1] This lecture was a shortened, somewhat toned-down summary of Fiedler's essay of the same title that later appeared in *Playboy* 12 (1969): 151, 230, and 252–58; rpt. in Leslie Fiedler, *Collected Essays*, 2 vols. (New York: Stein, 1971), 2: 461–85.

fessor of literature. While respondents Reinhard Baumgart, Jürgen Becker, and Helmut Heißenbüttel gave mixed reviews, others such as Peter O. Chotjewitz and Martin Walser voiced opposition to Fiedler. Rolf Dieter Brinkmann, however, applauded these new directions in literature. His contribution to the series, "Angriff aufs Monopol: Ich hasse alte Dichter,"[2] enthusiastically follows Fiedler's advice for a new style of literary criticism. Even if some might question the aesthetic merit of Brinkmann's essay, there can be no doubt it is irreverent. In fact, Brinkmann's response is as much a commentary on Fiedler as a relentless attack on anyone who objected to this radical new stance on literature. Fiedler's importance for Brinkmann can be understood in terms of an upstart American challenge to European literary traditions. Pop art is significant, he argues, for having developed not in Europe but in the United States. Like Fiedler, Brinkmann stands as a proponent of a literature of ecstasy, as evidenced by his fervent praise of William S. Burroughs's *Naked Lunch* (1959). Borrowing terminology from Marshall McLuhan, he describes the effects of innovative literary trends in the U.S.A. as "Implosion" — specifically a breakthrough into the psychic realm. Furthermore, Brinkmann seizes the opportunity to deride his literary elders for not sharing this pop-oriented sensibility, charging that Germany is limping along behind the trend-setting U.S.A. In light of his highly confrontational tone, Brinkmann's participation in the Fiedler debate can be viewed as a conscious effort to distance himself from the West German literary establishment.[3]

Fiedler's appearance on the West German literary scene was but a prelude to further postmodern influences from the United States.

---

[2] *Christ und Welt*, 15 November 1968. Brinkmann takes the subtitle for his essay from a line in Gregory Corso's poem "I am 25." See Gregory Corso, *Gasoline and The Vestal Lady on Brattle* (San Francisco: City Lights, 1958), 36.

[3] Brinkmann's outsider status is often linked to an incident that occurred two days after the publication of his "Angriff aufs Monopol" in *Christ und Welt*. On 17 November 1968 at the *Akademie der Künste* in West Berlin during the program "Autoren diskutieren mit ihren Kritikern" Brinkmann attacked critics Marcel Reich-Ranicki and Rudolf Hartung with the outburst: "Wenn dies Buch ein Maschinengewehr wäre, würde ich Sie über den Haufen schießen!" Quoted by, among others, Jochen Wüllner in his retrospective essay "R. D. Brinkmann — Der Autor als Kameramann," *guckloch* 4 (1985): 122.

The late 1960s were politically charged throughout the Western world. Moreover, the image of America was at a postwar low in Germany, especially among writers, intellectuals, and students. These factors account for negative reactions to Fiedler's lecture as, for many, his pop aesthetics came across as politically irresponsible. The prevailing attitudes within the German literary community thus made the reception given three new American anthologies all the more surprising. The first to appear was Ralf-Rainer Rygulla's collection of underground poetry entitled *Fuck You!* (1968).[4] To a certain extent, this collection picks up where the Corso/Höllerer and Paetel anthologies left off. Many of the same authors appear, plus a number of new names from the post-Beat Generation. Rygulla follows an approach similar to his precursors both in introducing new writers and in educating German readers on recent cultural trends in America. The major difference, however, is the blatant apolitical editorial stance. Here we do not find the "other" America of poets in Lowenfels's *Where is Vietnam?*, those whose activism and dissension reflect the ideals and responsibilities associated with a participatory democracy. Instead the focus is on an America seemingly devoid of responsibility. Rygulla promotes this American counterculture crusade as the total negation of societal values, with emphasis on its anarchic traits rather than those of any political ism. Granted, his afterword does point to elements of political protest, but it features a mode of dissent transgressing the accepted norms through the flagrant use of obscenities.

As evident in the title, Rygulla's collection of poems aggressively confronts the reader. While an offensive tone is the mark of such entries as Charles Bukowski's "Men's Crapper," Tuli Kupferberg's "Bayonet Drill," and Ed Sanders's "Coca-Cola Douche," others — especially poems by Ted Berrigan, Edward Dorn, Frank O'Hara, Jack Spicer, and Philip Whalen — are simply clever or humorous, underground in the sense of antiliterary. Sanders's call for a "total assault on the culture" characterizes the aim of this

---

[4] Ralf-Rainer Rygulla, ed., *Fuck You! Underground Gedichte* (Darmstadt: Melzer, 1968), with its title taken from Ed Sanders's *Fuck You: A Magazine of the Arts*. This collection expands upon an earlier small press publication also edited and translated by Rygulla: *Untergrund Gedichte: Letzte amerikanische Lyrik* (Berlin: Oberbaumpresse, 1967).

radical contingent of poets, a phrase likewise setting the tone for *ACID* (1969),[5] an anthology of not only poems but also short stories, essays, manifestos, interviews, comics, and photographs. Unlike *Fuck You!*, *ACID* generated a fair amount of attention in the West German press; moreover, its reprint history confirms its standing as a source book for German devotees of the underground scene. While one reviewer concentrates on the book's titillating qualities, another examines *ACID* as a good collection of bad literature offering the reader a "Nonstop-LSD-Trip."[6] Although opinions on the texts in the anthology are at best mixed, remarks concerning both the editors' monumental efforts in compiling this 419-page tome and Brinkmann's informative afterword, "Der Film in Worten,"[7] are for the most part positive.[8]

The significance of Brinkmann's afterword, however, lies not in his informative analysis of the American underground culture, but in what it reveals about the formation of his own poetics. Equally important is how he continually pits the new American scene against the reigning forces in contemporary German literature. For example, Brinkmann regards the European standards of the traditional essay as aristocratic. Therefore, he adopts a free-associative collage style for his afterword, a technique complementing the contents of the anthology. In other sections of the afterword the American-European dichotomy takes on more aggressive overtones. Brinkmann makes an overt effort to set himself apart from the main body of German literature by criticizing select figures. A primary target is Hans Magnus Enzensberger, whose 1962 essay

---

[5] Rolf Dieter Brinkmann and Ralf-Rainer Rygulla, ed., *ACID: Neue amerikanische Szene* (Darmstadt: März, 1969 and 1975; rpt. Reinbek bei Hamburg: Rowohlt, 1983).

[6] See Karl Krolow, "Angst, daß Genet nur Spaß macht," *Die Tat*, 14 June 1969; and Jost Nolte, "Aufstand gegen die Grammatik?" *Die Welt*, 8 Jan. 1970.

[7] The title is from a statement by Jack Kerouac reading in the original: "Bookmovie is the movie in words, the visual American form." See No. 26 of Kerouac's "Belief & Technique for Modern Prose: List of Essentials," in *Evergreen Review* 2.8 (1959): 57.

[8] See Holger Masata, "Die Befreiung des Gedankens," *Publik* 31, 1 Aug. 1969; Reinhard Priessnitz, on the other hand, takes issue with Brinkmann's afterword in "Meinetwegen, fuck you!" *Neues Forum* 17.3 (1970): 257–58.

"Die Aporien der Avantgarde" labeled the maxims in Kerouac's "List of Essentials" as naive.[9] Brinkmann's purpose is to provide a counterpoint to politically engaged writers of the 1960s. For instance, whereas Enzensberger solemnly proclaims the "death of literature,"[10] Brinkmann attempts to revitalize German letters with a model program based on a politically aloof American underground.

Brinkmann identifies a number of features distinguishing the literary scene in the United States. First, he sees American literature moving to assimilate other art forms, particularly painting, photography, and music. Second, he points to an adaptability on the part of American writers enabling them to switch literary genres. His examination of genre classification leads to third observation, a preference on the part of American writers for poetry. The new breed of American authors is noteworthy, he claims, for an aesthetics of everyday life and a pronounced short-term memory. Accordingly, poetry becomes the preferred mode of expression, having proved itself to be the most flexible literary form and the genre best suited for capturing the nuances of fast-paced contemporary lifestyles.

In contrast to the theoretical tone of the afterword to *ACID*, Brinkmann reveals a more practical side in the seventy-five "Notizen" comprising the preface to *Silverscreen* (1969).[11] Once again, he accents differences between America and Europe, voicing his preference for the antitheoretical nature of stateside poetry. The contemporary American poem, he argues, presents images rather than ideas, functioning not as a discourse on problems of language or politics but more as a snapshot capturing scenes from daily life. This precept rings no doubt of a specific American poet, but Brinkmann appropriates William Carlos Williams in unique fashion,

---

[9] See Enzensberger, *Einzelheiten* (Frankfurt am Main: Suhrkamp, 1962), 290–315, especially 305–6.

[10] See Enzensberger, "Gemeinplätze, die Neueste Literatur betreffend" in *Kursbuch* 15 (1968): 187–97.

[11] Brinkmann, ed., *Silverscreen: Neue amerikanische Lyrik* (Cologne: Kiepenheuer & Witsch, 1969). Both the preface to *Silverscreen* and the afterword to *ACID* are reprinted in Brinkmann's posthumously published *Der Film in Worten: Prosa, Erzählungen, Essays, Hörspiele, Fotos, Collagen 1965–1974* (Reinbek bei Hamburg: Rowohlt, 1982).

declaring in "Notiz 56" that pop art begins with Williams's poem "This Is Just To Say."[12] Spontaneity also functions as a key to composition, just as accessibility to all readers is the mark of the successful poem. Furthermore, Brinkmann attributes a sense of democratic ideals to literature as writing poetry is an act from which no one is excluded. Finally, his apolitical stance is defined as a move "from politics to metapolitics"[13] in order to lead an aesthetically charged life, a concept best understood when viewed in conjunction with Brinkmann's commentary on the 1960s Poetry Project at St. Mark's Church in the Bowery section of New York City. Here he finds the ideal milieu for realizing his goals — a setting where public readings are regularly staged, literary journals are published, and poetry broadsides are distributed on the streets. The St. Mark's Poetry Project, then, becomes the scene he attempts to transplant in Germany.

The März publishing house and its founder Jörg Schröder took an active role in supporting these efforts.[14] Representative of what Brinkmann learned from his American counterparts is his long poem "Vanille,"[15] including five pages of the author's "Anmerkungen" explaining the poem's genesis, methodology, and various quotations borrowed by the poet. "Vanille" reflects Brinkmann's penchant for literature with a heightened visual component as the text is interspersed with photos and illustrations; in fact, the title page is superimposed on a photo of the movie star Raquel Welch frolicking on a beach in bell-bottom pants and bikini top. Sexual allusions occur throughout the poem, and its content is best described as "a collage of ready-mades" including newspaper headlines, excerpts from poems, diary entries, commentary on current cinema, and instructions from a

---

[12] See Williams, *Selected Poems: Enlarged Edition* (New York: New Directions, 1968), 55. Brinkmann's "Notiz 56" quotes the poet Harold Norse as cited in the essay "The Image and Poetry" by critic Nicolas Calas from *Art in the Age of Risk* (New York: Dutton, 1968).

[13] See "Notiz 64," where Brinkmann quotes Herbert Marcuse from a special issue, "Ecstatic Revolution," of the London magazine *Running Man* 3–5 (1969).

[14] See "Interview mit einem Verleger," *März Texte 1* (Darmstadt: März, 1969), 283–96.

[15] In *März Texte 1*, 106–44.

package of birth-control pills.[16] In this regard "Vanille" is a found poem, a point underscored by the poet inserting the phrase »objet trouvé« in boldface, oversize print at the midpoint of the text. Its free-form style led another critic to label "Vanille" a long "Americanized" poem since it displays much of what Brinkmann promoted as editor and intermediary for the contemporary American literary scene.[17] American influences extend beyond form to content, in particular an allusion to Andy Warhol — IM ANFANG WAR DIE DOSE — and his trademark Campbell's soup can. There is also mention of the American poet John Ashbery and a quote from his poem "Our Youth." Nevertheless, to cite Ashbery as an influence on Brinkmann at this point would be misleading, as the reference is more an example of incorporating found material into the text.[18] Finally, and to com-plement the author's explanatory notes, the appendix to *März Texte 1* contains a copy of one of the proof pages of "Vanille" with Brink-mann's hand-written instructions for deletions and changes in type, line spacing, and indentation — an inside look at how poet and pub-lisher strive to bridge the gap between author and reader and to foster a brand of literature with nothing to hide.

The poem "Vanille" mirrors Brinkmann's efforts to create an en-vironment — à la the St. Mark's Poetry Project — compatible with his literary aspirations. In 1969, along with Ralf-Rainer Rygulla and Rolf-Eckart John, he brought out *Der Gummibaum: Hauszeitschrift für neue Dichtung,* one of the first in a group of hectographic journals

---

[16] See R. Hinton Thomas and Keith Bullivant, *Literature in Upheaval: West German Writers and the Challenge of the 1960s* (Manchester: Manchester UP, 1974), 156.

[17] See Martin Grzimek, "Über den Verlust der Verantwortlichkeit: Zu Rolf Dieter Brinkmanns poetischen Texten," in *Neue deutsche Lyrik: Beiträge zu Born, Brinkmann, Krechel, Theobaldy, Zahl u.a.* (Heidelberg: Arbeitskreis Linker Germanisten, 1977), 98–129, here 107.

[18] Ashbery later had a marginal influence on Brinkmann, in particular the poem "Sommer (Aus dem Amerikanischen)" in *Westwärts 1 & 2: Gedichte* (Reinbek bei Hamburg: Rowohlt, 1975), 23, an example of a surface transla-tion with Brinkmann's text playing off the poem "Summer" from Ashbery, *The Double Dream of Spring* (New York: Dutton, 1970), 20. As to what Brinkmann did with Ashbery, see Joachim Sartorius, "Die Oberfläche des Sommers oder Was Brinkmann mit Ashbery machte," in *Akzente* 32.3 (1985): 196–98.

representative of the West German literary underground. Other such publications worthy of mention are *Der fröhliche Tarzan* edited by Rolf-Eckart John as well as Jürgen Theobaldy's *Benzin*.[19] Their endeavors reflect both the practice of self-publishing associated with Whitman's *Leaves of Grass* and the role of American "little magazines" in providing a forum for young writers, specifically, an alternative to the highly selective, slick periodicals of the literary establishment. In addition, these underground publications regularly contained translations of American poets of the Beat and post-Beat Generations.[20]

Besides his role as promoter of a new American scene in poetry, Brinkmann is also renowned as Germany's foremost pop poet. His pop phase is most pronounced in *Die Piloten* (1968),[21] a collection with an antiliterary bent evident at first glance as Brinkmann's self-made collage adorning the book jacket is reminiscent of The Beatles's *Sgt. Pepper's Lonely Hearts Club Band* album cover.[22] In addition, its three sections of poems are introduced by American comic strip characters mouthing the likes of "Ich bin ein Dichter. . . . Spiel besser die Leier als C. F. Meyer!" (216) As to the contents, one critic remarks that movies, comics, and commercial products dominate,[23] — a point clearly supported by selected poem titles: "Der nackte Fuß von Ava Gardner," "Ra-ta-ta-ta für Bonnie und Clyde etc.," "Cartoon: 29.8.

---

[19] For a documentation of Germany's underground press scene, see J. Wintjes and J. Gehret, ed., *Ulcus Molle Info-Dienst: Jahrgänge 1969–1974* (Amsterdam: Azid, 1979).

[20] See Jürgen Theobaldy, "Wie und warum ich Benzin herausgab," in Günther Emig, ed., *Verzeichnis deutschsprachiger Literaturzeitschriften* (Heilbronn: Emig, 1981), 7–13.

[21] Rolf Dieter Brinkmann, *Die Piloten: Neue Gedichte* (Cologne: Kiepenheuer & Witsch, 1968); rpt. in Brinkmann, *Standphotos* (Reinbek bei Hamburg: Rowohlt, 1980), a collection containing all poems originally appearing in the nine volumes of verse published by Brinkmann between 1962 and 1970. Subsequent page-citations for poems reprinted in *Standphotos* will be given parenthetically in the text.

[22] See Helmut Salzinger, "Pop mit Ra-ta-ta-ta," *Der Tagesspiegel*, 23 Feb. 1969 and Anton Krättli, "Ganz leer sein, um zu begreifen," *Neue Zürcher Zeitung*, 10 Apr. 1981, who calls *Die Piloten* the most important book of German pop poetry.

[23] See Christel Buschmann, "Gegen feinsinnigen Hokuspokus," *Die Zeit*, 6 June 1969.

mit x,y,z," and "Chiquita-Banana-High." With the publication of *Die Piloten* Brinkmann established a brazen antiliterary trend in German poetry and opened the door for poets to explore new modes of expression. Peter Handke also warrants mention as a pop poet, and like Brinkmann he has ties to Hollywood films and popular music. Handke's poetry of the late 1960s exhibits American influences with distinctive pop overtones, a trait conspicuous in "Warner Brothers und Seven Arts zeigen:"[24] — a poem listing the actors, film crew, and production credits for the movie *Bonnie and Clyde* (1967) in simulation of the scroll-like fashion in which these particulars appear on the screen. The choice of an American gangster film emblematic of cinematic changes in the 1960s is no coincidence. Just as Warren Beatty defied Hollywood's old guard and studio system, Handke bucks German literary traditions with a text identifiable as a poem only because it appears in a volume of poetry. Beyond its pop attributes, "Warner Brothers and Seven Arts zeigen": is also the prototype found poem, a classification suggesting the very nature of pop art; that is to say, in spite of various precepts and claims, pop art can be defined as the art of finding art on the street.[25]

The influx of pop art created new avenues for German poetry of the late 1960s. These inroads likewise led to changes in the image of America. As a case in point, let us consider a group of poems addressing one of the milestones of the era: the space race, specifically American efforts to land a man on the moon. The first example is Nicolas Born's "Feriengedicht [Juli 1969],"[26] a poem, as the title and first line explain, recounting the author's vacation during July of

---

[24] Peter Handke, *Die Innenwelt der Außenwelt der Innenwelt* (Frankfurt am Main: Suhrkamp, 1969), 119–21; see also 36–38 for Handke's verse adaptation of a song in "Der Text des rhythm-and-blues." For an in-depth look at Handke's image of America, see his novel *Der kurze Brief zum langen Abschied* (Frankfurt am Main: Suhrkamp, 1972).

[25] See Heinz Ohff, ed., *Pop und die Folgen: Die Kunst, Kunst auf der Straße zu finden* (Düsseldorf: Droste, 1968). For further examples of late-1960s found poems see Peter Handke, *Deutsche Gedichte* (Frankfurt am Main: euphorion, 1969) and Horst Bienek, *Vorgefundene Gedichte: Poèmes trouvés* (Munich: Hanser, 1969).

[26] Nicolas Born, *Das Auge des Entdeckers: Gedichte* (Reinbek bei Hamburg: Rowohlt, 1972), 81–86; rpt. in Born, *Gedichte 1967–1978*, 163–69.

1969. Born employs a number of maxims outlined in Höllerer's "Thesen zum langen Gedicht," as this is a long poem relying on free-association and featuring the banalities of everyday life on holiday. The setting is somewhere in a southern region with mention of the sea, a mountain range, and a desert; the precise locale, however, is not specified. The content plays off a day-night dichotomy conveying more a state of mind than any fully developed story line. Interspersed throughout are allusions to the Apollo 11 moon shot and astronaut Neil Armstrong. Crucial here is the manner in which Born relates how the moon landing not merely captured worldwide attention during the summer of 1969 but established a sense of collective consciousness among humankind. The tone of the poem is matter of fact, the focus ever shifting, as if to remind us that a vacation is a time for letting the mind wander. Rather than elaborating on specifics of space travel, Born opts for the passing remark: "Armstrong gibt eine neue Position durch." In the one direct quote from outer space, he chooses not the famous first words spoken from the moon's surface, but a simple one word statement: "Armstrong: «Okay!»" — the quintessential American word in the English language. Likewise, ostensibly reporting the return of the lunar module to the mothership, Born reduces tensions and exhilarations to the minimum — "NACH DEM KRITISCHEN MANÖVER/ BEIFALL IN HOUSTON" — thus undercutting any sense of high drama associated with the delicate operation. Moreover, the closing reference to the moon landing and its aftermath, — "die Lichter gehen aus die Sterne drehen ab/ das Banner gefriert im «Meer der Ruhe»" — provides both contrast to a vacation land climate and corollary to the end of a holiday.

Brinkmann, however, takes a different approach in "Der Mond, der Präsident und die amerikanische Prärie: Populäres Gedicht Nr. 11" (218):

> Der amerikanische
> Mond über dem
> Kapitol in Washington D.C.
> ist ganz aus reinem
>
> Kunststoff, eine
> endlose Variation
> auf ein altes Thema
> wie man deutlich sieht.

> Der Präsident
> sieht ihn sich
> täglich einmal
> an und läßt ihn
>
> dann wieder verschwinden.
> Einsam über einer Prärie
> ganz in der Nähe geht
> er aber wieder auf. Dieses
>
> Mal ist es der echte Mond
> mit dem Abbild des Prä-
> sidenten auf der Rückseite.

Although pre-dating the moon landing, this poem anticipates the event. Not mentioned but implied, the Apollo program, much like a work in progress, provides a counterbalance to the poem itself. Rather than praising American know-how, Brinkmann mocks the extraterrestrial, imperialistic drive of the United States. In this fantasy world of pop culture, nothing is real. The moon, grand prize in the superpower space race, is purely synthetic, a plastic plaything for the president reminiscent of how Charlie Chaplin used a globe as a prop in his film *The Great Dictator*.[27]

In Günter Herburger's pop parody "Die jungen Amerikaner, die, statt zu flippern, schießen"[28] the Apollo astronauts are not highly skilled space-age explorers but overgrown school boys:

> wenn auf dem Weg zum Mond
> die Jungens in der Kapsel aus der Bibel vorlesen und sagen
> wie schön die Erde ist, blau, weiß und grün, so schön sei sie,
> ein Edelstein im schwarzen Weltall, aber dann sind die Jungens
> wieder lustig, und wir hören, wie ihr Puffreis, genau derselbe
> Reis
> wie unser Puffreis, vor den Mikrophonen knistert.

---

[27] See Sibylle Späth, *Rolf Dieter Brinkmann* (Stuttgart: Metzler, 1989), 53.

[28] Günter Herburger, *Training: Gedichte* (Neuwied and Berlin: Luchterhand, 1969), 54.

On one level, these lines generate a special tension between form and content resulting from the incorporation of an American free-verse style in a poem ridiculing one of America's greatest technological achievements. On another more pop-oriented level of consumer consciousness, Herburger uses the collective *we* to link the poet with the common folk, not only undercutting any elitist sense of art but also identifying the pop poet as a good consumer. Finally, that a writer with heretofore Marxist leanings would turn to such a carefree, frivolous mode demonstrates the extent to which American influences had infiltrated German poetry.[29]

The pop spirit exploited by both Brinkmann and Herburger appears all the more striking and preposterous when compared to the solemn mood expressed in Walter Höllerer's "Sätze,"[30] a poem in which the sentences of the title are the contrasting quotations of Apollo 10 astronaut Tom Stafford and an unnamed old man whose world is falling apart.

> «wie diese Fortschritte in der
>   Zukunft aussehen werden,   kann nur
> unsere Phantasie überlassen bleiben.   Aber
>   wenn wir unsere Energien sammeln und
> unsere Vorauschau richtig anwenden, dann
>   sind die Ziele unbegrenzt».   Tom Stafford
>   auf dem Rückflug zur Erde . . . «dieses Leben ist
> furchtbar», sagte der alte Mann, dem die Welt
>   zerfiel . . . «auf dem Höhepunkt meiner Kraft
> möchte ich sterben»

Whereas Stafford, quoted during the return flight to earth, presents an optimistic worldview characterized by faith in the future, the old man sees life as dreadful. Höllerer's use of the Stafford quote expands the concept of America as the land of unlimited opportunities. Within the context of a mission to place a man on the

---

[29] See Hans Bender, "Die Entwicklung der Lyrik seit 1945 in der Bundesrepublik," in Weissenberger, 25–37, especially 30–31, on Herburger's *Training*, in particular its boxboard cover likeness of an American football player wearing a helmet with facemask.

[30] Walter Höllerer, *Systeme: Neue Gedichte* (Berlin: LCB, 1969), 45.

moon, the notion of progress is imbued with fantasy. A new set of parameters takes over, and with the proper application of energies and resources a people can begin to strive for unlimited goals. Decidedly unlike his pop counterparts, Höllerer's realm is the abstract, that of ideas not things, and his tone somber. Moreover, he refuses to mock the myth of America's pioneer spirit in exploring the new frontier of outer space, and thus Höllerer stands as a holdover from the 1950s in an age otherwise characterized by the rise of trivial myths.[31]

Although pop poetry was a short-lived phenomenon in Germany, changes initiated by Fiedler's Freiburg lecture were long term. The late 1960s signal a move away from an elitist concept of literature and reflect both a populist propensity and an identification with an emerging youth culture. The preoccupation with sex and obscenities on one hand and a fascination with "Gadgets & Gimmicks"[32] on the other, led to wholesale dismissals of pop art and labels such as "Junk Culture."[33] Such verdicts, however, overlook significant considerations associated with the development of pop culture, in particular a democratization of art.[34] The three anthologies of American poetry discussed earlier in this chapter certainly contributed to this trend. Although notable as documents of an era, the combined contents of these collections reveal less about the overall literary climate in the United States than about the tastes of the editors. *ACID* and *Silverscreen*, however, are all-important in understanding the American influences on Rolf Dieter Brinkmann, especially that of Frank O'Hara. Brinkmann is frequently mentioned in connection with O'Hara, whose *Lunch Poems* he published in translation along with the essay "Die Lyrik Frank

---

[31] See Renate Matthaei, ed., *Trivialmythen* (Frankfurt am Main: März, 1970), in particular the contributions by Peter O. Chotjewitz (115–27) and Uwe Nettelbeck (151–79).

[32] Felix Pollak, "The Popeye Papers," *The Smith* 5 (1965): 4.

[33] Hans Platschek, "Tautologie der Gegenstände," in *Merkur* 18.1 (1964): 33–42, here 37.

[34] Erasmus Schöfer, "Demokratisierung der Künste," in *kürbiskern* 2 (1969): 292–97; see also Jost Hermand, "Pop oder die These vom Ende der Kunst," in *Basis I*, 94–115; and Jost Hermand, *Pop International: Eine kritische Analyse* (Frankfurt am Main: Athenäum, 1971).

O'Haras."[35] Other signs of this connection can be found in the preface to *Die Piloten* in which Brinkmann voices displeasure with German poetry and proclaims his affinity with O'Hara, to whom he dedicates his book. Statements in this preface have lead many critics and reviewers to cite O'Hara as the driving force behind Brinkmann's poetry. This view, though accurate to a degree, is misleading, for it overlooks other significant influences operating in Brinkmann's poetry. In fact, a look back at Brinkmann's earlier poetry will reveal two other American poets shaping his work, William Carlos Williams and Robert Creeley.

Even though he first made a name as a prose writer with the best-selling novel *Keiner weiß mehr*,[36] Brinkmann had been publishing poetry in limited editions since 1962. These early collections draw primarily on European traditions; however, by 1964 American influences are evident.[37] Enzensberger's translation of Williams had appeared in 1962, and there is reason to believe Brinkmann was familiar with this book, as *Le Chant du Monde* offers a number of Williamsesque glimpses of everyday life.[38] While many of these poems fall flat due to a static mood, Brinkmann is more likely to succeed — and displays truer allegiance to Williams — when his verse takes on a dynamic quality. An example of a more vibrant poetic point of view is provided by "Wechselt die Jahreszeit" (68):

---

[35] Frank O'Hara, *Lunch Poems und andere Gedichte*, trans. Rolf Dieter Brinkmann (Cologne: Kiepenheuer & Witsch, 1969). Brinkmann's afterword, "Die Lyrik Frank O'Haras," is reprinted in *Der Film in Worten*, 207–22.

[36] Rolf Dieter Brinkmann, *Keiner weiß mehr* (Cologne: Kiepenheuer & Witsch, 1968).

[37] Brinkmann's first book of poems, *Ihr nennt es Sprache* (Leverkusen: Willbrand, 1962), bears the dedication "dem roten Rühmkorf," an allusion to this poet's "Schäfer-Lied." See Peter Rühmkorf, *Irdisches Vergnügen in g* (Reinbek bei Hamburg: Rowohlt, 1959), 66. The title of Brinkmann's second collection, *Le Chant du Monde* (Olef/Eifel: Hagarpresse, 1964), suggests a holdover of the French influence on German poetry of the 1950s.

[38] See Brinkmann, *Standphotos*, in particular the poems "Dann" (36), "Natur morte" (50), "Photographie" (52), "Kühl" (53), "10 Uhr 20" (54), and "Geschlossenes Bild" (57).

Die
straffen Brüste
siebzehnjähriger
pullovertragender
Mädchen sind
schöner im
Regen, wie
sie versteckt
unter den leichten
Nylonmänteln hüpfen
beim Überspringen
von Pfützen auf dem
Bürgersteig. Wer denkt
dann noch an
gewagte Metaphern
angesichts so vieler
Ausdrucksmöglichkeiten
für einunddasselbe
Bild?

Noch
ehe der Nachmittag
vergeht vor lauter
Regenschirmen, hohen
Schuhen und
Südwestern
wechselt die
Jahreszeit.

Brinkmann expands the concept of the poem as snapshot in that he links a series of isolated images by means of a technique akin to film editing. Such trivial objects as nylon raincoats take on amplified meaning by displaying the contour of that which attracts the poet's attention. The allure of female anatomy is a trademark of Brinkmann's poetry, and even if his somewhat prurient preoccupation bespeaks a juvenile sensibility, the rhetorical question closing the first stanza offers a mature counterbalance. Likewise the craft displayed here hints of a seasoned poet, especially the manner in which Brinkmann telescopes the passage of time and his fluid syntax eases the choppy line breaks.

By 1966/67 Robert Creeley appears to have displaced Williams as the dominant American influence on Brinkmann.[39] In that Creeley owes much to Williams, this step is but a logical progression. Brinkmann's affinity with Creeley manifests itself on several different levels. First, selected poems display a distinctive appearance on the printed page with short lines broken so as to evoke a series of energy particles. Second, colloquial speech is used in an attempt the hold the tangible and intangible in flux through language. And finally, certain cryptic allusions lend a quality of "mythical anonymity" to sensory awareness.[40] While *Die Piloten* is exemplary for its pop poetry, there are also signs of Creeley. For instance, poems such as "Tritt" (209) and "Noch einmal" (206) rely on a visual feature in order to convey meaning not only through language but also through their appearance on the printed page. In effect, the stanzas suggest vertebrae and the complete poem a spinal column; thus, the text carries an added sense of delicacy if not vulnerability.[41] While "Tritt" uses direct address and a colloquial voice in the manner of Creeley, "Noch einmal" offers an intimate look at interactions between husband and wife:

> Meine Frau
> auf einem
> Bein, nackt

---

[39] See the collections *&-Gedichte* (Berlin: Oberbaumpresse, 1966), rpt. in *Standphotos*, 91–110, and Brinkmann's first book of poems issued by a major publishing house, *Was fraglich ist wofür* (Cologne: Kiepenheuer & Witsch, 1967), rpt. in *Standphotos*, 111–58.

[40] See Hans Dieter Schäfer, "Rolf Dieter Brinkmann" in Weisenberger, 391–403, especially 394–95 and his discussion of the poem "Anwesend" (*Standphotos*, 114)). Schäfer borrows the term "mythische Anonymität" from Klaus Reichert's observation on Creeley's poetry in the afterword to Creeley, *Gedichte*, 164. Furthermore, Schäfer considers Creeley's influence on Brinkmann much stronger after the 1967 publication of Creeley in German translation.

[41] Cf. Hans-Jürgen Heise, "Einer nennt es Sprache," *Rheinischer Merkur*, 5 Dec. 1980; see also Gerhard W. Lampe, *Ohne Subjektivität* (Tübingen: Niemeyer, 1983), 95, who claims this stylistic mode borrows from the calligraphic techniques of concrete poetry.

das andere
Bein auf
den Bade-
wannenrand

aufgestützt
fragt nach
der Uhrzeit
wie spät

und ich sehe
den kleinen
Fleck Haar

zwischen ih-
ren Schenkeln
für sie eine
Stelle wie

jede andere
zum Waschen
und denke
warum nicht

während sie
noch einmal
fragt, nackt

das Standbein
gewechselt.

Here Brinkmann, like Creeley, exhibits a deft touch with his discerning eye for gestures, especially those made by one's partner.[42] In addition, "Noch einmal" punctuates how the faculties of sense perception can be mutually exclusive, for in this vignette heightened visual awareness operates at the expense of auditory attentiveness.

Before moving on to a discussion of O'Hara's influence on Brinkmann, let us consider another small-press release, *Godzilla*

---

[42] "Noch einmal" bears a thematic link to Creeley's "Something." See Robert Creeley, *Words* (New York: Scribner's, 1967), 35.

(1968).[43] This publication is unique as Brinkmann's one book of poetry with thematic unity. Each of the seventeen poems collected here addresses a topic synonymous with the late 1960s, the new sexuality. Adding to the book's homogeneous makeup, the poems are typeset on photographs for magazine advertisements, for the most part close-up shots of young women in bikinis. Brinkmann and Rygulla incorporated the same pop technique with several poems in *ACID*; for instance, Tom Clark's "Sonett" is printed upon a photo of a woman provocatively lowering the shoulder strap of her negligée. Clark's variation on the Petrarchan form is sexual in content: a clinical précis of the female orgasm reading as if lifted from the files of Masters and Johnson. In light of these factors, then, it is no coincidence that Brinkmann's *Godzilla* bears a motto from another poem appearing in *ACID*, Clark's "After Abélard."

Unlike Clark, however, Brinkmann does not adopt an erudite scientific vocabulary. Whereas he once demurely discussed the breasts of seventeen-year-old girls, in the poem "Celluloid 1967/68" (169) he raves about "die Titten von Jane [*sic*] Mansfield." Such language is more the rule than the exception in *Godzilla*. For instance, "Meditation über Pornos" (162) begins with the four-time repetition of the line "Diese Fotze ist gut." Equally impudent is "Godzilla telefoniert so gern" (173), where Brinkmann draws on the Freudian link between sex and death by means of an obscene phone call. Another document of its era, *Godzilla* not only shows Brinkmann following in Fiedler's footsteps but also reflects how the 1960s concept of camp embraced aspects of pornographic fantasy.[44] Still other American influences in *Godzilla* can be found in "Andy Harlot Andy" (165):

> Von einem bestimmten Augenblick
> an hört man auf, nur eine Banane

---

[43] Rolf Dieter Brinkmann, *Godzilla* (Cologne: Hake, 1968); rpt. in *Standphotos*, 159–82.

[44] Susan Sontag reached German readers with "Anmerkungen zu »Camp«" in *Akzente* 13.6 (1966): 501–21, and the two-part series on "Die pornographische Phantasie" in *Akzente* 15.1 & 2 (1968): 77–95 and 169–90, respectively. Her selected essays were published as *Kunst und Anti-Kunst*, trans. Mark W. Rien (Reinbek bei Hamburg: Rowohlt, 1968).

zu essen. Er ist Jean Harlow in
Verkleidung und sieht so scheu

aus, wenn die Seide raschelt. Die
Bedeutungen wechseln ständig hin
und her. (Einmal ist es eine Banane, einmal nicht!) Mein Leben ist

auf einmal um eine Idee kürzer
geworden, sagt er und zittert mit
den schwarzen Augenwimpern auf
derselben Stelle. Es folgt eine

andere Banane. Er zieht ihr mit
Bedacht die Schale ab und lutscht
sie auf. Die Bedeutungen wechseln
ständig. Er sagt: was wir sehen, ist

nicht das, was wir sehen und fängt
von vorne an. (Einmal ist es eine
Banane, einmal nicht!) Und auf dem
selben alten Sofa wie vorher sitzt

Jean Harlow in Verkleidung. Sie möch-
te endlich kommen, kann es aber nicht.
Sie muß zum Schluß erst noch eine Banane essen, die sie nicht mehr finden
kann.

The title plays off Andy Warhol's 1964 underground film *Harlot* in which the transvestite Mario Montez, disguised as Jean Harlow, sits before the camera eating one banana after another. Brinkmann's poem mirrors the content of the film and the principal features of Warhol's cinematic style: a minimalist plot both repetitive (an actor eating a series of bananas) and ambiguous (questions of gender identity). *Harlot*, however, relies on a special interplay between repetition and ambiguity, in that while a banana is undeniably a phallic symbol, its repeated use throughout a seventy-minute film negates any inherent symbolic potency. The film, then, teases the viewer with its one-dimensionality by piquing the senses while simultaneously thwarting the intellect. In "Andy Harlot Andy" Brinkmann's strength is his restraint. He deftly captures the gist of Warhol's surface art by recounting the bare essentials of the film without interpreting its meaning.[45] What Warhol's film means is not the question, for what we see is not what we see. With meaning in a constant state of flux, interpretation — rather than acting out one's sexual fantasies — is taboo.

The New York scene, with artists like Warhol and poets like O'Hara, played a crucial role in the formation of Brinkmann's poetics. Although he certainly drew on Warhol's pop aesthetics and the notion of surface art, perhaps most important in terms of what Brinkmann learned from Warhol was the business of art: consumer-oriented marketing techniques and how to turn provocation into self-promotion. As to O'Hara, the clearest indications of his influence on Brinkmann can be found in two sources, Brinkmann's essay "Die Lyrik Frank O'Haras" and his preface to *Die Piloten*. A close look at the former offers insight into what makes O'Hara's brand of American poetry so appealing. For Brinkmann, O'Hara represents a contemporary New York blend of late-nineteenth-century Parisian surrealism with the expressionism of Berlin following the First World War. As a central figure in the New York school of poetry, O'Hara displayed qualities distinguishing him from many contemporaries. Unlike the Black Mountain poets, he had no programmatic theory of poetry. Without theory, neither subject matter nor style is predetermined. Thus, spontaneity becomes the key to composition.

Brinkmann is also drawn to O'Hara's extraliterary impulses, in particular contact with the New York art scene. Both his personal and professional interests in painters and painting brought a special energy to O'Hara's writing. The blending of art forms creates new possibilities for language, and, as Brinkmann notes, O'Hara was a pioneer in collaborating with painters and incorporating the techniques of pop art or action painting into his poetry. With regard to the latter, Brinkmann recognizes O'Hara the poet as taking an active role within the poem itself. According to his analysis, O'Hara's poetry gains its vitality by renouncing literary exclusivity and including all possibilities, especially common, everyday occurrences. This is most evident in

---

[45] See Gerd Gemünden, "The Depth of the Surface, or What Rolf Dieter Brinkmann Learned from Andy Warhol," *The German Quarterly* 68.3 (1995): 235–50, here 241.

what O'Hara himself called his "I-do-this, I-do-that" poems. The *Lunch Poems* exemplify this style and place the poet in action within his milieu, the streets of New York City. The surroundings may be nonliterary, even trivial, but the poet is the key in determining what is to be taken in and then rendered in return. For Brinkmann, the subjective interests of the poet are much more important than any theory of poetic language. The poet's role is that of a writer of poems, but also a participant, observer, actor. The premise is that poetry will simply flow from a willing encounter with one's environment.

If Brinkmann's essay "Die Lyrik Frank O'Haras" outlines what he admires in this American poet, then the preface to *Die Piloten* lays claim to what he as a poet shares with O'Hara. Though more frivolous in tone, the preface picks up on several matters discussed in the essay. Paramount is the emphasis on everyday life, indeed a preference for the ordinary and commonplace with the only requirement being for the poet to have a discerning eye. Along related lines, Brinkmann embraces O'Hara's penchant for the poem as snapshot, a trademark suggesting not only common traits but also a common mentor, William Carlos Williams. Brinkmann's reference to O'Hara as a passionate fan of the movies is telling for it does more than remind us that both poets were fascinated by the big-screen world of Hollywood. More importantly, this remark underscores one area in which Brinkmann both recognized and approached O'Hara's poetic sensibility. Their various poems on films and film stars do more than pay tribute to the industry. In fact, in spite of all the naming of names, their movie poems are more about movie-goers than movie-stars. Neither poet is seeking to escape into a celluloid fantasy world. They are not duped, as they clearly see through the mythic spectacle regardless of how stunningly staged. And therein lies the enchantment: the challenge to maintain the thrill in the face of an acknowledged illusion.[46]

The preface to *Die Piloten* rings of O'Hara's bold prose style. From the outset Brinkmann establishes his position with regard to traditional poetry by announcing his preference for rock 'n' roll,

---

[46] This distinction also applies to pop stars in general; cf. Gemünden, 243 and his discussion of "Graham Bonney oder das komplizierte Gefühl" and "Nachtrag zu dem Gedicht über Graham Bonney etc." in *Standphotos*, 233–34 and 279–80, respectively.

and central to his argument is the frequently quoted declaration, "Man muß vergessen, daß es so etwas wie Kunst gibt! Und einfach anfangen." (186) This statement, as well as the spirit permeating the overall preface, is best understood when compared to the opening of O'Hara's "Personism: A Manifesto."[47]

> Everything is in the poems. . . . I don't believe in god, so I don't have to make elaborately sounded structures. I hate Vachel Lindsay, always have; I don't even like rhythm, assonance, all that stuff. You just go on your nerve. If someone's chasing you down the street with a knife you just run, you don't turn around and shout, "Give it up! I was a track star for Mineola Prep."

Brinkmann's directive "forget art!" must be viewed in light of O'Hara's "You just go on your nerve." Each statement is a flat denial of literary theory and schooled aesthetics, to say nothing of how a writer confronts a blank sheet of paper. Both O'Hara and Brinkmann represent a posture that openly scoffs at speculative doctrine. By forgetting art and going strictly on nerve, they repudiate the importance of any guiding principle, whether as impetus for creative expression or justification of the end product.

Although the preface to *Die Piloten* touts Brinkmann's kinship with O'Hara, this claim — in light of the total body of each poet's work — is misleading. "Personism," written in 1959 for Donald Allen's *New American Poetry* but then withdrawn for not complementing O'Hara's earlier poems selected for inclusion, is doubtless a parody and most likely of Charles Olson's "Projective Verse." Its witty nonchalance is a sign of O'Hara's objections not only to what he perceived as the pretentious manifestos of the Black Mountain poets, but also to poetic theory in general.[48] Moreover, it is the only such example of O'Hara elaborating on his poetics. Brinkmann, on the other hand, exhibits a near obsessive need to explain his poetry and himself. His numerous forewords and afterwords to books of poetry plus notes and remarks to specific poems all indicate that he, unlike O'Hara, was neither willing nor able to let the poems stand on their own. A glaring example of this compulsion is his "Ein unkon-

---

[47] In *The Collected Poems of Frank O'Hara*, ed. Donald Allen (New York: Knopf, 1971), 498–99.

[48] Marjorie Perloff, *Frank O'Hara: Poet Among Painters* (Austin: U of Texas P, 1979) 16–17.

trolliertes Nachwort zu meinen Gedichten," a posthumous publication written in 1974 that reads as counterpoint to Brinkmann's earlier claims. In retrospect, the rejection of poetic theory had proven more a handicap than an aid to his creative expression: "Hätte ich eine Theorie anzubieten, ein Weltbild, eine Ansicht, eine Ideologie, wäre mir zu schreiben leichtergefallen."[49] As a result, his poetry frequently relies on a fragmentary form or a series of disjointed free associations. Moreover, this statement rescinds the notion expressed in the preface to *Die Piloten* that poetic theory hampers expression.

O'Hara steadfastly adhered to the opening sentence of his tongue-in-cheek manifesto: "Everything is in the poems." Just as Brinkmann was never able to follow this credo, he likewise failed to capture O'Hara's unique style of verse. In comparing Brinkmann with his other American models, we can conclude that he borrowed specifics from Williams and Creeley, for example the poem as a snapshot and short lines, but from O'Hara he took the general, especially the notion that anything is possible and everything allowed. Although Brinkmann's poetry occasionally reflects aspects of O'Hara's poem "Biotherm,"[50] he was unable to re-create the engaging style of his "I-do-this, I-do-that" poems. An isolated example of Brinkmann imitating this form is "Heute" (328–29), a poem employing recognizable features yet failing to match O'Hara's trademark charm. With its prosaic language and lack of sharp poetic imagery, there is little to raise the story line above the mundane. Because he was clearly out of his element with the O'Hara variety of occasional poem, it is no wonder Brinkmann avoided future attempts.

O'Hara's influence on Brinkmann is strongest in the years 1968 to 1970, especially in *Die Piloten* and *Gras*.[51] Appearing in between these two major publications was *Standphotos*,[52] the small press edition from which the posthumous Rowohlt collection takes its title.

---

[49] *Literaturmagazin* 5 (1976): 228–48, here 235, an essay originally intended as the afterword to Brinkmann's *Westwärts 1 & 2*.

[50] See *Collected Poems of Frank O'Hara*, 436–48.

[51] Brinkmann, *Gras* (Cologne: Kiepenheuer & Witsch, 1970); rpt. *Standphotos*, 299–361.

[52] Brinkmann, *Standphotos* (Duisberg: Hildebrandt, 1969); rpt. *Standphotos*, 281–97.

Standphotos also shows signs of O'Hara, but in a more indirect fashion. One of the eleven poems appearing here is "Hommage à Joe Brainard aus Tulsa, Oklahoma" for the New York artist with whom O'Hara collaborated and whose "C-Comics" Brinkmann used as illustrations in *Die Piloten*. In addition to Brainard, *Standphotos* also includes a poem for Ron Padgett, actually two poems: the English and German versions of "Reading Ron Padgett's Great Balls of Fire" (285–86 and 289–90). Padgett, one of many O'Hara disciples, appeared in both *ACID* and *Silverscreen*, and assisted Brinkmann in the compilation of the latter. The American influences on *Gras* are evident from the title alone — not to be understood strictly in the botanical sense of the lexical motto with which Brinkmann introduces the forty-one poems. The title is both a tribute to Walt Whitman's *Leaves of Grass* and an allusion to drug-culture slang for marijuana. Equally significant, Brinkmann celebrates the Whitmanesque tradition in American poetry with poems in a variety of styles.[53] Titles such as "Die Aloe" (357) and "Nachmittags" (358) reveal a new mode of expression for Brinkmann, the prose poem. "Samstagmittag" (308) and "Die Hand" (351) suggest Williams, while others recall Creeley, in particular "Der leere Stuhl" (316) and "«Le fils de l'homme»"(322). O'Hara's influence can be seen in the movie-star tribute "Mae West macht mit 75 immer noch weiter" (326–27) and especially "Gedicht «Für Frank O'Hara»" (309–315), a poem much in the style of "Biotherm."[54] Finally, "Nach Guillaume Apollinaire" (354) carries an indirect American connection, that is, a reminder of another translation project by Brinkmann and how Apollinaire served as an identity figure for the American poet Ted Berrigan.[55]

---

[53] See Lampe, 108–14; Späth, *Brinkmann*, 59; and especially Sibylle Späth, *"Rettungsversuche aus dem Todesterritorium"* (Frankfurt am Main: Lang, 1986), 229–30, who views the title as a sign of the drug-induced fantasies in the poems. Späth also points to American influences in Brinkmann's experiments with form and structure in *Gras*, in particular a multiplicity of poetic forms reminiscent of the stylistic variety in *ACID* and *Silverscreen*. See also Schäfer, "Brinkmann," 399, who claims Brinkmann is striving for formal pluralism in *Gras*.

[54] See Schäfer, "Brinkmann," 399, who calls this style "Flächenkomposition."

[55] Cf. Späth, *Rettungsversuche*, 239–40. See also Ted Berrigan, *Guillaume Apollinaire ist tot. Und anderes*, trans. Rolf Dieter Brinkmann (Frankfurt am Main: März, 1970).

By the time *Gras* was published, the novelty once associated with Brinkmann's pop poetry had faded. Reviews now voiced skepticism with his "do-it-yourself poems,"[56] even calling him a "Vorgartenzwerg der US-Pop-Szene."[57] Walser leveled a more pointed critique, arguing that the fanfare generated by Brinkmann's American anthologies and his own pop poetry was indicative of the newest form of fascism.[58] With the fading of late-1960s counterculture euphoria Brinkmann withdrew from the literary scene and did not publish again until the appearance of *Westwärts 1 & 2* in 1975. Thus, the period 1962 to 1970 provides a fixed block of time in which we can observe the American influences at work in the development of both his poetry and poetics. The willingness to experiment is a constant in Brinkmann's writing; in fact, these early years can be viewed as a series of exercises in which he samples diverse American forms of poetry.[59] Nonetheless, attempts to imitate these masters often miscarried due to various shortcomings. For example, the strength of William Carlos Williams lies not just in his visual acuity but rather in how this is given expression through idiomatic speech patterns; Brinkmann, however, shows a growing predilection for the vulgar rather than poetically charged colloquial language.[60] Likewise, although a number of poems bear the external contours of Robert Creeley's work, Brinkmann seldom matches his tender lyrical tone. In brief, while Creeley's mark is delicacy, Brinkmann tends to be heavy-handed. Furthermore, Brinkmann came to view Creeley's use of language as too formal, hence restrictive, which explains why he turned to the spontaneous style of poetry written by O'Hara.[61] Finally, a close comparison of

---

[56] See Jürgen P. Wallman, "Jedermann-Gedichte," *Nürnberger Nachrichten*, 6 Jan. 1971.

[57] See Yaak Karsunke, "Ins Gras gebissen," *Frankfurter Rundschau*, 27 June 1970.

[58] Martin Walser, "Über die Neueste Stimmung im Westen," *Kursbuch* 20 (1970): 19–41.

[59] See Heise, "Einer nennt es Sprache," who contends that Brinkmann constantly required an identity figure whose style he would adopt as his own.

[60] See Jürgen P. Wallman, "Ein wüster, alltäglicher Alptraum," *Die Tat*, 3 Oct. 1975.

[61] See Schäfer, "Brinkmann," 397.

the poetry of Brinkmann and O'Hara reveals more differences than similarities. For instance, even though O'Hara had a strong interest in pop art, he is not a pop poet and does not share Brinkmann's aesthetic ties to Andy Warhol.[62] Moreover, Brinkmann's efforts to create a German variant of O'Hara's poetic sensibility more often than not fall short, and there is evidence to suggest that he simply did not understand the veritable sophistication of his mentor.[63] In the final analysis, Brinkmann assimilated a vast variety of influences, foreign as well as native. We can see how he dabbled, so to speak, in assorted styles, trying out one before discarding it for another. The years 1962 through 1970 show that no single author or school ruled for an extended period of time, a sign that Brinkmann's attention span — like the postmodern memory he endorsed — was strictly short term.

[62] As art director for *Kulchur* in 1962 and 1963 O'Hara wrote three "Art Chronicles." In *Kulchur* 3.9 (1963) O'Hara wrote that pop artists such as Warhol and Robert Indiana "tend to make their art *out of* vulgar (in the sense of everyday) objects, images, and emblems," while Claes Oldenburg "makes the very objects and symbols themselves, with the help of papier-mâché, cloth, wood, glue, paint and whatever other mysterious materials are inside and on them, *into* art." O'Hara's "Art Chronicles" are rpt. in *Standing Still and Walking in New York*, Donald Allen, ed. (Bolinas, CA: Grey Fox, 1975). See also Perloff, 87.

[63] See Harald Hartung, "Pop-Lyrik am Beispiel von Brinkmanns 'Piloten,'" *Replik* 4/5 (1970): 57–62, especially 61–62. See also Hartung, "Pop als ›postmoderne‹ Literatur: Die deutsche Szene: Brinkmann und andere," *Die Neue Rundschau* 82.4 (1971): 723–42.

8: Travel Destination America: Image and Influence through the mid-1970s

Although Rolf Dieter Brinkmann eventually distanced himself from the American scene he once so zealously promoted,[1] he can be credited for maintaining a positive fascination with the United States at a time when its image suffered badly in Germany. The early 1970s show German poets following Brinkmann's lead in looking westwards for inspiration. As a result, the image of America proved its resilience in spite of the ongoing war in Vietnam, disclosures of CIA activities, and the Watergate scandal. This chapter will open with a look at a number of American travel poems in order to examine the post-1968 portrayal of the U.S.A.

To begin, let us consider Nicolas Born's "Landschaft mit großem Auto,"[2] a landscape portrait typical of the travel poem genre:

> Mit so einem großen Auto müssen wir hindurch
>   tot   oder lebendig
> im Nacken eine Musik
>   die nie aufhört
> süße Luft von Montana bittere Luft von Missouri
> unsere Mäntel wehen als wären wir auf der Flucht

The opening lines show how Born's use of language and free verse form serves to enhance content. First, by foregoing punctuation and interspersing an isolated word or brief phrase into otherwise long lines he establishes a unique rhythmic flow. Second, the contrasting

---

[1] See Brinkmann, *Rom, Blicke* (Reinbek bei Hamburg: Rowohlt, 1979), 325, 385; Brinkmann, *Erkundungen für die Präzisierung des* Gefühls *für einen Aufstand: Reise Zeit Magazin (Tagebuch)*, (Reinbek bei Hamburg: Rowohlt, 1987), 321; and Brinkmann's "Brief an Hermann Peter Piwitt, 22.7.1972," in *Literaturmagazin* 36 (1995): 92–101, here 100.

[2] Born, *Auge des Entdeckers*, 77; rpt. Born, *Gedichte 1967–1978*, 158.

adjectives (dead/living and sweet/bitter) widen an already expansive landscape. And third, he complements background sounds by means of alliteration; for example, the repetition of *w* in "wehen als wären wir" simulates wind, while the recurrent bilabial nasal phoneme initiating the *m*-words (*mit, müssen, Musik, Montana, Missouri,* and *Mäntel*) echoes the hum of a motor.

A dual awareness of surroundings and self is a primary feature of the travel poem. That is, the poet makes use of the senses, assimilating a variety of external stimuli, to trigger self-reflection. Born, however, employs the first person plural, thus creating a less self-centered perspective.

> wir tanken voll
>   Hundefänger streunen
> wir in den Seitenblicken der Cowboys
> wir im spendablen Schatten eines Flugzeugs
> wir außerhalb des Schußfeldes von Chicago
>   wir schütteln William Fulbright die Hand
>   wir geistern durch Arkansas
> wir besuchen das Grab eines Dichters zu Lebzeiten
> Grün rundum   nur mit einem Stich ins Gelbe
> die Demonstration rennt in die Flammen von Phoenix
>   Arizona rotbraun der Weltraum schwarz

Just as these lines span vast stretches of the continental United States, subject matter moves beyond geography to bridge such diverse types as dogcatchers, cowboys, gangsters, senators, poets, and protestors. Anaphora adds rhetorical effect, underscoring the sense of gratitude and respect in references to international educational exchange or the act of paying homage to a literary hero. In parallel fashion, allusions to Chicago and Phoenix play off mythic aspects of American culture and history.

As if dwarfed by the vast landscape through which they drive, Born's travelers exhibit the diffident demeanor of self-conscious foreigners:

> wir sind ein Punkt der sich westwärts bewegt
> wir sind nicht Amerikaner
>   gehören aber auch dazu
> ein Sheriff zwingt uns zum Anhalten

nein wir haben keinen schwarzen Hitchhiker
   mitgenommen
wir sind keine Pferdediebe allerdings Deutsche
unsere Höflichkeit ist die Höflichkeit von Ausländern

With the landscape dominant and the passengers subordinate to the large automobile in which they travel, the human element of this poem is reduced to a point in motion, traceable as if on a map. The passing mention of a sheriff, a black hitchhiker, and horse thieves adds an intriguing subplot to an otherwise loose travel narrative; furthermore, the topic of law and order gains potential for controversy when race is added to the mix. The polite reserve of these foreigners, however, suggests more than a passive desire for anonymity. Throughout this poem ego is held in check; hence, the digression on horse thieves does not serve as a point of departure for socio-political commentary.

Following this diversion, the final seven lines hurry the poem to its conclusion:

wir werden schneller

wir meinen wir sausen

eingepackt in süße Luft

und in eine Musik die nie aufhört

altern wir ganz langsam

vielen Dank Pentagon

für diesen statistischen Verzögerungseffekt

The increase in velocity heightens self-consciousness and brings about changes in perception. Seemingly intoxicated by speed, sweet air, and non-stop music, the travelers experience a time lag affecting the aging process: the faster they travel the slower they age. Rather than veer off into sci-fi fantasy, however, Born undercuts this sense of alienation by concluding with an ironic aside to the American military establishment.

A more critical though self-deprecating tone can be found in Born's "Bilanz mit Zwischenfall,"[3] an episodic travel poem debunking American myths by linking the fate of a Thanksgiving-day turkey

---

[3] See Born, *Auge des Entdeckers*, 73; rpt. Born, *Gedichte 1967–1978*, 154.

to that of Native Americans. Once again the poet paints a topog-
raphical portrait, but this time casts doubt on the natural beauty of
the scenic vistas: "das Land ist frisch eingesprüht/ für den größten
Farbfilm aller Zeiten." While landscape panoramas typify Born's
American travel poems, other poets turn to cityscapes in verse for
their portrayals of life in the United States. In "Wir sind alle verrückt,"[4] Johannes Schenk presents the visiting writer on a tour of
Chicago where, by means of poetic license, Bertolt Brecht meets
Upton Sinclair in the city's legendary stockyards. Jürgen Becker observes urban life in America with "In der Nähe von Andy Warhol,"[5]
a poem literally taking focus on a New York City street scene:

> als er dann wankte und umfiel,
> der Schwarze auf dem Union Square,
> hob ich ans Auge die Kamera
> und sah im Sucher, daß
> er liegen blieb
> zwischen den gehenden Leuten.

Adopting a minimalist style, Becker dispenses with typical travel
poem details; instead, he relies on a camera to add the tourist
touch. Within six lines this poem exposes a society failing to come
to the aid of a man in need. The detail of his skin color makes the
incident an issue and raises questions of racial prejudice in the
U.S.A. The title, however, creates an additional set of parameters.
The reference to Andy Warhol is both spatial and thematic. On a
literal level Becker locates the scene in the vicinity of Warhol's new
factory at 33 Union Square between East 16th and East 17th
Streets in Lower Manhattan. On a thematic level the mention of
Warhol suggests an in-crowd celebrity set and pop culture indiffer-
ence to goings-on in the real world. For Becker, then, the scene
captured here becomes an unstaged happening, with reluctance on
the part of passersby to get involved symptomatic of an individual-
istic attitude pervading city life in America. Finally, Becker's mini-
malism matches Warhol's own aesthetics, and the poet's use of a

---

[4] See *Dimension* (1983): 432–35; from Johannes Schenk, *Zittern* (Berlin:
Wagenbach, 1972).

[5] Becker, *Gedichte 1965–1980*, 72.

camera viewfinder to frame the nonaction of this scene corresponds to Warhol's portrait-style of film making.

A minimalist style combining the theme of flight to America is found in Dieter Leisegang's "Stille Teilhabe."[6]

> Ich habe ein Stückchen Land gekauft
> Bißchen Wüste New Mexicos
>
> 1km², der Preis: 1000 Dollar
> Aber, zu fern, drauf zu leben
>
> Zu fern für ein Grab, gerade
> Gut genug, mir zu gehören
>
> (Solch stillem Teilhaber)
> Von fern —

These four couplets and abrupt conclusion exemplify the poet's place in contemporary German literature. Atypical of his generation, Leisegang advanced the postwar German tradition of hermetic verse by assimilating a touch of American empiricism.[7] Never having visited America, he adds a new twist to the standard travel poem by assuming the role of a foreign investor in real estate exploiting the myth and enchantment of a far-off land with its wide-open spaces. Leisegang relies on irony throughout this poem, from the diminutive constructions "Stückchen Land" and "Bißchen Wüste" to the parenthetical self-characterization "Solch stillem Teilhaber." The allusion to a grave site takes on added significance in light of Leisegang's suicide on 21 March 1973, approximately six weeks after the composition of this poem. In retrospect, then, "Stille Teilhabe" reads like a postscript to the poet's brief literary career. The investment for purposes of neither residence nor burial represents Leisegang's ties — "from afar" — to modern American poetry. Moreover, the purchase of a plot of land in New Mexico's desert suggests an ideal setting for a poet generally ignored by German literary circles to play out his role as a sleeping partner.

---

[6] Leisegang, *Lauter letzte Worte*, 193.

[7] See Klaus Weissenberger, "Die Voraussetzungen der Gegenwartslyrik," introduction, Weissenberger, 21.

Another variation on the standard travel poem is Erich Fried's dramatic monologue "Amerikanischer Tourist in Tijuana."[8] Here Fried takes the notion of the ugly American one shocking and abhorrent step further:

> Hundert Dollar für einen Sitz in der zweiten Reihe
> Dafür hätte ich den Präsidenten im Weißen Haus sehen können
> Aber nein, nur in diesem stinkenden mexikanischen Puff
> um aus nächster Nähe einer Kastration beizuwohnen

While sparing no details, the account of this incident is surprisingly low-key if not blasé. The even tone follows from the motto — "it was (you may say) satisfactory," from Eliot's "Journey of the Magi" — and corresponds to a business-like attitude rating the lurid show in terms of monetary value: "Immerhin/ hundert Dollar war das schon wert: das erlebt man/ nicht alle Tage." Finally, a bizarre sense of poetic justice is offered in the closing stanza by presenting the victim in his previous role as child molester:

> Nur jetzt vorige Woche habe ich in dem gleichen Lokal
> in einer stinknormalen Show mit einem Geschäftsfreund
> denselben Kerl gesehen wie er drei Kinder fickte
> Also war das damals wieder ein glatter Betrug.

In spite of Fried's apparent fixation on the most horrendous subject matter, his purpose is to direct attention away from the stage and onto the audience. If, as the final stanza shows, the American tourist is a Tijuana regular, then the poem proves the business law of supply and demand by showing that such spectacles are staged to suit the wanton desires of dollar-paying customers from north of the border.

For other poets, America and Mexico offer topics less reprehensible and venues more exotic. For example, Christoph Meckel's "Landschaften, die sie durchfahren"[9] presents Mexican landscapes in a style reminiscent of Höllerer's "Thesen zum langen Gedicht." Here, the opening stanza:

---

[8] Fried, *Die Freiheit den Mund aufzumachen*, 49.

[9] *Akzente* 22.4 (1975): 289; rpt. in Christoph Meckel, *Liebesgedichte* (Berlin: Anabis, 1977).

Landschaften, die sie durchfahren, gemeinsam und ohne
besondres Gepäck; an Wintertagen im Buick
auf steigenden Ebenen: Mexikos Horizonte
klar, und leuchtend, und raumlos, und unentrinnbar
der Staub und die Glocken, im Abend der Regenzeit
und weiß gebautes Gebirge im Wind, in der Luft.
(«Erinnerst du dich? Wir durchquerten den Kiesfluß
langsam umfuhren wir den toten Skunk auf der steinigen
Straße nach Zacatecas, Stadt des Staubs und der schmutzigen
Apotheken — und immerwieder zurück
an die Küste, immerwieder in irgendein altes
Encantada-Hotel, das wir kannten
von früher her, aus einer bessren Beleuchtung —»)

Although American influences are rare in Meckel's poetry, this poem literally features an American vehicle and the long lines and rolling rhythm of Whitman. There is also a discerning balance and interplay of form and content in that the extended poetic lines complement an expansive landscape and wide horizons. Likewise, the rhythm builds in momentum parallel to the accumulation of visual details during the drive.

American influences also mark Meckel's "Jugend."[10] Although not an American travel poem, "Jugend" displays the exuberance of Kerouac's *On the Road* and pays homage to an international Beat Generation.

Brother what a life that was! Wir rannten
den melodischsten Pfeifen hinterher
scharrten nach den Knochen der Toten, den gleissenden
Knochen weggeworfener Engel, ja
wenn irgendwas wahr ist: wir schwammen in
    Rotweinflüssen
und die Räusche balgten sich um uns, und die Sommer —
Haufen Azur zwischen Nacht und Nacht —
überfielen uns im Schlaf, es weckten uns Feste
satt und ohnmächtig verschwanden wir in den offenen Himmel.

---

[10] Christoph Meckel, *Wen es angeht: Gedichte* (1974; Munich: Heyne, 1979), 8–10.

Brother what a life that was! Rumstreuend
trunken und nichts sonst
Wind und Kognak oder sonstwie sonstwas
vorüber an den Bungalows unserer Bosse
sterblich wie Zwieback, die die Tempel ersetzen
für eine Weile, unsterblich wie Zwieback
im Auge immer Atlantis, die Horizonte des Tieflands
Ebenen, darauf der Himmel saß, ein fetter Türke
Frauen betrachtend an Abenden aus Heu und Anis
schlaflos in einem Hotelbett, schnelle Liebe
oder in einem Gehölz, wo das Gürteltier pflügt.

The euphoria here predates a 1960s political awareness, and the
poem celebrates memories of youth in a distinctive fashion with its
opening exclamation, in English, acknowledging the enormous influence of American culture and counterculture since the 1950s. In
addition, this poem recalls the anthologies that introduced the
American Beat Generation to Germany. In other words, Meckel's
"Jugend" mirrors the reckless abandon Paetel associated with Beat
writers and embodies the rebellious voice for which Höllerer had
longed in postwar German verse:

Haben wir nicht nach einem Heiland gerufen: O Lazarus, Buddha
o Alkohol, o Syphilis, o Erbrechen
Gerechtigkeit!
Haben wir nicht geheult nach Göttern: zeigt euch
in der blutfarbenen Mandorla, stimmt ein
in den zähneklappernden Jubel!
Haben wir unsere Väter nicht ausgepfiffen
während die Erde in den Mittag fuhr, haben wir
unseren Frauen und Träumen nicht Kinder gemacht
Sack und Asche verweigernd, ungetrost
und nüchtern am Ende raufend um den Rest der Welt!

Furthermore, "Jugend" not only borrows the wide-ranging lines of
Ginsberg, it bears a strong likeness to his poem "Ready to Roll."[11]
Both subject matter and diction are analogous in the two poems,

---

[11] See Allen Ginsberg, *Reality Sandwiches* (San Francisco: City Lights, 1963), 64.

especially references to alcohol and sex as well as the frequent exclamatory outbursts.

The seraphic tone of "Jugend" is broken in the middle of stanza three by the question "Stimmt das?" With this query Meckel reaffirms "Jugend" as a poem that reminisces, and its refrain "Brother what a life that was!" underscores the transitory nature of ecstasy and the fleeting side of youth. However, this intrusion does not doubt the reliability of memory, but the propriety of a life style. And if adulthood poses the question, then youth provides the resounding answer in the closing stanza:

> *Brother what a life that is!* In die Gräber mit uns
> wenn wir den Himmel nicht gestürmt haben auf Treppen
> voll azurner Scherben.
> In die Gräber mit uns, auf der Stelle, restlos
> wenn Wut und Jubel verstummt, weil uns ein
> Gähnen kommt an den Abenden
> und wenn wir je die mördrische Treppe räumen.

The answer is a confirmation of the youthful prerogative to live life to its fullest. The change of verb tense in the refrain is an attempt to negate the ephemeral quality of joy. At the core of "Jugend" lies a clear and distinct concept of happiness. Meckel addresses this topic in *Suchbild*, noting that happiness is established as a human right in the United States.[12] In spite of Meckel's slight misrepresentation of the U.S. Constitution, this is the idea of happiness employed in "Jugend." America's revolutionary spirit amended the Enlightenment notion of life, liberty, and property, consequently establishing the *pursuit* of happiness as an inalienable right. This same ardor permeates Meckel's poem. The collective *we* tran-

---

[12] See Christoph Meckel, *Suchbild: Über meinen Vater* (1980; Frankfurt am Main: Fischer, 1983), 116: "Es gibt verschiedene Definitionen von GLÜCK, die nicht viel besagen. Das GLÜCK gilt als günstige Fügung des Schicksals (die übliche Formel) und wird beschrieben als Seelenzustand, der sich ergibt aus der Erfüllung von Wünschen, die für den jeweils einzelnen wesentlich sind. In politischen und philosophischen Systemen wird das Verlangen nach GLÜCK bejaht als sittlich berechtigter Antrieb menschlichen Handelns. In der Verfassung der Vereinigten Staaten ist GLÜCK als ein Recht jedes Menschen festgelegt."

scends, indeed transgresses, the traditional literary sense of *carpe diem* by pressing for more than today. Here youth demands to exercise those rights, seizing the pursuit of a life of happiness in a distinctively American way.

To conclude this section, let us return to Rolf Dieter Brinkmann, who in 1974 served as writer in residence at the University of Texas at Austin. Brinkmann recounts his journey to America in "Westwärts,"[13] a long poem capturing both the realization of certain dreams and a sense of disillusionment. The narrative line of this poem is set by the travel route from London to New York, and — once stateside — over Washington, D.C., and Nashville, Tennessee, to Austin, Texas. The lyric persona, however, does not narrate the journey as a conventional travel report; the story is communicated by means of poetic moments noted at various stations along the way. Consistent with Brinkmann's poetics as culled from his American models, "Westwärts" employs the present tense throughout its three sections. Passages where the preterit tense occurs indicate flashbacks in which the past is viewed through the ongoing here-and-now perspective of the narrator. The following excerpt shows how Brinkmann blends the two time frames and moves forward in the present by looking back at the past:

in London steige ich um.

Ein kalter Wind weht durch die Halle. Das

Transparent schaukelt, Fortschritt, Frieden
Kartoffeln im Komputer.

Dann werde ich durchsucht.
Mich fröstelt.
Am Gebäude wächst eine Wiese vorüber.

Auf einmal, da war ich, an dieser Stelle, in meinem Leben.

Einige Zeilen weiter hob das Flugzeug ab. Die nächste Zeile
hieß, eine matschige Winterdämmerung in New York, bleiche
rosa Wolken fern und

---

[13] Brinkmann, *Westwärts*, 42–47. Subsequent references to poems from this book will be cited parenthetically in the text with the abbreviation "Ww" followed by page number.

> nah ein Neger in Uniform vor der Tür,
>   der mit dem Kleingeld spielt.
>
> Beobachtung: ich schaute
>
> auf das Flugfeld und hatte plötzlich das Gefühl, ich
>   hatte keine Vergangenheit mehr.

By noting how individual lines of the poem mark the passage of narrative time, Brinkmann underscores a self-conscious recognition of recording the events of the journey. The New York airport intensifies self-awareness, and the strategically isolated line "Beobachtung: ich schaute" signals the here-and-now with such power that the lyric persona is forced to acknowledge loss of his past.

Arrival in America marks a new chronological sequence. The parenthetical command "Anschnallen!" indicates the end of the layover in New York and resumption of air travel as passengers fasten their seatbelts. Until this point the poem has operated on a visual level; now the acoustic component emerges with "Ei läi in äh Field/ off tohl Grass samwär" — Brinkmann's phonetic rendering of the English text of the song "Spill the Wine" by Eric Burdon and War.[14] The announcement "der Unterhaltungsteil hat/ angefangen" confirms a change in mood, and indeed the text takes on a more relaxed, entertaining character, even when addressing the topics of human interaction and love:

> Die beste Entfernung für zwei Personen ist,
>   ein Meter zwanzig zu suchen,
>
>   überdrüssig der Bäume,
>   überdrüssig der Stadt,
> Musik: Oh, sweet
> nothing   Washington ist nichts
>   anderes, beim Drüberfliegen,
>   nachts, als eine Menge Funzeln in der
> und wie fällt man in   Dunkelheit,
>   die Liebe?
>
>   und hier bin ich wieder,
>
>   abgeschnallt.

---

[14] According to Burglind Urbe, *Lyrik, Fotographie und Massenkultur bei Rolf Dieter Brinkmann* (Frankfurt am Main: Lang, 1985), 164, reference to this song suggests a drug-induced change in perception.

The passage is vintage Brinkmann with the poet at his dissociative best blending visual impressions with musical accompaniment while pondering an abstract concept *and* still maintaining the narrative line. Furthermore, his reference to Washington, D.C., hints of disappointment as from on high the faint lights convey nothing of the majestic grandeur associated with the nation's capital.

Evidence that the past has not been left totally behind is found in the lines "& ich kaue/ ein belegtes Brötchen aus Köln// über Nashville, Tennessee." Such a sidelight not only casts the world as a global village in this the jet age, but the very act of eating a sandwich made in Cologne also takes on defiant — albeit piddling — overtones as these lines are placed alongside the interdiction "Fleisch einführen/ verboten." Brinkmann's homeland likewise surfaces in the ensuing contemplative interlude:

> Zur Problematik des
> Dichterischen heute dachte ich die Frage, wer
> mag schon die Bauern Südoldenburgs besingen?
> (. . . grünt Natur, fressen Tiere
> darüberhin)
> Meine erstaunliche
> Fremdheit!
> Die nächsten Kapitel wurden überflogen.

The question of who is to extol the virtues of Brinkmann's rural heritage is legitimate; nevertheless, the lyric persona reacts with disdain at the thought of traditional nature poetry, reducing it to an anachronistic endeavor in the postmodern era of transatlantic flights. Furthermore, the alleged strangeness of the lyric persona is surprising only in the most ironic sense. The further westward the journey proceeds, the greater the feeling of homelessness, a condition affirmed by the response to the query "wo kommst du her?" — "Direckt aus/ der Mitte von nirgendwo." The poem is the vehicle by which passengers reach their destination:

> Natürlich nicht!   Die Wörter
>   ziehen uns weiter,
>   westwärts,
>   wohin? (Wer ist
>   wer?) Und

Romananfang:
(my heart went
    boom)   die Mythologie der vier Himmels
als ich über den dichten   Richtungen bricht zusammen,
    Rasen ging.
                     in verschiedenen Farben.

This artifice, in which words pull the passengers to their goal, corresponds to a form of locomotion where travelers are fully dependent on the means of conveyance — here, an airplane and flight crew. Thus, there is a loss of identity as expressed in the parenthetical question "Wer ist/ wer?" Final arrival is a new beginning — "Romananfang" — accompanied by an emotional boost voiced in the Beatles quote: "my heart went/ boom." Disorientation and fatigue, however, counter the elation; and Brinkmann provides a masterful rendering of jet lag with "die Mythologie der vier Himmels/ Richtungen bricht zusammen,/ in verschiedenen Farben."

The conclusion of the first section of "Westwärts" finds the lyric persona in temporary lodgings:

Hier ist eine Wüste, dachte ich im Motel, nächste Zeile.
Eine tote Palme stand neben dem Swimming Pool.

(Villa Capri
Motor Hotel, 2400   Kleenex aus dem Schlitz
N. Interregional
Highway, Austin   in der Wand, zum Abwischen der Liebe
Texas 78705   wessen?

Der Aufwischneger bringt Bierdosen.

A dead palm tree next to a swimming pool is not a welcome greeting to a weary traveler. In addition, this image underscores the futility of man's attempt to create an oasis in the desert. Instead of time and date, motel name and address add a personal touch — minutiae stressing the now static position of a lyric persona long underway. Furthermore, the notation of the address serves to locate the self in new surroundings and is the first step in an attempt to re-establish personal identity lost en route. The lines "Kleenex aus dem Schlitz// in der Wand" make use of imagist technique in capturing a distinctive detail of American motel room décor. Beyond stylistic proficiency this allusion takes on special meaning in Brinkmann's work, specifically the use of Kleenex in a sexual — here, autoerotic — context.[15] Moreover, the sexual allusion in these lines parallels the barren setting outside the motel room, in that here sex is not an act of procreation, just as the swimming pool does nothing to augment the fertility of its surroundings. Finally, the passing mention of the "Aufwischneger" is particularly depersonalizing as Brinkmann identifies this figure strictly according to race and his mop-up job, then places him in a servile role. These details are not incidental, since the only human beings who warrant notice and mention in the first section of "Westwärts" are black men.

Section two is traditional in both form and content. The setting is a park and the narrative line of a travel poem is replaced by a discourse on love, societal restraints, and language.[16] Section three returns to a free-form style, but does not depend on the narrative line of a journey. The lyric persona now occupies a static position around which sounds and images whirl. Brinkmann is less concerned with the myth of the American West than the present-day reality of his Texas environs. Although there is a sense of the wide-open spaces of America's legendary frontier,

> Da bin
> ich
>
> in diesem enormen
> Raum

most other references lack mythic proportion. Brinkmann is moved more by curiosities, showing that he has an eye for bumper stickers —

> „Think Trees"
> „I break for Animals"

---

[15] Cf. Urbe, 166 who claims that Kleenex (or *Tempotaschentücher*) in Brinkmann's work are a sign of hygiene, particularly a means of wiping away traces of repressed sexuality.

[16] The setting evokes George's poem "Komm in den totgesagten park." See Stefan George, *Das Jahr der Seele*, vol. 4 of *Gesamt-Ausgabe der Werke*, 18 vols. (Berlin: Biondi, 1928), 12.

— and an ear for the

> kosmische
> Rock'n'Roll Musikstation
> in der Nacht.

Besides pop culture and round-the-clock shopping, Brinkmann pays homage to modern American poetry and Hart Crane's *White Buildings* with the translated quote "die Äpfel, Bill,/ die Äpfel."[17] Like Crane, Brinkmann addresses the interplay between art and nature, even if the American West he experiences is littered with "Dreck." Furthermore, the reference to this poem by Crane is telling due to its freely associative, dynamic language and the explosive utterance as quoted by Brinkmann. In short, Crane surfaces here as another in the progression of Brinkmann's American influences.

The end of the Texas sojourn is signaled by the unanswered question "Würde ich zurückkommen?" Brinkmann remains vague even with the concluding lines:

> Wohnwagen, Schlangen
> > Gras, schwarze große Vögel,
> > > krächzende Automaten im Februar.
> Ich starrte auf die Buchstaben,
> > > > > das war der Westen,
> > > > als ich den leeren, weiten Parkplatz überquerte.

There is little evidence to suggest Brinkmann is fascinated by the size of this empty parking lot. In fact, this final image first takes on definitive meaning in "Westwärts, Teil 2" (Ww 48–60), which relocates the lyric persona "Zurückgekehrt in dieses/ traurige, alte Europa." Only then do we comprehend the true upshot of Brinkmann's American experience as expressed in the line, "Merkwürdig, wie leer ich zurückkam."

To better understand the cause for this strange feeling of emptiness let us turn to Brinkmann's "Gedicht" (Ww 41), a travel poem recording impressions left by a train journey in the U.S.A.:

---

[17] From the poem "Sunday Morning Apples" addressed to the poet's painter friend William Sommer; see *The Collected Poems of Hart Crane*, ed. Waldo Frank, 2nd ed. (New York: Liveright, 1946), 67.

Zerstörte Landschaft mit
Konservendosen, die Hauseingänge
leer, was ist darin? Hier kam ich

mit dem Zug nachmittags an,
zwei Töpfe an der Reisetasche
festgebunden. Jetzt bin ich aus

den Träumen raus, die über eine
Kreuzung wehn. Und Staub,
zerstückelte Pavane, aus totem

Neon, Zeitungen und Schienen
dieser Tag, was krieg ich jetzt,
einen Tag älter, tiefer und tot?

Wer hat gesagt, daß sowas Leben
ist? Ich gehe in ein
anderes Blau.

Brinkmann's portrayal of this ruinous landscape draws on methods retained from American models. The opening lines evoke the sense of a camera-eye surveying the scene and singling out pertinent details for commentary. An absence of humankind suggests a ghost town; and the adjectives *zerstört*, *leer*, and *tot* plus the annoying sensations associated with dust all contribute to a negative setting. The poetic moment on which the poem hinges is the passage from stanza two to three where the lyric persona moves out of a dream-world. The ensuing allusion to a Spanish dance — literally peacock dance — brings both color and motion to the scene. In addition, the visual transmission is "zerstückelt" thus linking individual images in the choppy fashion of a motion-picture projector. Finally this stately court dance conjures up music, here slow and tedious, a mood corresponding to that expressed in the variation on lines appropriated from the American song "Sixteen Tons."[18] In such manner, Brinkmann charges the purely visual with enhanced

[18] The original reads: "another day older and deeper in debt." Altough the setting is not specifically identified, "Gedicht" is generally acknowledged as an American travel poem. See, e.g., Späth, *Rettungsversuche* 269–70, who also underscores the significance of Tennessee Ernie Ford's "Sixteen Tons" for Brinkmann's generation.

meaning, further evidence for viewing his poetics as a combination of photography and popular music.[19]

This selection of travel poems from the early 1970s reveals a number of particulars in the development of postwar German poetry. American influences, growing since the early 1960s, have by now firmly taken hold. How thoroughly these American influences had permeated German verse can be seen in the work of Meckel, a poet generally known for following in the French tradition.[20] Brinkmann remains the German poet most closely associated with America, and the volume *Westwärts 1 & 2* shows — in spite of his ongoing preoccupation with rock 'n' roll music — that he had freed his poetry from a pronounced pop proclivity.[21] More significantly, the image of America in select travel poems signals the end of what had once been his American dream. With the closing lines of "Gedicht" taking the lyric persona into "another blue," there is a strong hint of Brinkmann renouncing American influences and returning to his European roots, in particular the poetic vision of Gottfried Benn.

As for other poets, the image of America remains vibrant and multifaceted. The critical edge characteristic of 1960s protest poems has noticeably dulled, yet remains present to varying degrees in the poems of Becker, Born, and Fried. One factor stands out in several poems discussed here, that is, an eye for Black America. It is no coincidence that the incidental unnamed Americans appearing in many of these travel poems are black. Although such references often carry socio-political connotations, repeated allusions remind us that for the German travel poet, America offers unique opportunity for contact with an exotic array of peoples. Finally, since the early 1970s German writer-in-residence programs have grown steadily at colleges and universities throughout the United States. As a result, more and more German authors have had occasion to

[19] Urbe, 19. See also Hansjürgen Richter, *Ästhetik der Ambivalenz* (Frankfurt am Main: Lang, 1983), who views the poetics of *Westwärts 1 & 2* as exemplary of the postmodern era.

[20] See Uwe-Michael Gutzschhahn, *Prosa und Lyrik Christoph Meckels* (Cologne: Oberbaum, 1979).

[21] See Jürgen Theobaldy, "Schreckensbilder aus Wörtern," *Frankfurter Rundschau*, 24 May 1975.

experience America first hand. This has affected not only the image of America in German poetry but also the reception of American poetry in Germany.

Even with the image of America undergoing setbacks, German interest in American poetry continued to grow during the early 1970s. Backlash against the imperialist policies of American government and business brought special status to American poets with ties to the underground. The anthologies *Fuck You!*, *ACID*, and *Silverscreen* did much to further this trend, though not without precipitating negative side effects. From the late 1960s through early 1970s a preoccupation with the American underground scene made it difficult for academic poets to gain a foothold in German-speaking countries. In fact, one could argue that mainstream American poetry suffered due to unfounded ties to mainstream American society. A review of those books of American poetry published in German translation from roughly 1965 to 1975 shows two camps of poets. In addition to poets discussed earlier, we can list the following: in one group Archibald MacLeish, John Berryman, James Laughlin, Robert Lowell, and William Carlos Williams; in the other John Giorno, Gerard Malanga, Michael McClure, Ron Padgett,[22] and Charles Bukowski — all of whom appeared in *ACID*. Although Williams could be considered

---

[22] MacLeish, *Journey Home*, trans. Hans-Jürgen Heise (Darmstadt: Bläschke, 1965). Berryman, *Huldigung für Mistress Bradstreet*, trans. Gertrude C. Schwebell with an afterword by Walter Hasenclever (Hamburg: Hoffmann und Campe, 1967). Laughlin, *Die Haare auf Großvaters Kopf*, trans. Eva Hesse (Zürich: Arche, 1966). Lowell, *Für die Toten der Union*, trans. Curt Meyer-Clason (Frankfurt am Main: Suhrkamp, 1969); see also Meyer-Clason's translations of selections from Lowell's *Notebook 1967/68* in *Neue Rundschau* 81.1 (1970): 30–33; and from the GDR: Lowell, *Ein Fischnetz aus teerigem Garn zu knüpfen*, trans. Karl Heinz Berger (Berlin: Volk und Welt, 1975). Williams, *Neue Orte*, trans. Gertrude C. Schwebell (Darmstadt: Bläschke, 1966); and Williams, *Paterson*, trans. Anselm and Josephine Hollo (Stuttgart: Goverts, 1970). Giorno, *Cunt: Gedichte*, trans. Rolf-Eckart John et al. (Darmstadt: März, 1969). Giorno was the superstar of Warhol's film *Sleep*. Malanga, *Selbstporträt eines Dichters*, trans. Rolf Dieter Brinkmann (Frankfurt am Main: März, 1970). Malanga was another of Warhol's film factory superstars. McClure, *Dunkelbraun*, trans. Heiner Bastian (Frankfurt am Main: März, 1970). Padgett, *Grosse Feuerbälle: Gedichte, Prosa, Bilder*, trans. Rolf-Eckart John et al. (Reinbek bei Hamburg: Rowohlt, 1973).

a bridge figure linking these two disparate groups, there are clear distinctions with regard to their respective audiences. Moreover, developments in German poetry during this period indicate which poets exercised the strongest influence. The rebel voice and counterculture stance are the attributes attracting the greatest attention in German literary circles, a point underscored by the continued interest in poets first introduced by the Corso/Höllerer and Paetel anthologies. Both Lawrence Ferlinghetti and Allen Ginsberg[23] remained central figures, and Kenneth Koch, a pivotal poet of the New York school even if not featured in Brinkmann's late-1960s anthologies, gained individual recognition later in the 1970s.[24] The above-listed names raise questions regarding reception, in particular why certain poets of merit fail to generate much interest while others attract a following. With, say, Berryman and Lowell the issue is one of timing. The comparatively solemn nature of their subject matter, especially topics out of American history, plus the formal structure of their verse rang obsolete in an era of pop and protest. The more capricious style of those poets promoted by Brinkmann and Rygulla was more accessible; moreover, it signaled a clear break from the hermetic poetry of past generations. In conclusion, if Ginsberg and Ferlinghetti show the most staying power of American Beat poets introduced in the early 1960s, who of the American poets promoted by Rygulla and Brinkmann in the late 1960s established long-term recognition in German literary circles? Frank O'Hara is the first name to come to mind, and his status as a leading figure in contemporary American poetry has not diminished; O'Hara's disciples, however, have faded from the forefront. In light of publication volume alone, Charles Bukowski stands apart as the American writer who benefited most from the reception of counterculture American poetry in Germany. Having been born in Germany no doubt contributed to interest in his writing,

---

[23] Ferlinghetti, *Ausgewählte Gedichte*, trans. Alexander Schmidt (Zürich: Diogenes, 1972). Ginsberg, *Planet News*, trans. Heiner Bastian (Munich: Hanser, 1969, 2nd printing 1970); *Indische Tagebücher, März 1962-Mai 1963: Notizhefte, Tagebuch, Leere Seiten, Aufzeichnungen*, trans. Carl Weissner (Munich: Hanser, 1972); *Der Untergang Amerikas*, trans. Carl Weissner (Munich: Hanser, 1975).

[24] Koch, *Vielen Dank*, trans. Nicolas Born (Reinbek bei Hamburg: Rowohlt, 1976).

and through the 1970s "Buk" reached German readers through a variety of publications, both poetry and prose.[25] Moreover, his popularity illustrates how Fiedler's Freiburg address anticipated changes not only in literary styles but also reception.

Sylvia Plath, whose bilingual edition of *Ariel* appeared in Germany in 1974, presents a more complicated case study in reception.[26] Following her 1963 suicide at the age of thirty, Plath was recognized in both America and Great Britain as one of the major contemporary poets of the English language. Yet neither Fried's translations nor the positive reviews[27] led to an enthusiastic following in Germany; and unlike other Americans she did not serve as a model for German poets. That Plath lacked either a Beat or pop sensibility certainly played a role; likewise, allusions to Nazi atrocities as well as denunciation of both her father and the German language likely limited her prospects for attracting German readers.[28] The latter point is especially enigmatic in that she shared

---

[25] Among the books of poetry, see Bukowski, *Gedichte die einer schrieb bevor er im 8. Stockwerk aus dem Fenster sprang*, trans. Carl Weissner (Gersthofen: Maro, 1974); *Flinke Killer*, trans. Carl Weissner and Rolf-Eckart John (Cologne: Palmenpresse, 1977); *Western Avenue*, trans. Carl Weissner (Frankfurt am Main: Zweitausendeins, 1979). Bukowski also appeared in and co-edited with Carl Weissner the anthology *Terpentin on the rocks: Die besten Gedichte aus der amerikanischen Alternativpresse, 1966–1977* (Augsburg: Maro, 1978).

[26] Sylvia Plath, *Ariel*, trans. Erich Fried (Frankfurt am Main: Suhrkamp, 1974).

[27] See Günter Blöcker, "Im Kreislauf der Zerstörung," *Frankfurter Allgemeine Zeitung*, 5 Oct. 1974; Rolf Vollmann, "Wie man vielleicht besser leben könnte," *Stuttgarter Zeitung*, 10 Oct. 1974; Werner Vordtriede, "Der Weg des Todes," *Die Zeit*, 25 Oct. 1974; Rudolf Hartung, "Selbstmörderisch eins mit dem Ritt," *Süddeutsche Zeitung*, 8 Feb. 1975; and Kyra Stromberg, "Das existentielle Wagnis," *Frankfurter Allgemeine Zeitung*, 7 Feb. 1976.

[28] A brief biographical note is in order here. Plath's Germanic heritage (mother of Austrian ancestry and father born in East Prussia) plays a crucial role in her poetry. Selected poems are especially critical of her father; see, in particular, "Daddy" in which Plath identifies her father with the Nazis and herself with Jewish victims. Such charges have led to various misunderstandings. For instance, in his review of the bilingual edition of *Ariel*, Alexander Schmitz, "Am Vater verzweifelt," *Die Welt*, 21 November 1974, falsely suggests that Plath's father played an active role in the Nazi regime. In truth, Otto Plath, born in 1885, was fifteen when he came to the United States,

common ground with German writers of the '68 generation: the struggle to come to terms with one's German heritage. This commonality clearly did not extend across international borders, and is compounded by the difficulties of translating Plath's American English into German. As Lowell writes of the *Ariel* poems, "The voice is now coolly amused, witty, now sour, now fanciful, girlish, charming, now sinking to the strident rasp of the vampire. . . . "[29] — all factors leading to problems in translation as well as reception. In addition, Fried provides neither preface nor afterword to his translations. Although Plath's autobiographical novel *The Bell Jar*[30] had appeared in German six years earlier, without a biographical sketch or background information to specific poems of *Ariel* the foreign reader is at a distinct disadvantage.

To better understand how the reception of American poetry affected developments in German poetry, let us look at selected poets and specific trends of the 1970s. The documentation of the new American scene in *ACID* created a variety of new possibilities for German poets. References to rock 'n' roll have since become commonplace in German poetry, especially among poets who came of age during the 1960s and even among those otherwise known for political poems and controversial texts. A case in point is "Einsamkeit eines alternden Stones-Fans" by F. C. Delius.[31] Both rock music and drug culture jargon mark the early poetry of Paul-Gerhard Hübsch, as seen in the book title *Ausgeflippt* and his "tagesschau &

---

where he remained for the rest of his life. An authority on bees, he taught biology at Boston University until his death in 1940.

[29] Robert Lowell, foreword, *Ariel* (1965; New York: Harper, 1966), vii. Plath, although not a student of Lowell's, attended his poetry seminar at Boston University in 1959.

[30] Plath, *Die Glasglocke*, trans. Christian Grote (Frankfurt am Main: Suhrkamp, 1968).

[31] F. C. Delius, *Ein Bankier auf der Flucht* (Berlin: Rotbuch, 1975), 14–15. Frequently anthologized, this poem also appears in Theobaldy, *Und ich bewege mich doch*, 110–12; Hans Bender, ed., *In diesem Lande leben wir* (Munich: Hanser, 1978), 106–7.; and Volker Hage, ed., *Lyrik für Leser* (Stuttgart: Reclam, 1980), 95–96.

wetterkarte, das war der überblick,"[32] a poem daring to unite Elvis Presley, The Beatles, and Walt Disney with Novalis. Christoph Derschau emulates Beat poets by documenting a psilocybin trip in the poem "Hamburg 1975" and pays tribute to the New York school of poetry in "Frankfurt — Stuttgart am 10.4.1975," a poem using a quote from Ted Berrigan as its motto and references to Berrigan's poetry in the text. Moreover, this poem begins with strict adherence to the O'Hara formula for an occasional poem: "Es ist 16 Uhr 25: im Zug reist es sich angenehm."[33]

Charles Bukowski also serves as a model for German poets, especially Jörg Fauser. Like Bukowski, one of Fauser's preferred settings for his brand of lowbrow verse is a barroom. Consistent with the surroundings the language is unadorned and draws from a reserve of slang and profanity. His poem "Zum Alex nach Mitternacht"[34] reflects not only Bukowski's style but also the influx of Anglo-American popular culture on West German everyday life:

> Die Charles-Bronson-Imitation aus Knautschlack
> brütet über einer Cola in der roten Sonne
> überbelichteter Vorstadt-Träume; erledigte Rivalen,
> klatschende Klöten, Kadaver am Galgen, letzter Show-down,
> triefende Mösen, absolutes Finale
> in Technicolor.
> Der blondgefärbte schwule Ithaker mit den lila Denims
> gibt es endgültig auf, Mick Jagger nachzuäffen,
> Mann ohne Publikum, Publikum
> ohne Mann.
> Paß auf, daß du im Lokus nicht ausrutschst
> und dir deinen
> parfümierten Schwanz brichst.
> Dieses miese Loch, Bastard

---

[32] See Paul-Gerhard Hübsch, *Ausgeflippt* (Neuwied: Luchterhand, 1971); and Heinz Piontek, ed., *Deutsche Gedichte seit 1960: Eine Anthologie* (Stuttgart: Reclam, 1972), 264. After renouncing drugs and converting to Islam, this poet is known as Hadayatullah Hübsch.

[33] See Christoph Derschau, *So hin und wieder die eigene Haut ritzen . . . : Ausgewählte Gedichte* (Frankfurt am Main: Fischer, 1986), 39–50 and 33.

[34] Jörg Fauser, *Die Harry Gelb Story* (Gersthofen: Maro, 1973), 13.

eines desolaten Hippie-Sommers, sag dem letzten
Taxifahrer Gute Nacht, sweet Mary,
vor die Wahl gestellt zwischen deinen
abgekauten Titten und dem Nichts
wähle ich deine Titten.
Die Einsamkeit macht uns alle fertig, sagt Klaus
und drückt Janis Joplin, Whisky und »Me and Bobby McGee«,
der Joker rattert, Maschinengewehr, Baader geschnappt,
chant d'amour et de la mort, so'n Mordsdusel,
der Apparat spuckt lauter Markstücke aus
und wir bestellen nochmal
ein Magengeschwür.
Alles was da hängt
ist Fleisch.

Unlike Meckel's "Jugend," Fauser's poem is not a celebration of counterculture lifestyle. Here the characters merely go through the motions of what once meant fun-filled interaction with fellow members of the in-crowd. Now loneliness prevails as the good times of the early hippie summer are past and the atmosphere has turned desolate. Even the name of Red Army Faction leader Andreas Baader, surfacing amidst the din, fails to generate more than passing notice. Here the mood is beyond resignation, the attitude thoroughly cynical or, to borrow the slang of this milieu, "abgefuckt."[35] Perspective is ego-centered but in a singularly self-destructive fashion. For instance, ordering a drink means naming not one's pleasure but one's pain, and the reference to an ulcer points to the chronic effects of this life style.

Fauser's "Zum Alex nach Mitternacht" exemplifies the radical changes in German poetry since 1968. To sprinkle one's text with English words and Anglo-American pop culture personalities seems to have become a prerequisite. Furthermore, since the publication of *ACID* propriety is no longer a guiding principle, and in certain circles shock poesy is the norm. Signs of these changes are most evident in the poetry of Wolf Wondratschek, one of the more

---

[35] Theobaldy/Zürcher, 146;. see also Michael Buselmeier, "Das alltägliche Leben: Versuch über die neue Alltagslyrik," in Buselmeier and Grzimek, eds., *Neue deutsche Lyrik*, 30.

commercially successful poets of the 1970s. Let us consider the title poem "Chuck's Zimmer"[36] from his best-selling collection of poetry and songs:

> Chuck wacht auf
> Die Erde ist leer
> Hunde streunen um die Kommode
> Neben dem Plattenspieler liegt eine Art Schlagzeuger
> In der andern Ecke liegt der Rest
> Die Mädchen die Haferflocken essen sind auch da
> Alles komplizierte Menschen denkt Chuck
> Steigert seine Aufmerksamkeit
> Und stößt buff buff die ersten Sätze aus
> Steht auf um zu duschen
> Hinter der fünften Wand begegnet er einer Frau
> Sie wünscht sich angefallen zu werden
> Breitbeinig wie im Märchen
> Und unglaublich obszön
> Um ihr Herz das sich nach der Liebe sehnt auf der
> > tätowierten Seele
> eines alten kostbaren Teppichs verbluten zu lassen
>
> Too late
> To be legal
> Too late
> To be legal

The depiction of Chuck's room is, in a word, hip. The quasi-narrative mode imbued with a surrealistic touch glides smoothly from one curious detail to the next. Although the enumeration of varied particulars contributes to a heightened sense of attention, the mood is undercut by a hint of resignation in the English-language refrain "Too late/ To be legal." Further evidence of Chuck's carefree manner can be found in "Warum Gefühle zeigen?"[37] with its title — an implicit shrug of the shoulders — reading as a synopsis of

---

[36] Wolf Wondratschek, *Chuck's Zimmer: Gedichte*/Lieder (Frankfurt am Main: Zweitausendeins, 1974), 24–25. Rpt. in Wondratschek, *Die Gedichte* (Zürich: Diogenes, 1992), 36–37.

[37] Wondratschek, 48–49.

Wondratschek's poetics. *Chuck's Zimmer* highlights developments in German literature since Fiedler's Freiburg lecture: a style of poetry marked by flight into an artificial world in reaction against elitist, hermetic verse and politically engaged literature.[38] Such poems propagate an aesthetic of the trivial and a secondhand consciousness with a lyric persona living vicariously through movies and music. More significantly, Wondratschek achieved surprising sales figures with poetry, and in this regard his popularity makes him a true pop poet as he reaches beyond the usual three percent of the populace with interests in contemporary literature.

The poets discussed in the preceding pages embody an antiliterary style flourishing in the early 1970s. Their ties to specific American poets and the Anglo-American sphere of pop culture are evident at first glance. Since German poetry underwent radical changes after 1968, we cannot speak of these poets as fringe figures to the literary scene — the younger set had become firmly established in its own right, not in spite of but rather due to its break with tradition. One poet who remains difficult to classify is Jürgen Becker. His experiments with language and poetic forms predate changes that have been in vogue since 1968. Moreover, the American influences at work in his poetry are more subtle and serve him in the formation of a definitive style of his own. Becker provides convincing examples in praxis of what Höllerer postulated in theory with his "Thesen zum langen Gedicht." Since 1967 he has developed a class of long poem marked by an open stanza form and unique voice blending detached objective description, personal recollections, and quotations from literary texts, popular songs, and conversations. Becker's mastery of this technique allows not only different layers of time to exist simultaneously, but also influences to surface unobtrusively. For example, his "Berliner Programm-Gedicht; 1971"[39] with its typographically stepped lines is reminiscent of William Carlos Williams's *Paterson* as well as Charles

---

[38] Hiltrud Gnüg, "Wolf Wondratschek — Erfolg eines Lyrikers," *Neue Zürcher Zeitung*, 18 Jan. 1979. See also Volker Hage, "Über Wondratscheks *In den Autos*," in *Gedichte und Interpretationen: Gegenwart*, ed. Walter Hinck (Stuttgart: Reclam, 1982), 396.

[39] Becker, *Gedichte*, 41–55.

Olson's "The Kingfishers."[40] As a result, his discerning camera-eye and sharply tuned ear convey a multidimensionality to the poem by encompassing private, public, and even political spheres.

Although employing a different style, Nicolas Born evokes similar comparisons with contemporary American poets and poetics. His break with tradition as proclaimed in his first book of poems, *Marktlage* (1967), is carried on in subsequent work. The long poem "Da hat er gelernt was Krieg ist sagt er"[41] from *Wo mir der Kopf steht* (1970) bears likeness to the photo-realistic approach of Williams in that Born tells a story by means of a series of poetic snapshots. Accordingly, the complete text reflects Olson's theory of "Field Composition" and stands as emblematic of a new era in German poetry in which formal concerns no longer determine the content of a poem; rather, content dictates form.[42]

By 1975, three decades since the end of the Second World War, a new set of parameters had been established for the subject of America in German poetry. One poem reflecting the scope of changes taking place during this thirty-year period is Martin Walser's "Versuch, ein Gefühl zu verstehen,"[43] an all-encompassing attempt to come to terms with America. Walser's poem marks both a turning point and conclusion to the German debate on America initiated by the war in Vietnam. Divided into eleven numbered parts, this multifaceted poem reads — as the title indicates — like an essay, for in the truest sense of the word Walser presents a trial discourse on his concept of the United States. Along these same lines the text is an editorial commentary on the "Experiment Amerika," blurring its literary profile by taking on features of a historical, socio-political trea-

---

[40] See Hans Dieter Schäfer, "Jürgen Becker: Das Ende der Landschaftsmalerei," *Neue Deutsche Hefte* 21.3 (1974): 585–591, here 587.

[41] See Born, *Gedichte 1967–1978*, 80–84.

[42] Walter Hinderer, "Form ist eine Ausdehnung vom Inhalt. Zu Nicolas Borns Gedicht *Da hat er gelernt was Krieg ist sagt er*" in *Gedichte und Interpretationen: Gegenwart*, 374–85. As to the "Konfiguration Becker-Born," both similarities and differences between the two, see Ernst Ribbat, "Subjektivität als Instrument? Zu Jürgen Becker und Nicolas Born," in Jordan, Marquardt, and Woesler, ed., *Lyrik — Von allen Seiten*, 485–501.

[43] First published in *Tintenfisch* 8 (1975): 27–30; rpt. in Martin Walser, *Versuch, ein Gefühl zu verstehen und andere Versuche* (Stuttgart: Reclam, 1982).

tise. Finally, Walser's "Versuch" is also a travel poem in a prose-poem form, drawing on the author's lengthy, first-hand experiences in traversing America's spacious domain, recording impressions and contemplating implications. Above all, this long poem enjoys the privilege — indeed presupposes the necessity — of a retrospective pause to contemplate America and what it has become.

Part one identifies that feeling to be explained and the poem's operative mode:

> Wer erklärt mir mein Heimweh nach Amerika?
> Wie muß der Ton beschaffen sein, der von hier bis Texas reicht
> und so lange hält wie dort der schöne Himmel?
> Wohin mit den zierlichen Eichen, den Zedern, den unzähligen,
> die mir im Kopf nachgewachsen sind?
> Was anfangen mit unsterblichen Sätzen aus dem Supermarkt, die
> noch an sich haben die südliche Windung der Lippen, aus der sie
> entstanden?
> Warum bleibt mir die Tankstelle als wäre sie von Michelangelo?

Walser seeks to reach an understanding of this feeling of homesickness through a series of questions. The lyric persona of line one is not necessarily soliciting aid, but suggesting the universality of the problem at hand. The process of posing questions contributes a sense of caution, and the concern for tone expressed in line two hints of humility on the part of someone undertaking such a monumental task. This reflective consideration likewise shows an awareness of craft striving to assure that not only the poem's form but also its voice will correspond, that is, do justice, to its content. In effect, the initial question in the first line is answered by the series of questions that follow, with each illuminating an underlying fascination with wonders both natural and man-made. Walser's technique is no doubt a rhetorical device; nevertheless, his approach to the subject matter provides various points of departure for the reader. For instance, the mention of a gas station as if built by Michelangelo evokes the allure of Americana as captured by Edward Hopper in the painting *Gas* (1940).

Walser's attempt to understand this unique feeling depends on comparisons of America and Europe. If a German's claim of being homesick for America seems presumptuous, we must recognize an important distinction: one can become an American citizen and leave European traditions behind. Walser, however, turns the notion of homesickness on itself, understanding his malady not as longing for days past but instead a homesickness for the future. This, then, becomes the premise on which the poem turns, and Walser's recorded impressions and commentary must be construed in relationship to his own vision of America, a view of the future in terms of what America might become.

Walser's vision is not optimistic, as he is cognizant of America's storied past. Therefore, in part two he asks with a definite measure of skepticism:

> Habe ich mich täuschen lassen von der Würde, die das Ver-
> brechen annimmt, wenn es von den Großen Familien begangen
> wird?

He has, of course, not been deceived by the myths surrounding such families as the Rockefellers and Kennedys. Walser probes behind the surface images to reveal the reality of America's class structure and the tensions resulting from discrepancies between the haves and have-nots:

> Habe ich nicht erfahren, daß die Mittelstandskinder in der Pause
> nichts zu tun haben wollen mit den schwarzen Bus-Fahrschülern,
> deren Fahrpreis bezahlt wird für Demokratie?

Democracy is the underlying principle and driving force in the poem. For Walser this is less a notion of democracy in practice, as in the above-quoted example of bussing school children to achieve racial balance, than a formulation of the abstract and conceptual: the notion that true democracy will conquer capitalism. As a socialist, Walser employs a concept of democracy defined to suit his idealistic goals. In parallel fashion he adopts the poetic aura of the Good Gray Poet of Democracy in his pursuit of the ideal: "Vielleicht bin ich in Kneipen, Hörsälen, Kaufhäusern und an/ Stränden deiner Demokratie begegnet, Walt Whitman."

The repetition of "Vielleicht" in part six as well as the questions posed throughout the poem underscore the fact that Walser's American experience has not instilled a sense of certainty. As part seven reads:

> Amerika ist, glaub ich, wo sich noch keiner gewiß ist.
> Europa ist, glaub ich, wo Adenauer, de Gaulle und Beckett sich
> ganz sicher sind.

Once again, the approach is to define America in terms of its opposition to Europe. The uncertainty pervading the United States is contrasted by a European brand of politics and literature both of which are grounded in the policy of conservative statesmen and the pronouncements of a writer convinced of life's absurdity.[44] America, on the other hand, stands "wie für immer provisorisch." Hence, positive impressions play against an imminently threatening backdrop. For example, observations such as

> War es das Mädchen im Fernsehen, das für Franklin's Sparkasse
> Sätze auf ihren Lippen gänzlich zergehen läßt?
> War es das grüne Tennessee oder das weißblonde Texas?
> War es der beständige Himmel, die lückenlose Freundlichkeit der
> Leute, oder das pfingsthafte Brausen des überholenden Trucks?

are tempered by the predatory nature of New York City cab drivers, the CIA perjury scandal, and the media smog of the American communications industry.

In the end, Walser's "Versuch, ein Gefühl zu verstehen" cannot shake its own uncertainty and succumbs by necessity to the admission:

> Ich gebe also zu: ich bringe nicht zusammen dieses kapitalistische
> Amerika, von dem der Globus dröhnt, und das konkrete Amerika,
> das ich erfuhr.

Perhaps, to borrow Walser's operative word, the attempt is simply an impossible task. Within the prescribed guidelines, Walser has no choice other than to view America provisionally. He is forced to balance Hollywood heroes — "die lächerlichsten Götter, die je gemacht wurden, Chaplin, Monroe, Sinatra" — with the very foundations of American democracy — "das Bürgerschlößchen, das Jefferson sich gebastelt hat auf einem Berg in Virginia." In such fashion Walser counters those criticisms one might expect with an otherwise positive and at times nostalgic view of America, a trait that surprised many of his German readers.[45] Thus, an equivocating mood marks Walser's critical stance and complements his

---

[44] See Theobaldy, "Begrenzte Weiten," 402.

[45] See Willson, *Dimension* (1983), 15.

reluctance to pass final judgment. As a result, the reader is left with a series of questions and statements in which the last impressions rendered have the best chance of enduring:

> Ich wäre am Rio Grande, mischte Apachen-Echos mit solchen
>   von
> Auschwitz, ich wäre in Tennessee, das so viele Hügel der Sonne
> nachtreibt, und keiner heißt Hohenzollern,
> ich wär in Virginia, dem Land des Laubs, um zu vergessen,
> ich wär in Texas und lernte mich rühmen,
> ich wäre weit weg.

All in all, Walser's "Versuch, ein Gefühl zu verstehen" reads like a review of the long tradition of America in German poetry by providing a portrait of the New World as an inspiring vision of the future, a vast land worthy of praise and indeed a visit, but still a country not without its shortcomings.

Qualities shared with other poems previously discussed make Walser's "Versuch, ein Gefühl zu verstehen" the ideal poem to reiterate developments in the image of America in German poetry from 1945 to 1975. One consistent aspect of Walser's view of the United States is the concept of America as the future. With his premise, "Amerikaner kann man werden," Walser reminds us of émigré poets such as Waldinger or Gong and what their work brings to Germany's postwar literary tradition. Although Walser makes no mention of Vietnam, his reference to the Apache echoes recalls America's less than glorious past and imparts a sense of shattered ideals, as in Karsunke's "Kilroy war hier." Born in 1927, Walser displays the disappointment with America the superpower that is common to German writers of his generation. His ridicule of American film stars corresponds to both Brecht's Hollywood poems and Benn's derision of American musicals; likewise, his censure of capitalism mirrors the socio-economic critique of America as intoned by Enzensberger, Fried, and others. Finally, characteristic of a category of German poems since 1965, Walser adopts a hymn-like voice reminiscent of Walt Whitman. This stylistic trait is employed not only to address both Whitman and the democratic ideals of the United States, but also to celebrate the natural wonders of North America, a feature also found in landscape travel poems of Meckel and Born. Above all, Walser's "Versuch, ein Gefühl zu verstehen" reaffirms the centuries-old European tradition of viewing America as an experiment. For Walser, America carries meaning beyond the clichéd designation as a land of new beginnings and unlimited possibilities. His interests lie less in how one starts anew than in how to make the most of potentialities not realizable in Europe. Walser's station as socialist poet combines the functions of historian, social scientist, and political analyst. His task in the ongoing study of the experiment America is to probe the nation's past and present in order to better understand what the future might bring. Even if his chosen assignment inevitably leads to uncertainty, he will neither forego the investigation nor deem its efforts futile.

9: Casting Light on Mr. Hopper's America: From the Late 1970s through the 1980s

T HE YEAR 1975 marks a watershed with respect to this study. First and foremost, it signals the end of a ten-year period in German poetry — starting with the publication of Höllerer's "Thesen zum langen Gedicht" — during which American influences became firmly established while at the same time the image of America — due to the Vietnam War — experienced tremendous upheaval. That these two factors are inextricably bound, although often as opposing forces, contributed to the very tensions of the era. Second, in 1975 Rolf Dieter Brinkmann was struck and killed by an automobile in London, thus ending the life of the poet most closely linked to the United States; the added significance is that Brinkmann's death signals not only an end but also a beginning, that is, the start of a series of posthumous publications providing valuable insight into his literary career. Finally, Martin Walser's poem "Versuch, ein Gefühl zu verstehen" was first published in 1975 and served as a review of developments in the image and influence of America since the end of the Second World War.

The ever-changing nature of America's postwar image is reflected in select German poems from the latter half of the 1970s, especially those combining the conflicting viewpoints of enchantment and reproach. One example is Jürgen Theobaldy's "Bilder aus Amerika,"[1] a quasi-travel poem employing an imagined journey to the U.S.A. as its point of departure:

> Weil mich, kaum geboren
> in den letzten Wochen des Weltkriegs
> beinah ein Soldat mitgenommen hätte,
> hinüber nach Amerika, träumte ich

---

[1] Jürgen Theobaldy, *Zweiter Klasse: Gedichte* (Berlin: Rotbuch, 1976), 9.

oft davon, in Amerika aufzuwachen
mit Jeans und Tennisschuhen,
den Baseballschläger unter dem Arm.

The opening excerpt claims a basis for its image of America in dreams and imagination. But the picture of America is not that imaginative. Even though not a prose poem, it reads like a prosaic vignette, and the portrait Theobaldy presents suggests more the clichéd likeness of a Norman Rockwell painting or advertisements from a news magazine:

Ich träumte vom frischen Rasen
vor der High School, von rosa Zahnpasta
und Ananas aus der Dose. Amerikanisch
hätte ich sich sehr breit gesprochen,
und später wäre ich, so träumte mir,
im Cadillac vors Bürohochhaus gefahren.

This idyllic depiction of America provides a contrast to reality, as the poem is less about what might have been than what has tran-spired in the past decade. Therefore, the poet turns the spotlight on "die qualmenden Häuser/ in den Gettos der Schwarzen" and "die Nationalgarde im Kampfanzug/ gegen barfüßige Studenten." Theobaldy is conveying a political message, and within the poem's publication time frame he attempts to show that protest poems are still possible and relevant.

"Bilder aus Amerika" pits two diametrically opposed aspects of Jantz's fourfold myth of America against each other. The barefoot students represent America's golden primitivism, with the National Guard in riot gear and scenes of ghettos in flames as its monstrous counterpart. These images of the real America are clearly negative, and the end result is that the lyric persona scarcely dreams of the U.S.A. anymore, "nicht einmal Schlechtes." The addendum rings of resignation, a salient point of the times and earmark of the New Subjectivity. In Karsunke's "Kilroy war hier" we noted the late-1960s sense of irretrievable loss associated with America's tarnished image, and the aftereffects of that mood persist well into the next decade. Theobaldy is not only a representative poet of the New Subjectivity, he also served as its chief spokesperson. The move-ment had its detractors, among them Jörg Drews, who denounced

Theobaldy, Godehard Schramm, Klaus Konjetzky, Karin Kiwus, Rainer Malkowski, Michael Krüger, and Christoph Derschau for promoting "eine Art Prosa-Parlando-Gedicht."[2] Rather than attempting to mediate the dispute engendered by these charges, let us note that the development of an inward-turning subjectivity based on personal experience is unthinkable without considering the American influences on German poetry since the 1960s.[3] Moreover, these innovations contributed to changes in the literary marketplace. Although many critics found the New Subjectivity suspect, its popularity among the general public resulted in sales of poetry previously unknown.[4] Once again, we see offshoots of Fiedler's lecture with egalitarianism in the arts not only bringing about a change in readership but also taking the private sphere of the poet into the public realm of the reader.

Before moving to other trends of the late 1970s, let us look at two poets often linked to the New Subjectivity, Karin Kiwus and Ursula Krechel. Although not known for using America as subject

---

[2] Jörg Drews, "Selbsterfahrung und Neue Subjektivität in der Lyrik," *Akzente* 24.1 (1977), 89–95, here 94, which set off a lively debate on New Subjectivity (also labeled "Neue Sensibilität" or "Neue Innerlichkeit" as well as "Literatur der Selbsterfahrung" and "Literatur einer neuen Privatheit") featured in succeeding numbers of volume 24 of *Akzente*. Theobaldy responded with "Literaturkritik, astrologisch," (24.2: 188–91) to which Drews countered with his "Antwort auf Jürgen Theobaldy," (24.4: 379–82). In the meanwhile, others had joined the polemic: namely Hans Dieter Zimmermann, "Die mangelhafte Subjektivität," (24.3: 280–87) and Ludwig Fischer, "Vom Beweis der Güte des Puddings," (24.4: 371–79). Peter M. Stephan provided closing arguments in "Das Gedicht in der Marktlücke," (24.6: 493–504). The entire series is reprinted in Jan Hans, Uwe Herms, and Ralf Thenior, eds., *LYRIK-KATALOG Bundesrepublik* (Munich: Goldmann, 1978) 453–512. See also Hiltrud Gnüg, "Was heißt »Neue Subjektivität«?" *Merkur* 32.1 (1978): 60–75.

[3] See Lothar Jordan, "Eine Dichtung unter Einfluß," 153.

[4] See Judith Ryan, "»Your life jacket is under your skin.« Reflections on German poetry of the seventies," *The German Quarterly* 55.3 (1982): 296–308, here 297, who speaks of a "publisher's dream"; Volker Hage, "Hauptsache, du verstehst," *Frankfurter Allgemeine Zeitung*, 11 Oct. 1979, who regards the rebirth of lyric poetry as the literary event of the decade; and Jörg Drews, "Nach der »Neuen Sensibilität« — Überlegungen zur jüngsten Lyrik" in Jordan, Marquardt, and Woesler, eds., *Lyrik — von allen Seiten*, 159–180, here 160, who observes that as poetry sales rose, the average age of the reader fell.

matter in her poetry, Kiwus employs language indicative of her generation. Born in 1942, she published two books of poetry in the 1970s,[5] each featuring poems sprinkled with English words, phrases, and quotations. Kiwus downplays the significance of this practice, citing how the film industry, popular music, advertisements, and advancements in technology have made the English language, and especially American turns of speech, matter of fact for those growing up in postwar Germany.[6] Comparing this experiential backdrop with that described in 1953 by Gottfried Benn as "Was schlimm ist"[7] —

> Wenn man kein Englisch kann,
> von einem guten englischen Kriminalroman zu hören,
> der nicht ins Deutsche übersetzt ist.

—we see how the lines of demarcation had evolved for German poets of the 1970s. Not only knowledge of foreign languages, but also the very perception of foreigners — especially non Anglo-Saxons — had changed significantly in Germany since the early 1950s. Just as Theobaldy pays respect to the Black Panthers in "Die Freiheit für Bobby Seale," Ursula Krechel takes Angela Davis on her journey "Nach Mainz!"[8] Even though focusing on domestic politics in the postwar division of Germany, this poem shows how American women — and here a black woman — served as models for the feminist movement in Germany.

---

[5] Karin Kiwus, *Von beiden Seiten der Gegenwart: Gedichte* (Frankfurt am Main: Suhrkamp, 1976); *Angenommen später: Gedichte* (Frankfurt am Main: Suhrkamp, 1979).

[6] See Karin Kiwus, "Nachwort" to Kiwus, *39 Gedichte* (Stuttgart: Reclam, 1981), 65. The thirty-nine poems collected here are selected from the two previously cited volumes; the title, as clarified by the motto, is derived from Alfred Hitchcock's film *The 39 Steps*.

[7] See Benn, *Gedichte 1*, 264.

[8] Ursula Krechel, *Nach Mainz!* (Darmstadt and Neuwied: Luchterhand, 1977), 27–28. As to Angela Davis and her German connection, see Leroy Hopkins, "'Black Prussians': Germany and African American Education from James W. C. Pennington to Angela Davis," in David McBride, Leroy Hopkins, and C. Aisha Blackshire-Belay, eds., *Crosscurrents* (Columbia, SC: Camden House, 1998), 76–78.

The Vietnam poems of Erich Fried and others of the 1960s carried a distinct political message. By the end of the 1970s the German protest poem adopted a more subtle mode of expression. As seen in Max Rohrer's anthology *Amerika im deutschen Gedicht*, the topic of Native Americans in German poetry boasts a long and oftentimes sharply critical tradition. The late 1970s and early 1980s extend this legacy with F. C. Delius's "Denkmal für einen Indianer,"[9] Günter Herburger's "Der Traum des Indianers,"[10] and Hans-Jürgen Heise's "Indianerreservation,"[11] from 1977:

> Weizenfelder unter der Bogenlampe
> des Vollmonds / es ist nicht wahr
> hier zogen niemals Bisonherden vorüber
> hier nicht and anderswo
> auch nicht / hier stand immer nur
> dieser betrunkene Indianer
> an einem Glücksspielautomaten

By means of the genitive case Heise transforms the full moon into an arc lamp illuminating the wheat fields. Thus, the statement "es ist nicht wahr" functions in twofold fashion, both as commentary on the preceding poetic technique and as a transition to the forthcoming reflection on bygone days and herds of bison. The tacit message of this poem is not so much the problem of credibility in resolving modern-day reality with historical fact, but rather the plight of being locked into a present-tense truth where the drunken Indian exists as a relic frozen in the incipient demise of times past. The *Bogenlampe* and *Glücksspielautomaten* in the first and last lines bracket the natural setting, signaling how white society surrounds the reservation and destroys a once proud nation through the introduction of alcohol, gambling, and technology.

---

[9] See F. C. Delius, *Die unsichtbaren Blitze* (Berlin: Rotbuch, 1981), 16.

[10] See Günter Herburger, *Makadam* (Darmstadt and Neuwied: Luchterhand, 1982), 26–27.

[11] Hans-Jürgen Heise, *Gedichte und Prosagedichte 1949–2001* (Göttingen: Wallstein Verlag, 2002), 367, © Hans-Jürgen Heise.

Moreover, the cumulative effect of these seven lines produces a final image with the full moon spotlighting a game of chance with the player destined to lose.

Perhaps the most significant collection of travel poems written in German during the 1970s is Günter Kunert's *Verlangen nach Bomarzo*.[12] Born in 1929, Kunert is a unique figure in contemporary German literature. During the years prior to reunification he, like Sarah Kirsch, was worthy of the designation pan-German poet; that is, a poet of such standing as to be claimed by both German states. A skilled practitioner of the travel poem genre, Kunert also invites comparison with the American poet Elizabeth Bishop. *Verlangen nach Bomarzo* features poems set in continental Europe, the United States, and Great Britain. One of the more intriguing poems in the collection, "Über dem Atlantik," reveals a seldom considered aspect of travel literature. With its concluding lines "Zwischen den Kontinenten/ wird keiner heimisch" Kunert relates how the traditional land-based travel poem expresses the poet's desire to feel at home, no matter how far removed from one's homeland. The American travel poems incorporate a variety of perspectives and settings. For instance, in "Zehn Minuten vor Dallas" Kunert contemplates the multi-dimensionality of travel on modern expressways, the order within the apparent chaos of intersections, bridges, under- and overpasses. While the bright lights of Broadway by night prompt "Erinnerung an Babylon," Kunert revels in the once-a-week emptiness of "Downtown Manhattan am Sonntagnachmittag." And Chicago, for this travel poet, looms as the Holy Grail with its skyline a work of art available for nighttime view "Im nichtimaginären Museum." Aside from these urban portraits, the preferred setting for Kunert's American travel poems is the Southwest. "Von einem Spaziergang" depicts the exotic flora and fauna one might discover on a walk in Texas, "Sky-City" takes us to the plateau town of Acoma in New Mexico with its blend of Old and New World cultures dating back to 1620, and "South Padre Island" offers escape to a tropical paradise. Kunert is at his best when he turns to the distinctively American, whether people or place. For example, the following excerpt from "Truth or Conse-

[12] Günter Kunert, *Verlangen nach Bomarzo: Reisegedichte* (Munich: Hanser, 1978).

quences"[13] conveys a scene that gains depth when filtered through the perspective of a foreign visitor:

> Ein Rettungswagen
> mit rotierendem Rotlicht fährt vor:
> zwei graue Typen von Frauen in weißen Kitteln
> entsteigen und kommen
> uns nahe: es dürstet sie
> nach der trüben Flüssigkeit, denn:
> Gewohnheit ist alles und führt letzten Endes
> immer zum Patriotismus.
>
> Es fährt vor der Wagen des Sheriffs,
> es erscheint ein Bauch, geheiligt vom Colt,
> und unter dem Stetson die bleiche
> und dickliche Kugel gibt sich als Kopf aus.
> Nun sitzen sie wie verabredet
> zusammen und stimmen sich ab oder ein
> und wir ahnen:
> wir sind im Wirtshaus im Spessart
> in Neu-Mexiko: unter Blicken
> denen der eigene am besten ausweicht, wählen wir
> der Tapferkeit besseren Teil:
> von Namen des Ortes zu spät gewarnt.

Kunert shows a stranger's attention to the curious. Although playing an integral part in the scene, the poet maintains an objective distance and remains a silent observer. Kunert's craft is the ability to highlight distinguishing features of the characters and the roles they play. He relies on understatement to capture not only that touch of Americana expressed in a unique place name, but also the characteristic American link between people and place. By focusing on particulars of anatomy, dress, and demeanor, Kunert offers commentary on American politics and religion without even raising the respective topics. In contrast to the wry undertones of "Truth or Consequences," Kunert's "Unterwegs nach El Paso" explores the expansive emptiness of the American Southwest, to European travelers a stock rhetorical theme. For Kunert the key word is ex-

---

[13] Kunert, *Bomarzo*, 44–45.

pressed in the title — "Unterwegs"— for only by remaining en route through the endless stretches of withered vegetation can one avoid the imminent danger.

Just as Kunert's American poems are often marked by understatement, a similar sense of reserve can be found in the American travel poems of Reiner Kunze. Born in Oelsnitz in the Erzgebirge in 1933, Kunze was a citizen of the GDR until 1977. However, with the publication of his volume of prose sketches *Die wunderbaren Jahre* in West Germany in 1976 he was declared an enemy of the East German state and pressured to move to the West. One section of his book of poems *auf eigene hoffnung* is entitled "Amerika, der autobaum" and features nine North American travel poems.[14] Kunze is known for his short poems and epigrammatic, at times aphoristic style. The travel poems of "Amerika, der autobaum" provide pithy observances of America, and the title poem of this section shows how Kunze's clever wordplay captures the role of the automobile in American society. As we have seen in numerous examples, the American prairie is a topos for the travel poet, and Kunze's variation on this theme is found in "mit dem gastgeber durch die prärie."

> Fünfundfünfzig meilen in der stunde,
> und nahtlos der asphalt
>
> An den rändern blühende kakteen,
> büffel, eine herde esel
>
> Einmal einen eselsschrei
> in die hände nehmen dürfen
>
> Hundert schritte tun
> außerhalb einer tankstelle

On one level Kunze takes a standard, reportorial approach: the vantage point is a car traveling through the prairie, the driver obediently observing the speed limit in cruising along a strip of seamless asphalt. While the smooth drive adds a tactile touch, the visual element appears on the wayside in references to flora and fauna,

---

[14] Reiner Kunze, *auf eigene hoffnung: gedichte* (Frankfurt am Main: Fischer, 1981), 89–96.

here cacti in bloom, buffalo, and a herd of donkeys. The natural stimuli trigger a lyrical longing taking the poem to another level where nature is something elusive, a realm where creatures of the wild — not humankind — are granted special privilege. Hence, the poet yearns for access to this domain, for permission — if even just once — to take hold of a donkey's bray. Characteristic of Kunze's style, the poems of "Amerika, der autobaum" are laconic but not satiric. Like Kunert, Kunze has the keen eye for meaningful detail; the accompanying insights, however, are more suggestive hints than bold proclamations. Thus, the observations found in Kunze's America poems show the poet taking the first step, but then pausing and inviting the reader to take the next.

To close off the 1970s calls for a return look at Wolf Wondratschek, both his America poems and his connection to Rolf Dieter Brinkmann. The phenomenal sales record of Wondratschek's poetry dwarfs even that of Brinkmann, whose *Westwärts 1 & 2* topped the bestseller list following his death in April 1975.[15] Although Wondratschek admits to only a passing acquaintance, his elegy for Brinkmann strives to forge an alliance between the two poets.[16] Furthermore, repeated allusions to Brinkmann's American phase seek to advance Wondratschek's own ties to the American scene. In fact, his late-1970s poetry suggests that Wondratschek attempts to pick up where his compatriot had left off. Selected poems from Wondratschek's *Männer und Frauen* (1978), including those reprinted in the special American issue of *Dimension* (1983), show a singular style of travel poem along with a highly selective image of America. As if popular success guarantees immunity, "Ein Dichter in Amerika" presents a new status level for the visiting writer on a reading tour. Here we encounter a lyric persona who invites reproach, knowing full well that personal magnetism and popularity will prevail (to say nothing of

---

[15] See Drews, "Nach der »Neuen Sensibilität«," 179, who cites sales of 30,000 for *Chuck's Zimmer* through the mail-order house Zweitausendeins; see also "Brinkmann führt Besten-Liste," *Frankfurter Rundschau*, 21 June 1975. By 1980 *Westwärts 1 & 2* was in its fourth press run with sales approaching 14,000 copies.

[16] Wolf Wondratschek, "Er war too much für Euch, Leute" appearing along with Günter Herburger's "Des Dichters Brinkmann Tod" in *Die Zeit*, 13 June 1975. As to Brinkmann on Wondratschek, see Brinkmann, *Rom, Blicke*, 322.

the fact that controversy sells). A devil-may-care recklessness, mixing repulsive subject matter with a sexist pose, pervades the poem. The diction is self-assured, the content seductive. In similar fashion, Wondratschek's poems ostensibly paying homage to American writers — his pilgrimages to literary shrines as in "Tennessee Williams" or "Hemingway-Museum, Key West" — are less tributes to the master than a celebration of the disciple. Here we learn far more about Wondratschek than about his literary heroes. Following the Brinkmann mode, Wondratschek also venerates pop culture heroes. The poems "Bob Dylan Revisited" and "The Thrilla of [sic] Manila" say thanks to an American songwriter and recount the career highlights of Muhammad Ali. In such poems the poet is like a journalist with insider status and the insight both to recognize and to elucidate greatness. His "Schluß mit dem Mist und den Mythen um Marilyn Monroe" aspires to cut through the boorish empty talk surrounding a legendary sex goddess. The content consists of biographical tidbits communicated via a quatrain stanza form and a haphazard mix of rhyme schemes producing a sing-song rhythm. Nonetheless, the poem fails to rise above the mundane and succumbs to the very myths Wondratschek seeks to renounce. All in all, Wondratschek's America poems depend on a blend of resignation and nostalgia.[17] The lyric persona may play a number of roles but each bears kinship to the hardened hero of a Western film: an individualist, a survivor, a variant of the lonesome cowboy riding off into the sunset.

The 1980s opened a unique era in German poetry, atypical for the simple fact that little of note evolved in terms of new directions. This is a decade devoid of spokespersons or movements, nothing to compare with the poetic pronouncements of Höllerer, Born, Herburger, Brinkmann, and Theobaldy.[18] In the 1950s and 1960s editors and critics spoke of the need for German poets to look beyond national borders; by the 1980s the advice was superfluous as foreign influences had become a foregone conclusion. Instead of new collections of American poetry, the 1980s brought

---

[17] See Marcel Reich-Ranicki, "Wolf Wondratscheck oder Poesie in Jeans," *Frankfurter Allgemeine Zeitung*, 25 July 1981.

[18] See Hans Bender, ed., afterword, *Was sind das für Zeiten: Deutschsprachige Gedichte der achtziger Jahre* (Munich and Vienna: Hanser, 1988), 243.

reissues of anthologies from the 1960s.[19] The growth of international book stores and mail-order houses, as well as an increase in transatlantic travel, created a literary global village. Hence, the function of an intermediary — that role played by, say, Höllerer or Brinkmann — lost its urgency.

Interest in American poetry continued to grow through the 1980s. As in past decades, *Akzente* (edited since 1981 by Michael Krüger) played an important role. During the 1980s *Akzente* presented a variety of American poets, both new and established, including John Ashbery, Hart Crane, Robert Lowell, Robert Creeley,[20] Robinson Jeffers, William Carlos Williams,[21] Amy Clampitt, Emily Dickinson,[22] Wallace Stevens,[23] Elizabeth Bishop, James

---

[19] One small-press anthology, however, does warrant mention: Jürgen Schmidt, ed. and trans., *Lines of Feeling* (n.p. [Germany]: Altaquito, 1987), with poems by Peter Orlovsky, Michael McClure, Jack Kerouac, Allen Ginsberg, Gary Snyder, and Gregory Corso. Of the three 1960s anthologies reissued, see *Fuck you!* by Fischer in 1980, *ACID* by Rowohlt in 1983, and *Junge amerikanische Lyrik*, retitled *Lyrik der Beat Generation* by Heyne in 1985. The new title suggests how the term *Beat* continues to carry special significance in Germany.

[20] *Akzente* 29.6 (1982) opens with Ashbery's "Schattenzug" (481–88), trans. Joachim Sartorius, but otherwise focuses on Hart Crane with selected poems (497–511), trans. Jürgen Muck, who adds three poems for and a monograph on Crane (489–96); others with poems on Crane are Lowell (511), Günter Eich (519), and Creeley (519). Rounding out the testimonial are excerpts of commentary from Crane's contemporaries (512–17) and Harold Bloom's essay "Hart Cranes Gnosis" (520–36), trans. Jürgen Muck and Wolfgang Knellessen.

[21] See *Akzente* 30.5 (1983): 407–23, selected poems of Jeffers, trans. Eva Hesse, followed by her essay "Die Exzesse von Robinson Jeffers" (423–46). Also included in this issue are five poems of Williams (447–52), trans. Karin Schmitz.

[22] See *Akzente* 31.5 (1984): 449–55 for selections from Clampitt's 1983 publication of *The Kingfisher*, trans. Jürgen Muck. *Akzente* 31.6 (1984), an issue dedicated to Friedhelm Kemp, features his translations of poems by Emily Dickinson (518) and Wallace Stevens (533–40).

[23] See *Akzente* 32.1 (1985): 20–36, for poems and prose by Stevens, trans. Klaus Martens, who also provides the essay "Jemand baut eine Welt zusammen: Wallace Stevens" (37–49), commentary on Stevens by his contemporaries (50–52), and a selected bibliography (52–53).

Laughlin, Anne Sexton,[24] and T. S. Eliot.[25] Two additional names also warrant mention, the American novelist and short story writer Joyce Carol Oates for a poem on the Berlin Wall,[26] and the emigrant poet Felix Pollak.[27] The compendium of poets featured in *Akzente* over this ten-year period profiles not merely a diversity of styles and voices, but a cross-section of American poetry from the 1920s through the 1980s. We must also acknowledge the efforts of various translators as well as the illuminating essays accompanying their work. The diligence and scholarship exhibited are evidence of the respect achieved by American poets since 1945. Moreover, the 1980s show reception of American poetry moving beyond a preoccupation with the underground scene.

Aside from the contribution of *Akzente* to promoting American poetry during the 1980s, a number of American poets had books published in translation. The majority of these books were either updated editions of earlier publications or translations of new material by poets introduced in decades past: T. S. Eliot, Ezra Pound, William Carlos Williams, Wallace Stevens, Robert Lowell, Allen Ginsberg, and Robert Creeley.[28] Worthy of special mention is John Ashbery

---

[24] *Akzente* 33.4 (1986): 292–312, presents poetry and prose of Bishop, trans. Klaus Martens, plus his essay "Das Ich des Auges, oder die Lust an der Geographie: Elizabeth Bishop" (313–24); selected poems of Laughlin (325–37), trans. Eva Hesse, along with her essay "»Als ob ein Mann sein eigener Autor wär . . .« Gedanken über James Laughlin, Verleger und Dichter" (338–46); and selected poems of Sexton (347–65), trans. Barbara von Bechtolsheim, whose essay "Über Anne Sexton" (366–70) concludes the issue.

[25] See Eliot, "Poetische Fragmente und Gelegentlichkeiten" and "Scylla und Charybdis: Nachbemerkung" in *Akzente* 35.4 (1988): 343–74, trans. Rüdiger Görner.

[26] See Oates, "Ekstase von Langeweile an der Berliner Mauer," *Akzente* 30.2 (1983): 188–89, trans. Renate Lasker-Harpprecht.

[27] See Pollak, "Zwei Gedichte," *Akzente* 27.4 (1980): 341–42; and "Vier Gedichte," *Akzente* 33.4 (1986): 289–91, trans. Hans Magnus Enzensberger.

[28] Eliot, *Gesammelte Gedichte 1909–1962*, ed. with an afterword by Eva Hesse, trans. Hesse, Erich Fried, Hans Magnus Enzensberger, et al. (Frankfurt am Main: Suhrkamp, 1988). Pound, *Lesebuch: Dichtung und Prosa*, trans. Eva Hesse (Zürich: Arche, 1985). Williams, *endlos und unzerstörbar*, trans. Christine Koller, Gertrude Clorius Schwebell (Walbrunn: Heiderhoff, 1983); and *Kore in der Hölle*, trans. Joachim Sartorius, Walter Fritzsche, and Jürg Laederach (Leipzig: Kiepenheuer, 1988); see also Joachim Sartorius, ed., *Der*

who, even though known to select German readers since the late 1960s, did not gain a wide audience in Germany until the 1980s.[29]

The 1980s show how multifaceted the reception of American poetry had become in Germany. As a sign of both the wide range of voices and the strides made in overcoming prejudices against American poetry, let us complete our discussion of reception in this decade with Rita Dove. A former Poet Laureate of the United States, Dove is a leading figure in contemporary African-American literature with strong ties to Germany, having studied as a Fulbright scholar at the Universität Tübingen and being married to the German writer Fred Viebahn. The late 1980s saw the appearance of two books of her poetry in German.[30] The first, *Die morgenländische Tänzerin*, combines *Thomas and Beulah*, for which she won the Pulitzer prize for poetry in 1987, and selections from *Museum* (1983); the second, *Die gläserne Stirn der Gegenwart*, features additional selections from *Museum* as well as poems from her first collection, *The Yellow House at the Corner* (1980). Both volumes have been well received in Germany with critics noting Dove's unpretentious language, concise imagery, and eye for perti-

---

Mann mit dem roten Handkarren: Über William Carlos Williams (Munich: Hanser, 1987). Stevens, *Menschen, aus Worten gemacht*, trans. Karl Heinz Berger, Kurt Heinrich Hansen, and Klaus-Dieter Sommer (Berlin: Volk und Welt, 1983); *Der Planet auf dem Tisch*, trans. Kurt Heinrich Hansen (Stuttgart: Klett, 1983), a revised edition of the 1961 publication. Lowell, *Gedichte*, trans. Manfred Pfister (Stuttgart: Klett, 1982). Ginsberg, *Jukebox Elegien*, trans. Bernd Samland (Munich: Heyne, 1981); *Herzgesänge*, trans. Michael Mundhenk, Klaus Feiten, et al. (Hamburg: Loose Blätter, 1981); *Überlegungen zur Poesie*, trans. Jürgen Schmidt (Hannover: Apartment Edition, 1988). Creeley, *Gedichte*, trans. Klaus Reichert (Salzburg and Vienna: Residenz, 1988).

[29] Ashbery, *Selbstporträt in einem konvexen Spiegel*, trans. Christa Cooper and Joachim Sartorius (Munich and Vienna: Hanser, 1980); Ashbery, *Eine Welle*, trans. Joachim Sartorius (Munich and Vienna: Hanser, 1986).

[30] Dove, *Die morgenländische Tänzerin: Gedichte*, trans. Karin Graf (Reinbek bei Hamburg: Rowohlt, 1988); *Die gläserne Stirn der Gegenwart: Gedichte, amerikanisch und deutsch*, trans. Fred Viebahn (Eisingen: Heiderhoff, 1989); two poems by Dove had earlier appeared in *Akzente* 26.5 (1979): 577–78, trans. Fred Viebahn.

nent detail.[31] Moreover, the reviews point out that although Dove's poetry defies labels (neither feminist nor Afro-centric in the socio-political sense), her lyrical tributes to the makers of Black American history follow in the tradition of Gwendolyn Brooks.

Our review of 1980s reception of American poetry in Germany reveals the high level respect gained by New World poets in the course of the preceding forty years. In parallel fashion, German poetry of the 1980s shows the heights attained by American culture since the end of the Second World War. Granted, Hollywood remains a subject of ridicule, and American culture is more likely understood as pop art and pop music; nonetheless, American branches of traditional schools of painting have gained acceptance if not acclaim. A case in point is Edward Hopper, whose reputation is affirmed by Harald Hartung in the 1984 poem "Wann lasen Sie den Plato Mr. Hopper."[32]

> Er schleppt den Kohleneimer für den Ofen
> heizt selbst das Atelier
>   Sie kauft die Kleider
> bei Sears und Woolworth kocht Konserven (wenn
> sie kocht)
>   Er schmeckt der Küche Frankreichs nach
>
> Sie duldet neben sich kein anderes
> Modell
>   Er läßt sie nicht ans Steuer: das
> ist alles das ist nichts und ist wie Leben

---

[31] See Helmut Winter, "Hölderlin auf der Veranda," *Frankfurter Allgemeine Zeitung*, 21 Jan. 1989; Cornelia Staudacher, "Eine späte Würdigung," *Der Tagesspiegel*, 9 Apr. 1989; Heinrich Vormweg, "Bilder aus dem Leben der Armen," *Süddeutsche Zeitung*, 5/6 Aug. 1989; Helmut Winter, "Der Hund im Blumenbeet," *Frankfurter Allgemeine Zeitung*, 13 Feb. 1990; Alexander Schmitz, "Geträller," *Die Welt*, 24 Mar. 1990; and Ilka Scheidgen, "Afroamerikanische Lyrik," *der literat* 32.6 (15 June 1990): 172–73.

[32] Harald Hartung, *Traum im Deutschen Museum*, 149. A sign of the American influences on Hartung's poetry is the motto for this collection: "We are poor passing facts,/ warned by that to give/ each figure in the photograph/ his living name." — the final lines of "Epilogue," the poem closing Robert Lowell, *Day by Day* (New York: Farrar, 1977), 127.

Er malt das Licht so weiß wie eben möglich
das Licht des Morgens leere Straßenfluchten
und macht die Schatten schräger für das Licht

Sie sitzt im Sessel, liest
                    Er steht am Fenster
raucht schaut hinaus: *an einem andern Ort sein*
Oder sie liegt nackt und weist ihm den Rücken
Er auf der Kante hält das Buch
                    Er las
den Plato ziemlich spät, so meint der Maler

Auf seinem letzten Bild sind sie vereint:
Zwei Komödianten treten an die Rampe
Das Leben lächelt und das Scheinen scheint

This poem can be classified a portrait in verse. Although the title
suggests a dialogue with the artist, the text narrows to a third person perspective, thus lending the poem qualities of both a biographical sketch and an essay. Content draws heavily from the
German edition of Gail Levin's Hopper monograph,[33] and the
poem is as much an homage to Hopper as to his wife Jo, also an
artist. Hence, Hartung presents a study in and model of equilibrium
with a he-she dichotomy (enhanced by stepped lines) balancing two
artist personalities within the parameters of their shared private life.
The austere lifestyle depicted in the opening lines of the first stanza
reflects not only the non-ornamental grace of Edward Hopper's
paintings but also the division of labor and individual responsibilities in their daily routines. Much of the text, then, reads as a series
of anecdotal allusions highlighting personal history and various
idiosyncrasies. For instance, the final line of stanza one recalls Hopper's three visits to France between the years 1906 and 1910, a reference subtly hinting that the artist was more influenced by French
cuisine than early-twentieth-century movements then taking hold in
the Parisian art world. Moreover, this reference to France, where
Hopper enjoyed a brief romance, is followed in stanza two by men-

---

[33] Gail Levin, *Edward Hopper, 1882–1967: Gemälde und Zeichnungen*, trans.
Karin Stempel (Munich: Schirmer-Mosel, 1981); see also Gail Levin, *Edward
Hopper: An Intimate Biography* (New York: Knopf, 1995).

tion that after their marriage in 1924 Jo Hopper insisted on posing for nearly every female figure he was to paint, and so points to the tensions, sexual and otherwise, in their relationship. Indeed, stanza two introduces the problematic side of the marriage, drawing on the couple's penchant for automobile travel but with emphasis on his stubborn refusal to allow her to drive.

Stanza three moves from a chronicle mode to a treatise-like discussion of Hopper's style and technique. In the first line of this stanza Hartung borrows directly from Levin's text and a quote from Hopper regarding his painting *Second Story Sunlight* (1960).[34] The repetition of the word *Licht* in all three lines of this stanza accentuates the importance of light to Hopper: that light was his primary concern, how light, not color, guides the artist's eye.[35] References to morning light and empty streets with rows of buildings conjure up scenes from a number of Hopper's paintings such as *Manhattan Bridge Loop* (1928), *Early Sunday Morning* (1930), *Morning in a City* (1944), *Cape Cod Morning* (1950), and *Morning Sun* (1952). Finally, the adverbial use of *schräger* recalls Hopper's diagonal composition form and the sharp geometric lines dividing shadow and light in his work.

Stanza four offers lyrical allusions to specific paintings while at the same time punctuating nuances in the artists' personal relationship. From a thematic standpoint this stanza reflects how the Hoppers' shared love of reading has degenerated to a point where it no longer promotes personal interaction. The first three lines re-create the scene in *Hotel by a Railroad* (1952). Hartung views the male figure in this painting as longing to be elsewhere and reinforces the previous remark on Hopper's lingering taste for French food.[36] Moreover, the poet hints of a breakdown in communication be-

---

[34] See Levin, *Gemälde*, 65. As to the original Hopper quote ("an attempt to paint sunlight as white with almost no yellow pigment in the white"), see Levin, *Biography*, 540.

[35] See Levin, *Gemälde*, 44; and Levin, *Biography*, 407.

[36] The phrase in italics in line sixteen borrows from Levin, *Gemälde*, 49, and her discussion of *Hotel by a Railroad*. See also Wolfgang Braune-Steininger, "Porträt des Künstlers als alternder Leser. Zu Harald Hartungs Gedicht *Wann lasen Sie den Plato Mr. Hopper*" in Walter Hinck, ed., *Gedichte und Interpretation: Gegenwart II*, vol. 7 of 7 (Stuttgart: Reclam, 1997), 301–9, here 305–6.

tween the Hoppers, a suggestion furthered by reference to a second painting, Hopper's *Excursion into Philosophy* (1959). Here, Hartung takes certain liberties: for instance, whereas in the painting an open book lies next to the man sitting on the edge of the bed, in the poem the man holds the book in his hands. The slight shift in detail smoothes the transition to Hartung's paraphrase of a second Hopper quote — the artist's remark on Plato "reread too late."[37] Poetic license serves Hartung in multiple fashion. First, especially as complemented by the clarifying directive "so meint der Maler," this statement answers the question posed in the title; second, the reference strengthens the autobiographical aspect of the scene portrayed in the painting; and finally, the mere mention of Plato raises the content of the poem beyond lyrical portraiture to a higher, indeed aesthetic plane. The autobiographical aspects of the painting point to a retrospective review of the Hoppers' marriage, and returning to Plato too late in life brings the realization that Platonic love had passed the Hoppers by, that true beauty is found only in the ideal.

Stanzas one, two, and four spotlight specific chapters in the Hoppers' personal chronicle. Typographical spacing not only underscores the he-she polarity but also extends the poetic lines in a manner not unlike a painter's canvas being stretched over its frame. The resultant visual quality afforded these stanzas signifies the underlying tension in the Hoppers' relationship, a tension finally and fully resolved in Hartung's closing three-line stanza. Edward Hopper's final painting, *Two Comedians* from the year 1965, is the focal point of stanza five. (In corollary fashion the painting performs the function of a genre study in literary forms; that is to say, its comedic content conveys the message: all's well that ends well.) Just as Hopper's painting is a personal testament with the male comedian gallantly presenting his female counterpart to the audience, Hartung pays tribute to the life and smile shared by these inseparable companions. This final stanza, however, does more than merely honor the Hoppers. Stanza four had pushed content into the realm of philosophy, and the final line of the poem moves from the stage scene portrayed in Hopper's painting to a succinct statement on aesthetic theory. The adroit phrasing of "das Scheinen

[37] See Levin, *Biography*, 525.

scheint" plays off not only Plato's parable of the sun but also Eduard Mörike's poem "Auf eine Lampe" (to which the close of the preceding line "an die Rampe" provides a subtle subconscious rhyme). In addition, Hartung's substantive-verb pairing evokes the interpretation controversy over Mörike's poem initiated by Martin Heidegger and Emil Staiger.[38] Crucial with respect to this study is that the American painter Edward Hopper provides the point of departure for Hartung's excursion into the rich tradition of German literary history and aesthetic theory. Thus, the formal respect accorded by the use of "Mister" in the title is raised to the highest degree as Hartung places Hopper into a pantheon of names from the world of art, literature, and philosophy.

Even if this decade confirmed America's cultural rise in Germany, the election of Ronald Reagan in 1980 initiated a reassessment of European attitudes on American politics. The ensuing escalation in cold war rhetoric, the NATO policy of multiplying the number of land-based nuclear missiles in Western Europe, and speculation on the feasibility of a limited atomic war in Europe, all served to revive the protest movement and swell numbers in demonstrations throughout the Federal Republic of Germany. All this notwithstanding, there did not follow a wave of Pershing II protest poems. Although one might mention Walter Höllerer's poem "Philosophie der Neutronenbombe,"[39] the prevailing attitude of the era is captured by Harry Oberländer's "Das Achtundsechziger-Sonett"[40] with its suggestion that the glory days of 1968 are the stuff of legends locked in a time capsule. More

---

[38] See Emil Staiger, "Ein Briefwechsel mit Martin Heidegger," in Staiger, *Die Kunst der Interpretation: Studien zur deutschen Literaturgeschichte* (Zürich: Atlantis, 1955), 34–49. See also Braune-Steininger, 307–8 for a concise summary of this debate over Mörike's use of the verb *scheint*. Staiger claims that this verb is to be understood in the sense of the Latin *videtur*; Heidegger, on the other hand, attributes its meaning to *lucet* and further argues that the final two lines of Mörike's poem express Hegel's aesthetic theory in capsule form. According to Braune-Steininger, the Hegelian Hartung likely adopts the latter interpretation in his tribute to Hopper.

[39] See Walter Höllerer, *Gedichte: 1942–1982* (Frankfurt am Main: Suhrkamp, 1982), 224.

[40] See *Luchterhand Jahrbuch der Lyrik 1987/88*, 23.

thought-provoking portrayals of America are achieved not by fixing on the politics of the present but by looking back on events shaping recent history. One example is "Biologische Überlegenheit"[41] by Sabine Techel:

> Ethel Rosenberg braucht
> viermal soviel Strom wie
> ihr Mann bis ihr
>
> Kopf raucht und
> sie zu ihrem Schöpfer kommt
> um ihm einige Dinge zu erklären

Born in 1953, the same year the Rosenbergs were executed, Techel represents a generation born into and growing up during the cold war. The source for "Biologische Überlegenheit" can be determined with the help of the poem "duck and cover" on the preceding page of *Es kündigt sich an* and its line "to study this virgin target." Particulars in both poems can be traced to *The Atomic Cafe*, a 1982 documentary film recounting the early history of the atomic bomb. As one learns from this film, the phrase "duck and cover" is from a 1950s song instructing American school children on what to do in case of nuclear attack; "to study this virgin target" refers to how the cities Hiroshima and Nagasaki, not having sustained previous bomb damage, served as pristine sites for scientific investigations of the aftermath of an atomic blast. As a document of cold war attitudes shaping early postwar America, *The Atomic Cafe* achieved a cult status within certain circles in Germany. In "Biologische Überlegenheit" Techel turns to the film for an eyewitness account of the execution of the Rosenbergs, and the six-line text draws on selected excerpts from a newsreel report on death by the electric chair. The title, then, is as much an ironic aside as a conclusion based on the facts. Techel's choice of present-tense verb forms lends the sense of a live broadcast, heightening both the tension and the horror. The stanza break is especially effective. First, it subtly prolongs narrative time to reinforce a sense of the extended actual time needed to complete the electrocution of Ethel Rosenberg. Second, the stanza

---

[41] Sabine Techel, *Es kündigt sich an: Gedichte* (Frankfurt am Main: Suhrkamp, 1986), 30.

break sharpens the eerie image of smoke rising from her head and subverts the pontificating tone of the final two lines. As a result, the reporter's self-righteous tag line falls flat, and its use here depicts the media as dupes in the hands of McCarthyites. Finally, "Biologische Überlegenheit" can be read as a companion piece to a pivotal work in contemporary American literature. That is to say, this poem presents a factual backdrop to the poignant reflections on the Rosenbergs in the opening paragraph of Sylvia Plath's *The Bell Jar*.

If the 1980s brought no new movements or programs, one group of writers who gained increased attention during this decade are those from German-language regions of Rumania. Oskar Pastior, who was born in Hermannstadt/Siebenbürgen in 1927 and has lived in West Berlin since 1969, offers his own unique image of America with three poems in the 1983 special issue of *Dimension*. America's appeal is even stronger in the postwar generation, as seen in the poetry of Richard Wagner, born in 1952 in Lowrin of the Banat region. His poem "Hotel California"[42] features a dizzying array of images, wordplay, and mind games, a combination begging the question "was hatte das schon zu/ bedeuten." Wagner's self-assured use of language along with his controlled diction eases the reader's task in assimilating a multiplicity of recorded sensations. The reason for the title choice, however, remains unclear until the final three lines:

> Was war da der Morgen
> Was warn da die Leute hinter den Wörtern
> man ging auf und ab es läutete an den Türen
> Na und hieß es sind wir nicht Schlimmeres gewohnt
> Die Lebensläufe lagen verbogen hinter den Dingen
> Ungewöhnlich groß hingen die Schneeflocken in der Luft
> Die Eagles spielten Hotel California
> Das Radio steckte unauffällig in sich selbst
> Ruhig betrachtete ich mich aus meinem Zeigefinger

Two key words — *Schneeflocken* and *Lebensläufe* — occur in both the opening and closing sections of "Hotel California," thus serving to bracket the thematic content of the main body of the poem.

---

[42] Richard Wagner, *Rostregen* (Darmstadt and Neuwied: Luchterhand, 1986), 76–78.

Not only does this technique bring closure to the disparate elements operating in the text, but also repetition of the words themselves acts as a reminder that no two snowflakes or personal records are identical. In the final section the extraordinarily large snow flakes do not fall but hang suspended in the air. This curious detail, however, soon gains clarity. With mention of an American pop song on the radio, Wagner demonstrates how the intrusion of background music on visual impressions can bring the outside world to a standstill. The creation of a freeze-frame image turns all external sensation inward and, in this singular case, grants a calm clarity to the oftentimes disconcerting act of self observation.

In parallel fashion the 1980s provide new directions with regard to the German Democratic Republic. Due to changes in official policy during the late 1970s East German citizens gained increased access to various forms of Western culture. As a result, the 1980s brought a new dynamic to East German poetry, especially among the younger generation. For example, on one hand we can speak of certain Prenzlauer Berg poets with ties to the West but without official sanction of the East German state.[43] On the other hand we have Steffen Mensching and Hans-Eckhardt Wenzel, two young poets who made their literary debuts in 1984 and were enthusiastically promoted by GDR officials throughout the decade. In literary circles it was rare to hear one name mentioned without the other; likewise their public readings, often billed and staged as a duo, combined elements of a folk-rock concert, making them popular among younger audiences, especially the East German youth group, *Freie Deutsche Jugend* (FDJ). As such, they represented a conscious effort on the part of East German apparatchiks to incorporate Western influences, but strictly on their own terms. This backdrop helps explain why both Mensching and Wenzel remained largely ignored in the West, and suffered the scorn of more strident factions in the East. As to this study they illustrate what easing restrictions brought to the image of America in East German poetry. A telling example is

---

[43] For an insightful examination of the Prenzlauer Berg scene in East Berlin as well as how Wolf Biermann exposed Sascha Anderson as a *Stasi* informant, see Jane Kramer, "Letter from Europe," *The New Yorker*, 25 May 1992: 40–64; rpt. as "Stasi" in Jane Kramer, *The Politics of Memory* (New York: Random, 1996), 153–212.

Mensching's "Ist dir aufgefallen,"[44] a poem making use of Berlin's divided yet special status, as in the privilege accorded by the quadripartite agreement allowing Allied military personnel to visit the city's Soviet sector:

> Ist dir aufgefallen, daß der amerikanische
>> Soldat
>> im Buchladen
> an der Kasse ein Bilderbuch kaufte für Kinder
> ab fünf Jahre, mit bunten Affen und Nashörnern, daß er
>> dich anlächelte
> und an seinem Uniformknopf fummelte,
> als du zurücklächeltest, und daß dieser Augenblick,
>> eine Sekunde oder zwei,
> sehr seltsam war, so verzweifelt, utopisch, blödsinnig
> hoffnungsvoll zeitlos kurz entwaffnend

Mensching rejects the portrayal of an American soldier on a shopping spree, and there is no hint of a capitalist exploiting the East German marketplace with currency obtained by means of favored exchange rates. Instead, he adopts a plaintive tone in a direct address to, one presumes, a young woman. The awkwardness on the part of the uniformed soldier is, then, as much attributable to a certain sexual tension as to any inherently threatening political backdrop. For the poet, whose role as observer of the encounter forms a triangle, everything hinges on the exchange of smiles. This brief moment defies a simple description, hence the listing of adjectives in the last two lines as if in search of the definitive modifier. The final choice — *entwaffnend* — carries meaning on various levels through various perspectives. First, there is a figurative disarmament as the shared smile dissolves East-West tensions; second, the poet is disarmed while observing the simple humanity of two players on what serves as a world stage; and finally, the poem attempts to disarm forty years of propaganda in which the American soldier has been the symbol for an aggressive imperialist state. Nonetheless, the poem suffers from what it tries to undo. While its strength lies in its openness, hiding neither message nor emotion,

---

[44] Steffen Mensching, *Tuchfühlung: Gedichte* (Halle and Leipzig: Mitteldeutscher Verlag, 1986), 25.

this too is its weakness. Consistent with the article purchased — a picture book for children five and above — the poem operates on a child's level, orchestrating sentimentality much like a Disney film.

In the autobiographical poem "Von mir aus"[45] Mensching revamps not only America's image but also history and the foundations of East German literary aesthetics. Intermixed with memories of childhood illness, hands-on adolescent sex education, and particulars of Marxist-Leninist schooling, are allusions to Frank Zappa, Marilyn Monroe, and Charlie Chaplin. More telling is his behind-the-scenes look at the Yalta conference:

> Roosevelt klebte seinen Kaugummi unter den
> Verhandlungstisch
> vor fünfzig Jahren
> niemand hat es bemerkt nur ich der ich mich schon
> damals
> in Dinge mischte die mich nichts angingen

A comparable bravado is found in Mensching's fusion of high art with pop culture:

> Ich stellte die Teetasse auf die Ästhetik von Georg Lukács
> und hörte vom Krieg der Sterne
> von George Lukas im Sender Freies Berlin
> zwischen diese Fakten montierte ich eine Stahlstange
> daran ich
> einen intellektuellen Felgaufschwung übte
> immer auf eine einwandfreie Haltung achtend

The act of placing a tea cup on the bible of East German aesthetics while tuning in a Radio Free Berlin program on the film *Star Wars* flaunts all Marxist rules of beauty, art, and taste. Yet Mensching is fully aware of the preposterous nature of this deed, as he practices his mental gymnastics with careful attention to discipline and style so to raise the performance level beyond reproach.

We have seen the role of Frank O'Hara in West German poetry, and it is no surprise that his influence would eventually move to the East. In spite of an undeniable fascination with O'Hara, sel-

---

[45] Mensching, *Tuchfühlung*, 35–61.

dom have German poets captured the distinctive style of his *Lunch Poems*. An exception is Michael Wüstefeld's "Noch knistert,"[46] a poem introduced by a quote from O'Hara's "St. Paul and All That." The first half reads as follows:

> *die Sonne braucht nicht*
> *unbedingt unterzugehen,*
> *manchmal verschwindet sie bloß*
> Frank O'Hara

NOCH KNISTERT
unterm nassen Hemd ein
Neues Deutschland

Der überlange langsame Bus
ist warm und sein Gelenk quietscht
in dieser und in der nächsten Kurve
wie meine Halswirbel wenn ich mich umdrehe
nach meiner kleinen ErstenBlickGeliebten
die mir ins nasse Gesicht sieht
und verlassen hinterm Gelenk sitzt
hinter der schwarzen Harmonika des Busses
die die Töne nicht findet
hinter der ihre Augen sich wegdrehen
wenn es in ein Rechtskurve geht
überlege ich ob sie mein
Neues Deutschland
lesen will
sehe ihre Augen drehen sich wieder
traurig wie Leierkastenlieder
von ner Schallplatte
und weiß
die will nicht mein
Neues Deutschland
auch nicht
rote Zungenfahnen
die uns zum Hals raus hängen

---

[46] In Sascha Anderson and Elke Erb, eds., *Berührung ist nur eine Rander-scheinung: Neue Literatur aus der DDR* (Cologne: Kiepenheuer & Witsch, 1985), 81–82.

This first person account of unspoken love on a bus ride finds the lyric persona having been caught in an unexpected rain shower. The extra-long bus provides not only shelter but also a setting for experiencing love at first sight. Wüstefeld's description of the bus recalls O'Hara's use of language and his proclivity for appropriating objects to create or support a mood. Here, the black segment joining the double-length bus, while separating the man from the woman, is likened to an accordion playing its own squeaky song. However, neither the accordion can find the notes nor the lyric persona the words to reach this woman. As in O'Hara's best work, no detail is accidental; thus, it is no coincidence that the bus makes a right-hand turn before the poem makes a second reference to the copy of *Neues Deutschland*. The lyric persona's wet shirt has kept his newspaper crisp and dry, ready to fulfill a multilevel purpose within the narrative. On one hand it functions as an objective correlative to the omnipresent East German state. On the other, while establishing an aesthetic distance to the political backdrop, this copy of *Neues Deutschland* does nothing to bridge the gap between the two isolated individuals within the poem. The possibility that the woman may have an interest in reading the official party organ is summarily dismissed, and then punctuated with clever wordplay in the blasphemous reference to the East Block practice of hanging red banners of socialist solidarity from windows.

The bus continues its route as the poem its story, now with a direct reference to Frank O'Hara:

> Beim nächsten Schlagloch
> sehe ich so zu ihr rüber
> daß sich mein Rückenmark zusammenzieht
> Ich frag mich
> ob wir vielleicht soeben über einen toten Mann
> Namens Frank O'Hara drüber gefahren sind
> von dem ich ein Gedicht gelesen hatte
> bevor ich in den Bus einstieg
> das mir wie der erste Blick
> in die Gruben ihrer Augen
> wie Rotwein in den Becher
> dann ins Blut fiel
> Wenn der Bus hält trifft mich einmal

der Geruch ihrer langen Beine
wenn sie in meiner Nähe steht
wie ich in mir
und auf den Türöffner drückt
und aussteigt über den Bordstein
und auf dem Strich geht
den die Steinkanten auf den Fußweg zeichnen
ohne ihr Gesicht zu verlieren
das unterm Schirm unerkannt bleibt

wie du
Nasses Deutschland
dort draußen und unter meinem trocknen Hemd

The adjective *nächsten* in the first line above is a proficient means of injecting not so subtle commentary on streets in the GDR. Aside from its economy, the observation provides transition for a digression on the death of Frank O'Hara, in itself a prelude to the woman getting off the bus. With the narrative flow having reached its anticlimax, the function of the O'Hara quote gains clarity. Both "St. Paul and All That" and "Noch knistert" are poems of unrequited love, although the latter is more unrequited fantasy and the love interest a woman. On this rain-soaked day the sun has disappeared. In its place comes a woman, one moment there on the bus, the aroma of her long legs intoxicating the lyric persona, the next moment gone, a street-walker whose face disappears under the umbrella. Likewise the copy of *Neues Deutschland*, having failed to bring the two individuals together, just disappears. The stanza break and final three lines effect a reversal of elements with the crisp dry newspaper replaced by a wet country, and the once wet shirt having dried in the warmth of the slow-traveling bus.

To conclude our discussion of the 1980s, let us turn to *Overseas call: Eine USAnthologie*,[47] a collection of two hundred America poems by contemporary German-language authors. The title is taken from a song by the American songwriter Loudon Wainwright III, who also provided the song-motto for Brinkmann's *Westwärts 1 & 2*, and by quoting the song in its entirety as motto,

---

[47] Gerhard C. Krischker, ed., *Overseas call: Eine USAnthologie* (Eggingen: Isele, 1989).

Krischker lends a touch of pop culture to the text. Although the overall quality is uneven, selections by a number of poets previously discussed here — Hagelstange, Jandl, Fried, Ausländer, Karsunke, Brinkmann, Born, Kunert, and Walser — carry the collection. Moreover, this retrospective look at forty years of America poems provides a valuable companion piece to Max Rohrer's 1946 anthology, *Amerika im deutschen Gedicht*, in that the two publications bracket the era between the end of the Second World War and German reunification. Like Rohrer, Krischker relies on specific chapter groupings to organize his compilation. Here we find poems on American landscapes, New York City, the Wild West, American writers, artists, movies, and movie stars, plus antiwar protest poems. A review of the contents reveals several noteworthy attributes. Most striking is the incredibly wide variety of American travel poems written by German poets of the postwar era. The number of New York poems alone is staggering and a testament of what this city, analogous to the role of Rome in earlier centuries, has become for German writers.[48] Aside from many familiar poems, readers will find selected rarities — for instance, excerpts from Brinkmann's *Eiswasser in der Guadelupe Str.*, the posthumous publication recounting his days in Austin, Texas. One perplexing matter is the decision to present Martin Walser's "Versuch, ein Gefühl zu verstehen" in abridged form with selected parts interspersed throughout the anthology. One suspects an editorial desire to pair the chosen sections of the poem with the dominant mood of respective sections of the anthology. The major criticism to be voiced here, however, concerns neither selections nor arrangement, but what the editor chooses not to do. In lieu of a preface Krischker opts for Wim Wenders's long poem "Der Amerikanische Traum," while a German translation of Ishmael Reed's "This Poetry Anthology I'm Reading"[49] and a three-line epigram by Ludwig Fels serve as afterword. Unfortunately, Wenders musing on the American dream does little more than remind us why he is a filmmaker, and the two poems in place of an afterword fail to provide closure to the collection. The reader comes away from *Over-*

[48] See Jordan, "Dichtung unter Einfluß," 156, note 9.

[49] See Ishmael Reed, *New and Collected Poems* (New York: Atheneum, 1988), 74.

seas call: Eine USAnthologie well informed in terms of who wrote what; however, the notion of impetus, that simple question of why America has become such a popular subject in German poetry is not deemed worthy of discussion. Lacking a definitive essay addressing not only its genesis and methodology but also specific trends, perspectives, and developments, this anthology fails to reach its potential as a document of an era. Without an editorial overview, the whole is but the sum of its parts.

10: After the Wall: Luftbrücke und heavy metal sounnz

IF THE YEARS 1965 and 1975 marked turning points with respect to America's image and role in German poetry, then the fall of the Berlin Wall and subsequent reunification of Germany signals a reassessment of the same. From 1945 to the end of the cold war, America's image in Germany had been filtered through the perspective of a country defeated then divided. With the collapse of the Soviet Union came a new role for the United States in Europe, and without the tensions emanating from the coexistence of two diametrically opposed political systems, America's image and role in a reunified Germany must necessarily undergo some change. A special 1992 issue of *The German Quarterly* focusing on "1492–1992: Five Centuries of German-American Interrelations" offers a retrospective look encouraged not only by the arithmetic of a half millennium but also by changes in attitude following the end of the postwar East-West propaganda battle. This issue opens with Margot Scharpenberg's poem on Columbus, "Kind deiner Zeit,"[1] providing a German viewpoint on five hundred years of European-American interactions. Moreover, as a native of Cologne and resident of New York since 1962, Scharpenberg represents the German-language writer living in America. In addition to the previously discussed poets (Ausländer, Gong, Pollak, and Waldinger) we should also mention Richard Exner, Lisa Kahn, Gert Niers, Peter Pabisch, Ilse Pracht-Fitzell, Hans Sahl, and Christiane Seiler as notable contributors to the German-American literary tradition.[2]

---

[1] In *The German Quarterly* 65.3–4 (1992): 265–66.

[2] See *Litfass* 13.47 (1989), Uwe Heldt, ed., *Amerika, wie bist du? Deutschsprachige Texte aus USA ausgewählt von Irmgard Elsner*, and Lisa Kahn, ed., *In Her Mother's Tongue* (Denver: Emerson, 1983). See also Don Heinrich Tolzmann, ed., *German-American Literature* (Metuchen, NJ and London: Scarecrow, 1977); Jerry Glenn, "What is German-American Literature?" *Monatshefte* 86.3 (1994): 350–53; and Wulf Koepke, "German-American and Exile Studies: Still a Divided Stream?" *Monatshefte* 86.3 (1994): 361–66.

As to reception in the 1990s, *Akzente* once again plays an important role in presenting American poets in German translation. Although overshadowed earlier in his career, John Ashbery continues to gain prominence in 1990s Germany.[3] Also drawing attention in the 1990s are W. S. Merwin,[4] Mark Strand, Ann Lauterbach, and Charles Reznikoff.[5] Co-founder Walter Höllerer returned as guest editor in 1994 for a special issue marking the fortieth anniversary of *Akzente*. The issue reads as a greatest hits collection featuring an international array of writers who have appeared in this journal since 1954, and the American contingent includes Ashbery, Creeley, Ferlinghetti, and Ginsberg. The 1990s also show how the reputation of William Carlos Williams remains as strong as ever in Germany, with both biographical material and selections from his vast body of work continuing to appear in translation.[6]

Since the 1980s American women poets have gained increased recognition in Germany, especially Elizabeth Bishop and Anne Sexton.[7] African-American women poets have also received more attention, in the 1980s Rita Dove and in the 1990s Alice Walker.[8]

---

[3] See *Akzente* 40.3 (1993): 249–61, "Flow Chart," trans. Joachim Sartorius, followed by the translator's essay (262–63) "Wenn Frequenzen sich entsprechen. Zu John Ashberys Langgedicht »Flow Chart« (1991)."

[4] Selections from Merwin's *From the Rain in the Trees* (New York: Knopf, 1988) appear in *Akzente* 38.3 (1991): 266, trans. Alexander Schmitz.

[5] See *Akzente* 41.5 (1994): 479–87 (Strand), 488–500 (Lauterbach), 501–17 (Reznikoff).

[6] See *Akzente* 41.5 (1994): 524–25, Joachim Sartorius, "Zur Person: William Carlos Williams" along with a translation of his poem "Danse Russe." See also Williams, *Der harte Kern der Schönheit*, trans. Joachim Sartorius (Munich and Vienna: Hanser, 1991); and *Paterson*, trans. Karin Graf and Joachim Sartorius (Munich: Hanser, 1998).

[7] See, e.g., Anne Sexton, *Liebesgedichte*, ed. Elisabeth Bronfen, trans. Silvia Morawetz (Frankfurt am Main: Fischer, 1995); *All meine Lieben / Lebe oder Stirb*, ed. Bronfen, trans. Morawetz (Frankfurt am Main: Fischer, 1996); *Buch der Torheit. Das ehrfürchtige Rudern hin zu Gott: Gedichte*, ed. Bronfen, trans. Morawetz (Frankfurt am Main: Fischer, 1998).

[8] See the two-volume collection Alice Walker, *Ihr blauer Körper: Gedichte I* and *Ihre braune Umarmung: Gedichte II*, trans. Gerhard Döhler (Reinbek bei Hamburg: Rowohlt, 1993 and 1995). Reception, however, was not as enthu-

However, the most significant new development in the reception of American women writers is the rediscovery of Sylvia Plath. German readers now have better access to her poetry thanks to the translation of two biographies on Plath as well as selections from her diaries and correspondence.[9] In addition to selected prose works, two bilingual editions of her poetry have also appeared, the comparatively light-hearted *The Bed Book*, a children's book written in 1959, and *Three Women*, a verse drama for three voices broadcast as a radio play on the BBC in 1962.[10] Equally significant, these numerous publications have renewed interest in Plath's best known works, *Ariel* and *The Bell Jar*.[11] As a result, there has been considerable

---

siastic as that for Dove; see Steffen Jacobs, "Überall weinen die Leute," *Frankfurter Allgemeine Zeitung*, 21 Dec. 1995.

[9] Anne Stevenson, *Sylvia Plath: Eine Biographie*, trans. Manfred Ohl and Hans Sartorius (Frankfurt am Main: Frankfurter Verlagsanstalt, 1989); Linda Wagner-Martin, *Sylvia Plath: Eine Biographie*, trans. Sabine Techel (Frankfurt am Main: Insel, 1990); Janet Malcolm, *Die schweigende Frau: Die Biographien der Sylvia Plath*, trans. Susanne Friederike Levin (Hamburg: Kellner, 1994); and Frederik Hetmann, *So leicht verletzbar unser Herz: Die Lebensgeschichte der Sylvia Plath* (Weinheim: Beltz & Gelberg, 1988). As to diaries and letters, see Sylvia Plath, *Die Bibel der Träume: Erzählungen, Prosa aus den Tagebüchern*, trans. Julia Bachstein and Sabine Techel (Frankfurt am Main: Frankfurter Verlagsanstalt, 1987); and Aurelia Schober Plath, ed., *Sylvia Plath: Briefe nach Hause 1950–1963*, trans. Iris Wagner (1981; Frankfurt am Main: Fischer, 1992); and Frances McCullough, ed., *Die Tagebücher*, trans. Alissa Walser (Frankfurt am Main: Frankfurter Verlagsanstalt, 1997).

[10] Plath, *Das Bettbuch*, trans. Eva Demski (Frankfurt am Main: Frankfurter Verlagsanswtalt, 1989); Plath, *Drei Frauen*, trans. Friederike Roth (Frankfurt am Main: Frankfurter Verlagsanstalt, 1991). See also Plath, *Zungen aus Stein: Erzählungen*, trans. Julia Bachstein and Susanne Levin (Frankfurt am Main: Frankfurter Verlagsanstalt, 1989).

[11] The tenth edition of Erich Fried's 1974 translation of *Ariel* appeared in 1993, and in 1997 Suhrkamp published a new translation of *The Bell Jar* by Reinhard Kaiser. Reviews of Kaiser's translation point not only to how translations age quickly and therefore need to be redone for subsequent generations, but also to how Kaiser's translation better reflects the icy understated style of Plath's prose by capturing her subtle mix of suffering and comic. See Gisela von Wysocki, "Das Leben. Ein hektisches Dabeigewesensein," *Die Zeit*, 4 Apr. 1997; Wilhelm Kühlmann, "Die klare Sicht des Wahns," *Frankfurter Allgemeine Zeitung*, 15 Apr. 1997; and Angela Schader, "Mit reinerem Klang," *Neue Zürcher Zeitung*, 8 Aug. 1997. As to secondary literature, see Wolfgang

media attention to Plath, no doubt sparking an interest in those who may have overlooked her in the 1970s, to say nothing of a new generation of German readers. The various reviews reveal several particulars regarding Plath reception in the German-speaking world.[12] Her suicide not only invites an urge to examine the poems for evidence of why she took her own life but also places her in the ranks of a special class of writers. Invariably, names such as Virginia Woolf, Hart Crane, Ernest Hemingway, Georg Trakl, and especially Paul Celan surface in the commentary. In connection with Celan, Plath is presented as a poet — in the role of both victim and survivor — confronting the Holocaust. The likeness, however, has its limits. While Celan represents the hermetic tradition of poetry, Plath is more straightforward if not blunt; moreover, her verse can be remarkably giddy while macabre. The diaries, correspondence, and biographies do much to separate myth from reality and help the reader distinguish personal history from poetic license. In addition, these sources clarify issues surrounding the relationship of Plath and her husband cum literary executor, the English poet Ted Hughes. In this respect, Malcolm's study of the Plath biographies aids in mediating the personal biases of the biographers. The Plath renaissance in Germany marks a new era. The wealth of material now available in German translation will make it possible for Plath to achieve a status in German-speaking countries comparable to what she has maintained in England and America since the mid-1960s.

Werth, *Ikonographie des Entsetzens* (Trier: Wissenschaftlicher Verlag, 1990); Monika Steinert, *Mythos in den Gedichten Sylvia Plaths* (Frankfurt am Main: Lang, 1995); and Sabine Kruse, *Ted Hughes' Birthday Letters vor dem Hintergrund der Plath-Hughes-Kontroverse* (Essen: Die Blaue Eule, 1999).

[12] See Elke Schmitter, "Ein Panther stellt mir lauernd nach," *Die Weltwoche*, 1 Feb. 1990; Manuela Reichart, "Spaßwunderbetten," *Die Zeit*, 20 Apr. 1990; Elke Schmitter, "Karriere auf schiefer Ebene," *Der Spiegel*, 17 Dec. 1990: 193, 196–99; Eva Maria Alves, "Das Leben gedichtet, auf daß es erträglich werde," *Deutsches Allgemeines Sonntagsblatt*, 26 July 1991; Rudolf Walter Leonhardt, "Sie sind aus Wasser," *Die Zeit*, 30 Aug. 1991; Heinrich Detering, "Lauter kleine Wunder," *Frankfurter Allgemeine Zeitung*, 28 Sept. 1991; Hanspeter Künzler, "Die Tote und die Lebenden," *Neue Zürcher Zeitung*, 8/9 July 1995. See also Marianne Kneerich-Woerner, *Der Selbstmord* (Frankfurt am Main: Lang, 1988), a psychoanalytic investigation of suicide in literature with case studies of Plath and Heinrich von Kleist.

The 1990s are likewise significant for the appearance of two new international anthologies of poetry, *Luftfracht* and *Atlas der neuen Poesie*, edited by Harald Hartung and Joachim Sartorius respectively. *Luftfracht*[13] presents a global exchange of poetry, and its title — "Airfreight" — espouses poetry not as something light and airy but an art form of considerable mass and substance. The anthology features poetry of the half century between 1940 and 1990; occasionally poems will appear both in translation and in the original, especially pivotal works of an era. The poems of each of these five decades are grouped in a *Magazin* — a designation suggesting not a periodical publication but a place where goods are stored, as in sections of a library. Although there is no thematic link joining the poets presented here, neither a stylistic nor sociopolitical stance to be promoted, the editor's preface makes it clear that each of the poets selected represents the world language of poetry spoken during this fifty-year period. Hartung's editorial remarks admit the subjective nature of his choices and point to the foundation on which his collection rests: Hans Magnus Enzensberger's *Museum der modernen Poesie*. Hartung's goal and purpose, then, is to advance the tradition established thirty years earlier by Enzensberger. Just as the *Museum* met and fulfilled specific needs of its era, developments since 1960 call for a new collection, a revised overview.

Although each magazine of *Luftfracht* displays distinguishing traits, the overall compilation shows how one decade leads to the next. For example, selections from the 1940s highlight the concept of poetry versus antipoetry, thus setting the stage for the 1950s when the notion of world poetry began to lose both its Eurocentric and academic foundations. Similarly, the 1960s feature a special blend of pop and politics, while the 1970s usher in a revisionist epoch — ideologically, politically, culturally, and aesthetically. Finally, the concluding section, the 1980s, leaves us with a new world of poetry, an age in which poetry has truly become international. Just as Hartung's preface explains his editorial approach and organizational principles, the biographical sketches of the poets featured in *Luftfracht* say a great deal about factors influencing the

---

[13] *Luftfracht: Internationale Poesie 1940 bis 1990*, ed. Harald Hartung (Frankfurt am Main: Eichborn, 1991).

selection process. Here the reader learns not just pertinent facts about the writer, especially those lesser known non-Europeans, but also the special qualities — even quirks — making the poet worthy of cargo space in Hartung's transporter. Finally, the biographies and bibliographical references are intended to spark the reader's interest, to provide a starting point for learning more about the poets and poetry introduced here.

As to the Americans in *Luftfracht*, selections for the 1940s and 1950s feature names familiar to German readers, thanks either to Enzensberger's *Museum* or other previously documented sources. With the 1960s, however, in addition to those poets promoted by Höllerer and Brinkmann we begin to see more of the editor's take on contemporary American verse, in particular Robert Lowell. For Hartung, Lowell embodies unique aspects of America's history and literary tradition: a member of a patrician New England family with maternal ancestors dating back to the *Mayflower* pilgrims, academic ties on his father's side to Harvard College, and a literary lineage established by his great-great-uncle James Russell Lowell and distant cousin Amy Lowell. In addition, Lowell can claim an adopted family, particularly with respect to his literary career, as after breaking off his studies at Harvard he transferred to Kenyon College to study with John Crowe Ransom and later attended Louisiana State University where he studied with Robert Penn Warren and Cleanth Brooks. During these years Lowell also forged close friendships with Allen Tate and Randall Jarrell and came under the influence of the school of New Criticism. As for Lowell's poems in *Luftfracht*, Hartung turns to his later work, dedications to Eliot and Pound from *Notebook, 1967–68*, a collection of unrhymed sonnets, somewhere between the formal and informal in terms of structure, and written in a language often closer to prose than poetry. Although emphasizing the literary aspects of Lowell's poetry, Hartung also captures the intensely personal side of his writing, both directly (through a translation of the poem "Heavy Breathing"[14]) and indirectly. That is to say, by featuring poems of Sylvia Plath and Anne Sexton and then alluding to how both attended Lowell's poetry seminar at Boston University, Hartung pays tribute to the "Confessional School" of

[14] Number nine of sixteen sonnets in the cycle of poems entitled "Marriage." See Robert Lowell, *The Dolphin* (New York: Farrar, 1973), 59.

American poetry, a movement generally said to have originated with the publication of Lowell's *Life Studies* in 1959.

Lowell also plays a role in the politics of the 1960s as Hartung cites his protests against the war in Vietnam. In parallel fashion the inclusion of Erich Fried's "17.–22. Mai 1966" reminds us of how this poet revitalized the political poem in Germany. As to the pop qualities of the era, William Carlos Williams is the central figure for Hartung. Even if out of synch as to the time frame, Williams's poem "This Is Just To Say" (published in 1934 but included as a portent of pop art) appears bilingually; also included is "Suzanne," a poem about his grandchildren. Together, these two poems hail Williams as a grandfather figure for both American and German poets of the postwar period, especially in the development of a pop sensibility. As a result, the 1960s magazine reads in part as an international family tree of poets with the Americans appearing as offspring of Williams and their German counterparts as cousins. For instance, Kenneth Koch is represented by Nicolas Born's translation of "Variations on a Theme by William Carlos Williams," and his fellow New York poet, Frank O'Hara, appears with three poems, including "Poem" ("Lana Turner has collapsed") in both English and German. From O'Hara and a movie-star tribute we necessarily move to Rolf Dieter Brinkmann, here with "Eine übergroße Photographie von Liz Taylor," then back stateside to Paul Blackburn with selections from Brinkmann's *Silverscreen* anthology (within the greater context, a subtle hint at Williams's influence on Black Mountain poets). Hartung also fits Jürgen Becker into this Williams-centered pop art constellation as his "Gedicht über Schnee im April" plays off the aesthetics of Andy Warhol. The Williams motif is then closed off with the German version of Allen Ginsberg's "Death News," the poem recounting how Ginsberg, while in India at the Benares Hindu University, learned that Williams had died.

Jumping ahead to the 1980s magazine we find the poems of Rita Dove and Jim Jarmusch. Dove's appearance reaffirms her standing in Germany as established during this decade; Jarmusch, who is better known as a filmmaker, represents the postwar, indeed baby-boomer generation of American poets and their unique worldview. Furthermore, Jarmusch reflects the international flavor of the anthology, as his ties to Europe (work as a film assistant in Paris) and an eye for the curious ethnic mix of American society make him an ideal fit for this collection. With respect to editorial choices, however, of all the Americans in *Luftfracht*, John Ashbery is most significant. Other marquee names notwithstanding, Ashbery stands unique as the one American poet appearing in three magazines spanning four decades: the 1950s, 1970s, and 1980s. (Curiously, Ashbery does not appear in the 1960s magazine, the decade in which he established himself as a leading poet of the New York school, but the absence is explained by the fact that his poetry is neither pop nor political.) By presenting Ashbery in such fashion Hartung emphasizes not merely his staying power but also how he transcends schools, movements, fads, and labels. As a means of providing context for approaching Ashbery's poetry, Hartung cites his ties to New York painters as well as work as an editor of *ARTnews* and then features poems demonstrating how Ashbery's montage technique bears semblance to the attributes of abstract art.

Such subtle undercurrents are at work throughout *Luftfracht*. The inclusion of Felix Pollak, who appears in the 1970s magazine, illustrates how poets span cultures and reminds the reader of what the poet in exile means in terms of the world language of poetry. In the case of Pollak, Hartung's biography and bibliographical data are especially valuable to readers unfamiliar with his poetry. Though he published seven volumes of poetry in the United States, Pollak did not live to see the only book printed in his native tongue;[15] hence, *Luftfracht* renders an all-important service in introducing a long-exiled voice to a new generation of German readers. In addition to Pollak, two other names warrant consideration with regard to how poetry transcends national borders and negates distinctions according to nationality: Derek Walcott and Joseph Brodsky. For Hartung, Walcott is not merely a poet of the Caribbean and the Americas, but a poet who literally embodies the world language of poetry with the blood of many peoples running through his veins. Brodsky, born 1940 as Jossif Brodskij in Leningrad, was expatriated from the Soviet Union in 1976 and became an American citizen in 1977, living in the United States until his

---

[15] Felix Pollak, *Vom Nutzen des Zweifels*, ed. Reinhold Grimm (Frankfurt am Main: Fischer, 1989). In the early summer of 1987 Pollak returned to Europe for readings at several West German universities as well as in Vienna, his birthplace. He died in Madison, Wisconsin, in November 1987.

death in 1996. Writing primarily in Russian but also in English, Brodsky established an international reputation unrivaled among poets of the latter half of the twentieth century, receiving the Nobel Prize for literature in 1987 and being named United States Poet Laureate in 1991. It is therefore fitting that Hartung chooses Brodsky to close the 1980s magazine of his anthology.

As a final note on *Luftfracht*, let us consider the unique way in which the editor annotates his anthology. Along the bottom margin, Hartung occasionally includes what he terms *Begleitpapiere*, that is, accompanying excerpts from letters, journals, or essays, to provide a backdrop for the featured poem. For example, the 1950s magazine has Charles Olson's "I, Mencius, Pupil of the Master . . ." (in which Olson, the pupil, pays homage to his master, Ezra Pound) accompanied by a passage from Olson's "Projective Verse" — a deft means not only of acknowledging Olson's literary heritage but also reminding us of his influence, via Gerhardt and Höllerer, on German poetry since the 1950s.

Atlas der neuen Poesie[16] stands as a companion piece to *Luftfracht*. Like Hartung, Sartorius acknowledges Enzensberger and asserts the need to carry on the legacy established by his *Museum*. Once again the editor's preface speaks of a world language of poetry, and if Enzensberger was notable for introducing poets of the Western Hemisphere to German readers, then Hartung and especially Sartorius further this tradition by featuring poets of Asia and Africa in their anthologies. The organizational principle for Sartorius's collection is a world atlas, with the editor in the role of cartographer and poets grouped in portfolios according to the meridians of longitude on a map. As a continuation of Enzensberger's *Museum*, the anthology features poems from the years 1960 to 1994 with an emphasis on the final twenty years of this period. As to the editorial selection process, the principle of discovery supersedes that of homage. Therefore, when faced with a choice due to spatial limitations, Sartorius opts for the lesser-known rather than the well-established poet.

American poets appearing in *Atlas* are Elizabeth Bishop, John Ashbery, James Tate, Michael Palmer, Clark Coolidge, and Charles Simic. The inclusion of Bishop (1911–1979) is somewhat of an

---

[16] Joachim Sartorius, ed., *Atlas der neuen Poesie* (Reinbek bei Hamburg: Rowohlt, 1995).

anomaly, in that she represents a generation of poets predating most in the anthology. Likewise her poem "The Map," which opens the American portfolio, was written in 1946, clearly outside the time frame announced in the preface. On the other hand, Bishop is an ideal choice to bridge the gap between this collection and Enzensberger's *Museum*. Furthermore, both "The Map" and her signature poem "Questions of Travel" (1965) capture the very essence of the *Atlas*-concept promulgated by the editor. In his biographical note Sartorius cites Harold Bloom's designation of Bishop as a model for both her own and subsequent generations of American poets (Berryman, Lowell, and Ashbery); thus, just as Williams serves as a grandfather figure for Hartung, Bishop presides as matriarch of the American poets selected by Sartorius. As to the other Americans, Ashbery stands as the dean of present-day American poets and the American poet most closely associated with Sartorius the translator. The appearance of Tate is definitely welcome, as here is an American poet long overdue in reaching a German audience. The choice of Palmer and Coolidge highlights the diversity of American poetry and shows how Sartorius promotes discovery of lesser-known poets. Finally, Simic represents a unique voice in American poetry of the past thirty years. Born in Belgrade in 1938, Simic lived the war years in Yugoslavia before emigrating to the United States in 1954. In the late 1960s he emerged as a leading figure among a new generation of poets, and in the 1990s, this mystic of everyday life began to reach German readers.[17]

In his preface Sartorius outlines the characteristic features of poetry since 1960. Although this era, he claims, is distinguished by an absence of binding poetics, poetological convictions are often to be found hidden within poems; such poems, especially the so-called meta poems with their reflections on poetry and the act of writing poetry, are the primary sources for information on contemporary poetics. In addition, Sartorius outlines three primary tendencies in poetry written during the previous thirty years. First, there is a definite compensatory character in many poems; that is to say, the poem functions as an instrument to correct and adjust a world out of bal-

---

[17] See Simic, *Ein Buch von Göttern und Teufeln*, trans. Hans Magnus Enzensberger (Munich: Hanser, 1993); and Simic, *Die Fliege in der Suppe*, trans. Rudolf von Bitter (Munich: Hanser, 1997).

ance. Second, Sartorius sees an undeniable metaphysical attribute in select poems owing to a skepticism about language and certain mystical tendencies — in other words, poetry as a search for redemptive language. And third, there is poetry that refuses to take itself too seriously, poems that exhibit a playful quality in terms of both language and subject matter. Let us now turn to the American poets appearing in *Atlas* and consider how they correspond to these distinctions.

Like Hartung, Sartorius emphasizes Ashbery's ties to the New York schools of painting and poetry. His poems, often cryptic and at times seemingly impenetrable, can be likened to verbal collages. As to those particulars put forth by Sartorius, we can say Ashbery exhibits a propensity to explore the possibilities of language, especially in his use of conversational passages and experiments with syntax and perspective. Although not averse to occasional surrealist frivolities, Ashbery maintains balance through an elegant reserve. James Tate is also renowned for forays into the realm of surrealism, and his poetry often corresponds to the category of verse that does not appear to take itself too seriously; to read Tate's poems is, in a word, fun. In his biographical sketch, Sartorius turns to Ashbery and Donald Justice who speak of how Tate can startle and amaze, bewilder and titillate the reader. Sartorius also highlights his comic vein, portraying Tate as a master of farce who, in Chaplinesque fashion, finds comfort in gloom, mirth in the midst of melancholy. Like Tate, Charles Simic gained recognition in the late 1960s. The bio note on Simic accents the autobiographical side of his writing, his war-torn childhood and emigrant mentality, how his poetry is infused with an East-European laconism and disillusionment. For Sartorius, Simic writes poems that refuse to forget, a poetry steeped in memory, its language tinged with both pathos and sarcasm — and in this light, we see a compensatory quality in Simic's poems. Moreover, like Bishop, Simic enhances a sense of poetic globalism at work within *Atlas*.

Both Michael Palmer and Clark Coolidge can be termed language poets, and their poetry represents the second of the three categories delineated by Sartorius. Palmer's poetry demonstrates a keen interest in the power of language to both reveal and conceal. Although admitting to the inevitability of narrative in poetry, Palmer stresses that story line necessarily involves a certain degree of camouflage. Along parallel lines, Palmer's poems exhibit a concrete quality especially in his use of the image; yet for Palmer images are often deceiving and therefore demand, according to Sartorius, careful scrutiny. While other poets have ties to jazz music or abstract painting, Palmer has collaborated with dance companies. Complementing his poetry, as Sartorius points out, Palmer is also known for his critical essays and editorial work. As editor of *Code of Signals: Recent Writings in Poetics* (1983) Palmer promoted theoretical writing among experimental poets, and during the mid-1960s he co-edited the influential magazine *Joglars* with Clark Coolidge. Coolidge, who is also a geologist, can be termed experimental in his attempts to break away from standard syntax and to expand the limited vocabulary of traditional poetry. His ideal reader will suspend the demand for narrative or a linear progression, in that Coolidge conceives of the poem as words arranged as if in a geologic formation. An earmark of his poetry, in the words of Sartorius, are Wittgenstein-like language games. His texts are denaturalized, indeed deconstructed, so that the reader is required to reestablish the relationship between language and meaning. Finally, with the inclusion of Coolidge and Palmer in *Atlas* Sartorius is able to highlight a more theoretical side of American poetry, a tendency closer to German traditions and distinct from much of the American poetry promoted in Germany since 1945.

As more and more American poets gain recognition, American influences on German poetry become more matter-of-fact. Likewise, America becomes less compelling as subject matter for German poets, especially late in the twentieth century. What was once exotic has become commonplace, the political edge has dulled, and all in all there seems less urgency for German poets to address the United States in verse.[18] To illuminate how the image of America has evolved since 1945, let us consider "Selbstporträt mit Luftbrücke" by F. C. Delius.[19] The title indicates a lyrical self-portrait framed by a specific historical context — the Berlin airlift. The text, however, does not present a single likeness of its subject, rather a composite picture drawing on a series of photo-like images spanning the years 1948 to 1992. The *Luftbrücke* (literally air bridge) in this portrait functions like a winding road receding into a panoramic landscape background,

---

[18] See Ludwig Fels, "Black Spirit Brevier," in *Dimension* (1983): 118–45, especially 126.

[19] See F. C. Delius, *Selbstporträt mit Luftbrücke: Ausgewählte Gedichte 1962–1992* (Reinbek: Rowohlt, 1993), 146–47.

thus providing perspective for viewing the featured subject. This autobiographical poem is, then, a bridge in time taking the reader back to childhood days of the poet. Noteworthy is how references to the airlift are made without commentary on the political situation and its historical consequences. Instead the reader is shown "Rollfelder,/ wo die Kinder mit Händen nach Flugzeugen griffen,/ aus denen Kohlen, Rosinen, Schweinehälften fielen" — an image with the documentary quality of newsreel footage. Likewise, the pilots of these airplanes are not identified as American or British; consistent with a child's point of view, they are simply "die fliegenden Menschen." Furthermore, the allusion to aviation terminology — *"touch down"* — is neither a foreign language lesson nor occasion for comment on linguistic imports to postwar Germany. Such observations have long since become passé. For Delius this loanword serves his self portrait as a metaphor for life skills: "in der richtigen Sekunde/ am richtigen Ort mit angemessener Geschwindigkeit/ landen."

In spite of the fact that its content revolves around an historical event with international ramifications, "Selbstporträt mit Luftbrücke" is a domestic poem, that is, a poem about being German since the end of the Second World War. In terms of history, the airlift marks the postwar division of Germany and signals the nascent tensions of the cold war. The title also signifies the airlift monument on the *Platz der Luftbrücke* in front of the Tempelhof airfield in West Berlin. In addition to creating a time bridge spanning the years 1948/49 and 1992 this self-portrait places the poet between photographers and the monument itself. The effect is twofold: not only does it reinforce a sense of closure — the cold war over and Germany reunified — but it also shows how the poet is caught somewhere between the forces of history. In this sense, Delius delineates postwar historical developments in terms of their impact on a specific generation of Germans. Thus, as a self portrait — and particularly within the context of Delius's place in contemporary German literature — the poem can be read as an ironic portrayal of a generation of erstwhile revolutionaries turned moderate, a generation once rash and narcissistic, now circumspect and unassuming.[20] The world into which this generation was

---

[20] See Silvia Volckmann, "Ausflüge in die Romantik. F. C. Delius — *Selbstporträt mit Luftbrücke*," in *Gedichte und Interpretationen, Gegenwart II*, 261–69, here 269.

born and within which they came to adulthood has undergone a fundamental change. On a deeper level, then, this poem is a subtle reminder of how from 1945 to 1990 Germany — and especially Berlin — had been the rope in an east-west tug-of-war between the two superpowers. Finally, and as pertains to this study, "Selbstporträt mit Luftbrücke" exemplifies how by 1992 the image of America in contemporary German poetry — like the place of the United States in postwar German history — had faded from the forefront while being raised to the commemorative status of a monument.

While Delius presents a 1990s image of America within a historical context, Richard Wagner and Thomas Kling highlight the aesthetic and cultural status of America in post-reunification German poetry. If Hartung's "Wann lasen Sie den Plato Mr. Hopper" confirms the respect accorded this American artist in European circles, then Wagner's poem "Hoppers Nacht,"[21] is proof of how Edward Hopper's painting *Nighthawks* (1942) has achieved topos status throughout the world:

> Hoppers Menschen
> sitzen in der Bar.
> Es kommt mir kein Wort
> über die Lippen.
> Eine kleine weiße Schlange kommt
> mir über die Lippen.
> Sie verschwindet im Garten,
> wer mich kennt, weiß Bescheid.
>
> Auf hohen Stühlen
> sitzen Hoppers Menschen,
> und sie führen ein Gespräch,
> ohne ein Wort zu sagen.
> Sie reden und
> eine kleine weiße Schlange
> windet sich um sie herum.
> Der Barmann weiß Bescheid.
>
> [...]
>
> Er spielt mit einem Gedanken,
> während du mit einem Wort spielst.

---

[21] Richard Wagner, *Schwarze Kreide: Gedichte* (Frankfurt am Main: Luchterhand Literaturverlag, 1991), 92.

Dieses Wort is sperrig und schwarz.
Niemand geht darauf ein.
Das Gleiche noch einmal, sagst du.

Hopper's *Nighthawks,* as well known as any American painting except perhaps for Whistler's portrait of his mother (1871) or Grant Wood's *American Gothic* (1930), shares the distinction with these classics of being subject to parody. Unique to Hopper, however, is his ability to spawn literature: stories and poems about specific paintings or literary works evoking a mood deemed "Hopperesque."[22] Wagner's "Hoppers Nacht" follows this tradition and invites comparison with the poem "Edward Hopper's *Nighthawks,* 1942" by Joyce Carol Oates.[23] While Oates imagines the interior monologues of the couple seated at the counter, Wagner adds a touch of the surface-level surreal to Hopper's nighttime scene. Although he alters the original, Wagner does so without poking fun — unlike, say, Marcel Duchamp affixing a mustache to the *Mona Lisa.* Whereas Oates listens in, Wagner invites the reader to join in. The very title of his poem suggests not the painting per se but the night on which the scene in *Nighthawks* takes place; its content, then, prolongs the moment-in-time of a still life and conveys what may transpire as we move deeper into the night. Wagner's attention is drawn to the human element in Hopper's painting, and it is no accident that he uses the word *Menschen* twice. Unlike Oates who probes the psyches of stock characters, Wagner leaves the figures at the counter lost in their private reveries. In tune with the painting, Wagner depicts the humane interaction of human beings engaged in conversation without saying a word.

With its dramatic tension and hint of imminent violence *Nighthawks* recalls scenes in gangster movies or Hemingway's short story

[22] See John Updike, "Hopper's Polluted Silence," *New York Review of Books,* 10 Aug. 1995: 19–21, here 19, who mentions works by writers including Ann Beattie, Tess Gallagher, Thom Gunn, John Hollander, William Kennedy, Ann Lauterbach, Norman Mailer, Leonard Michaels, Joyce Carol Oates, and Mark Strand.

[23] See Edward Hirsch, ed., *Transforming Vision: Writers on Art* (Boston: Little, 1994), 64.

"The Killers."[24] Wagner adds a stroke of the sinister with a snake, and the mention of a garden implies a biblical link to the concept of original sin. Nevertheless, his designation of "eine kleine weiße Schlange" creates less a sense of impending evil than that of a curious freak of nature. Moreover, this reptilian touch points to Wagner's European literary roots, a blend of French symbolism and German expressionism, with his playfully demonic air suggesting a cross between Théophile Gautier and Georg Heym. He also displays kinship with Brinkmann's poetics: an albino snake slithering across Hopper's canvas smoothes the surface while adding depth to the image. Finally, his coy autobiographical aside, "wer mich kennt, weiß Bescheid," parallels the key-to-the-puzzle vein of "He, ich bin/ im Krieg geboren" voiced by Brinkmann in "Westwärts, Teil 2."[25]

By the final stanza "Hoppers Nacht" has become the domain of the counterman and reader. Oates, although concentrating on the man and woman, saves the counterman for her closing thoughts; with Wagner the counterman steps forth at the end of the second stanza and shares the final five lines with the reader. In Wagner's final stanza Hopper's original setting has dissolved into a nocturnal otherworld spreading into blackness. What makes *Nighthawks* so Hopperesque is its celebration of nighttime loneliness in a large city. Hopper imbues the American way of life with his distinctive American imagination. For Wagner, the American imagination is the power to transform. His final line lets you, the reader, speak, proclaiming a desire to repeat the experience, to relive the moment. And in the final line Wagner breaks the silence, employing street vernacular consistent with coffee urns, condiments, and an all-night lunch counter.

For our final poem, let us turn to Thomas Kling's "taunusprobe. lehrgang im hessischn"[26] quoted here in its entirety:

---

[24] See Levin, *Hopper*, 350, who notes "The Killers" was one of Hopper's favorite short stories, one he praised as "an honest piece of work" without the "sugar coated mush" of so much American fiction.

[25] See Brinkmann, *Westwärts 1 & 2*, 50.

[26] Thomas Kling, *brennstabm: Gedichte* (Frankfurt am Main: Suhrkamp, 1991), 45–46. The following discussion of Kling's poem draws from a lecture, one in a series on "Contemporary German Poetry 1945–1995," delivered by Jörg Drews at Washington University in St. Louis on 3 April 1996.

»Ich deutete abwärts: sie[h] das rätselgesicht«
(Stefan George, 1922)

ssauntz.   grölende theke.
ATEM-SCHUTZ-GERÄTE-TRÄGER-LEHRGANG was
für ssauntz! unter pokalen, fuß-
balltrophäen die azurminiträgerin the-
kenblond.—GERÄTETRÄGERLEHRGANG IN A.
springt kajal, dringt vor im kajal,
kajalflor zu heavy metal sounnz (vorhersage: grölender stammtisch), gerekktes
hinterzimmer-, jetzt gaststubn-»heil!!«.
di theknmannschaft,pokalpokal, trägt
501 trägt wildleder-boots, drittklassiger
western den sie hier abfahrn HEILHEILHEIL!!!!
flaumblonde unterschenkel, es kajalt von
gegnüber; di blonde matte. FUN!
                        AUGN — FUNK.
IN B: FUNKSPRECHBERECHTIGUNXLEHRGANG, IN
C: FOLGT (fig. 3) DI MOTORKETTNSÄGE-
UNTERWEISUN', wies kajalt! hinpfeilnd aufs
dartboard, gewitterland-, gewitterlandschaft
im gesicht. die theknmannschaft (»I. preis
im torwandschießn 1990«) verchromtes hufeisen
im laredo-jeep, yosemety dschosmetti-aufkleb
an ihren niederkalifornien-karren, da draußn
vor der kneipntür. pfännchen-scheiß über
hinkümmerndn topfpflanzn, hufeisnverchromt
man geht im bärenwiegeschritt (vorkraftkaum
laufn). der Große Feldberg, sendersender,
störfunk   ssaunnzz

The following will proceed according to the question, how — not
what — does this poem mean?[27] In terms of genre, "taunusprobe"
can be classified a performance poem following in the Beat tradition of poetry readings staged with jazz accompaniment. Our approach, then, will be to determine how this poem goes about
being a performance of itself. The title indicates setting, subject

[27] See John Ciardi, *How Does a Poem Mean?* (Boston: Floughton Mifflin, 1959).

matter, and diction. The setting (and its regional dialect) is more rural than urban with *Taunus* designating a section of the Rhenish *Schiefergebirge* (slate mountain range) in the German state of Hesse. The reference to "der Große Feldberg" in the penultimate line further specifies the setting as within range of radio transmission towers situated on the highest peak of the Taunus mountains on the outskirts of Frankfurt am Main. As to content, the reader can expect a rehearsal, a trial run, or the demonstration of skills associated with an apprenticeship program.

The opening word *ssauntz* is a quasi-phonetic rendering of the English word *sounds*. And what sounds! One opens the door to this poem and is greeted with a blast of sounds. Personification amplifies the noise with the wail of a bawling barroom counter at the opposite end of the first line. The context of a training course — or perhaps a celebration marking the completion thereof — surfaces in line two with mention of a protective breathing apparatus used, for instance, by the fire department; subsequent references, from parts A, B, and C of a training manual, cite additional devices and parody the bureaucratic language found in such instructional booklets. The barroom setting is established by allusions to soccer trophies, a dartboard, and a plaque for first prize in wall-soccer shootouts (a contest in which players kick soccer balls at a goal outlined on a wall). Moreover, decor and clientele reflect a milieu best described as *bundesrepublikanisch* (of the *West* German Federal Republic). Club team members and a table of regular customers generate not only a sense of familiarity and camaraderie within the pandemonium but also a distinctive political posture. Finally, the blonde in a blue miniskirt adds more than a touch of the erotic; although seemingly lost in the cacophony, visual acuity and tactile contrast prevail in the particulars of her close-cropped hairdo and pubescent lower legs.

Two other features in the first half of this poem deserve our attention: one, the use of the word *kajal* (and its variants); and two, the exclamatory *heil*. According to Duden, the noun *Kajal* is from the Sanskrit and refers to a cosmetic, generally black in color, applied around the eyes; the verb *kajolieren* derives from the French *cajoler*, to sing or call out like a bird in a cage or to persuade by means of flattery, as in the English derivative *cajole*. Kling's usage seems to draw on this myriad of meanings as well as a synonymous relationship with the verb *grölen*, to wail or to bawl. In addition, *kajal* contributes to the sound quality of the poem, serving to rhyme with the equally repetitious *pokal* and sustaining fluidity in the liquid consonant *l* recurring throughout the text. The cosmetic connotation of *Kajal* not only puts eye makeup on the blonde in the blue miniskirt, but also paints a black ring around the barroom scene itself:

> kajalflor zu heavy metal sounnz (vorher-
> sage: grölender stammtisch), gerekktes
> hinterzimmer-, jetzt gaststubn-»heil!!«.

Here the fascist undertones of heavy metal music surface in a riot of bloom. A passage of time can be deduced from the strategically placed hyphens and the adverb *jetzt* in the third line above. Moreover, the word *Vorhersage* indicates that one could have foreseen what would become of this table of regulars. Once confined to the back room, these blustery cronies have taken their straight-arm Nazi salute out of hiding and into the open, their shouts of "HEILHEILHEIL!!!!" now a bold counterpoint to the barroom bedlam.

This undercurrent of violent fantasy resurfaces in the second half of the poem in the form of a perverse joke. The indication of an illustrated diagram ("fig. 3") of a chainsaw, conjures up scenes of blood and gore as from the horror film *Texas Chainsaw Massacre*. Sounds and images mesh, the dartboard mirrors a face with an expression taking on the sultriness of an approaching storm. Accordingly, the image of a thundercloud-filled landscape moves the show outside the barroom as the poem advances to its conclusion. The scene outdoors, however, is no less bizarre than indoors. No form of fertilizer will help the potted plant found next to the barroom door, and the customers are so bestially drunk they can barely walk. Sounds persist, specifically broadcast sounds, but the signal is jammed. There is interference, disturbance in the air.

Kling's "taunusprobe. lehrgang im hessischn" highlights the evolution of German poetry since 1945. Although the American influences are pronounced, "taunusprobe" is equally Germanic with respect to its literary heritage. The motto from Stefan George[28] may

---

[28] See Stefan George, *Das Neue Reich*, vol. 9 of *Gesamt-Ausgabe der Werke*, 18 vols. (Berlin: Biondi, 1928), 54–55.

seem ironic in light of the poem's non-literary content. Yet just as George addresses problems in Germany during the years following the First World War, here Kling offers a picture of Germany after re-unification and suggests there is a riddle to be solved. Aside from the motto, Kling is working within a specific literary legacy, a poem about a night out at a local establishment much in the tradition of Gottfried Benn's "Nachtcafé." The coarse language and vulgarities plus liberties in spelling and word formation recall the stylistic inventions of Arno Schmidt in such novels as *Kaff auch Mare Crisium* or *Abend mit Goldrand*. The performance-oriented language likewise suggests Ernst Jandl, in particular his poem "wien: heldenplatz." Finally, the strategic word placements in the first and last lines borrow from the principles of concrete poetry. In light of the balanced opposition and reversal of *ö* and *au* sounds in these lines the reader can superimpose an x-pattern on the entire poem, a configuration intersecting mid-text at "AUGN — FUNK." Similarly, if identical vowel sounds denote a semantic correlation, then "s*au*nzz" are constant regardless of the spelling change, and the "gr*ö*lende theke" somehow contributes to the "st*ö*rfunk." Placing "AUGN — FUNK" between "FUN!" and Part B of the instruction manual on authorized radio communication creates meaning on a variety of levels. First, the *FUN* in *FUNK* is that on which the poem thrives. Second, "AUGN — FUNK" deftly enhances sexual content with the sparkle of eyes relaying a message just as a radio unit transmits a signal. Finally, the insertion of "AUGN — FUNK" at the midpoint of the poem underscores the visual element of the printed text while rejoicing in its oral performance. Crucial with regard to this study is how Kling incorporates a distinctively American quality into the poem with America's image and influence merging seamlessly as one. The text of "taunusprobe" is bare without its American imports: from heavy metal music, Levi-brand 501 jeans, and cowboy boots to American slang and that uniquely American vehicle adorned with a chrome-plated horseshoe and bumper sticker from Yosemite National Park. Nevertheless, these features are more minutiae than primary focus. Hence, these American items function like flavoring particles in colloquial speech, pertinent details adding a characteristic touch. The main thrust is strictly German, specifically post-reunification West German, incorporating a mood and spirit where Americana and Americanisms have become matter-of-fact.

Conclusion: Imago America

BOTH THE IMAGE of America in German poetry and American influences on German poetry have undergone significant changes since the end of the Second World War. The latter half of the twentieth century proves how American literature, and especially poetry, has gained respect in the German-speaking world. We recall how in the early postwar period American poets were generally ignored, how even though American prose fiction and drama served as models for a new generation of German writers, American poetry still suffered from long-standing European prejudices. While the 1960s and 1970s showed America at the forefront of foreign influences at work in German poetry, by the 1980s American poetry had played out its run as a highly visible, trend-like force exerting leverage on German poets. Indeed, if looking for signs of pronounced American influences on German letters after reunification, then one would turn to journalism, specifically the New Journalism as practiced by such American writers as Jimmy Breslin, Truman Capote, Norman Mailer, Gay Talese, and Tom Wolfe.[1]

As to reception, our concluding thoughts raise the question, who are the most important twentieth-century American poets in the German-speaking world? T. S. Eliot and Ezra Pound are the first names that come to mind, and their status for German readers remains ever strong. Pound has overcome the fascist stigma that led many German critics to act as if he did not exist during the early postwar period; in fact, the journal *Das Gedicht* and its jury of over fifty writers, critics, and scholars named Pound the top international poet of the twentieth century.[2] In addition to Eliot and Pound, other American poets of their generation have gained pres-

---

[1] See Erhard Schütz, "»Dichter der Gesellschaft«. Neuer deutscher Journalismus oder Für eine erneuerte Asphaltliteratur," in *Text + Kritik* 113 (1992): 63–71.

[2] See *Das Gedicht* 7 (Fall 1999–Summer 2000): 99–109, an issue also featuring "Slam Poetry aus Chicago" and poems by Marc Kelly Smith, Cindy Salach and Reggie Gibson.

tige, particularly William Carlos Williams, who in Germany now stands on par with his erstwhile better-known contemporaries.

Even though Williams's reception moved at a slow pace, his status in German literary circles is significant on two levels. First, he is unique in having established a literary foothold for the antipoetic in subject matter and the everyday idiom of the common folk in voice. And second, Williams is an all-important bridge figure linking his era to a variety of schools of poetry developing during subsequent generations. With his introduction to Ginsberg's *Howl* Williams encouraged recognition of Beat writers in mainstream America and thus facilitated, if not accelerated, their reception in Germany. Although he distanced himself from Eliot and cherished disagreement with Pound, Williams does bear connection to his former classmate at the University of Pennsylvania. In fact, we can speak of a Pound-Williams line in American poetry, a line leading directly to Charles Olson and the Black Mountain poets. Moreover, the enthusiastic praise of Williams for Olson's "Projective Verse" was crucial to establishing Olson's reputation both in America and later in Germany, thanks first to Rainer M. Gerhardt and then to Walter Höllerer, who helped make Olson a moving force in German poetics from the mid-1960s onward. Finally, there is a connection between Williams and Frank O'Hara, a lineage recognized and promoted by Rolf Dieter Brinkmann, that lies at the heart of German pop poetry. Just as O'Hara noted that of the American poets only Whitman, Crane, and Williams are "better than the movies,"[3] Brinkmann found the beginnings of pop art in the poetry of Williams. These factors, in addition to ongoing translations from his vast body of work, are paramount in acknowledging William Carlos Williams within the German-speaking world as the grandfather of contemporary American poetry.

American poets of the Beat Generation continue to enjoy special renown, especially Allen Ginsberg, whose death in 1997 was covered extensively by the German-language press. *Die tageszeitung* honored Ginsberg in special fashion with his poem "Return of Kral Majales" in Adolf Endler's translation, a memorial address, and excerpts from a 1996 interview — plus a front-page photo of a nude Ginsberg on the

---

[3] See O'Hara, "Personism," *Collected Poems*, 498.

beach of the Sea of Japan in 1963.[4] While the *taz* retrospective plays up his reputation as "Uncle Sam des Underground," other testimonials hail Ginsberg not only as groundbreaking poet and leader of the Beat Generation but also as a public persona in a variety of roles including political activist, prophet, and visionary.[5] Thus, while some refer to Ginsberg as an angry poet and vehement critic of the postwar American way of life, others cite him as the founder of flower power and leader of peaceful protest against the war in Vietnam.[6] As an icon of the counterculture Ginsberg is often linked to revolutionary days of the 1960s and the world of sex, drugs, and rock 'n' roll. Accordingly, the tributes highlight his ties to such figures as Bob Dylan and The Beatles as well as Timothy Leary and the drug culture; likewise Ginsberg is recognized as one of the first to openly proclaim his homosexuality.[7] Furthermore, Ginsberg is lauded as citizen of the world, a vagabond preacher with a penchant for the teachings of Zen Buddhism. In terms of his international reputation he is remembered for visits to Cuba, India, Cambodia, Japan, England, the Soviet Union, Poland, and East Berlin, as well as being crowned King of May 1965 in Prague before being expelled by the Communist authorities.[8] Aside

---

[4] Detlef Kuhlbrodt, "Hallo Nikita, hier ist Gott!," and "Das war eine Befreiung des Worts," interview with Werner Stiefele, *die tageszeitung*, 7 Apr. 1997.

[5] Helmut Räther, "Die Beat Generation verlor ihren Begründer," *Westfälische Rundschau*, 7 Apr. 1997; Günter Ohnemus, "Hungrig, hysterisch, nackt," *Die Zeit*, 11 Apr. 1997; and Hadayatullah Hübsch, "Allen Ginsbergs Echo zieht weiter," *Der Literat* 39.5 (1997): 18.

[6] Martin Oehlen, "Im Rausch der Worte," *Kölner Stadt-Anzeiger*, 7 Apr. 1997; Bernhard Schulz, "Der Untergang Amerikas," *Der Tagesspiegel*, 7 Apr. 1997; and Reinhard Tschapke, "Vom ekstatischen Hippi zum sanften Buddhisten," *Die Welt*, 7 Apr. 1997.

[7] Werner Stiefele, "Nein, zornig war er nicht!" *Stuttgarter Zeitung*, 7 Apr. 1997; Thomas E. Schmidt, "Geheul — und andere politische Aktivitäten," *Frankfurter Rundschau*, 7 Apr. 1997; Peter Mohr, "Beat-Poet Ginsberg gestorben," *Saarbrücker Zeitung*, 7 Apr. 1997; Wolfgang Platzeck, "Am Puls der Zeit," *Westdeutsche Allgemeine Zeitung*, 7 Apr. 1997; see also Kuhlbrodt, Oehlen, Schulz, and Tschapke.

[8] Willi Winkler, "Wutgeheul als Gassenhauer," *Süddeutsche Zeitung*, 7 Apr. 1997; Rainer Bratfisch, "Und vergeßt nicht den Wahnsinn," *Berliner Zeitung*, 7 Apr. 1997; Christian Linder, "Sänger der Beatniks," *Rheinische Post*, 7 Apr. 1997; see also Kuhlbrodt, Räther, Schmidt, and Tschapke.

from his ties to Beat writers such as Kerouac, Burroughs, Ferlinghetti, and Corso, reviewers delineate his literary heritage with reference not only to Walt Whitman and William Carlos Williams but also to William Blake.[9] We are thus reminded of how his poetry embraces both the oral tradition and American idiom but with a unique visionary twist. In terms of the oral quality of his poems, in particular his recitative style, reviewers even go so far as to hail Ginsberg as a precursor of rap music.[10] Finally, although his reputation as clown — the protestor as court jester — remains strong, the image of Ginsberg in his later years takes on a more reserved capacity. Hence, he is portrayed as a late-twentieth-century pillar of academia owing to his position as distinguished professor of literature at Brooklyn College.[11] Interestingly, the *Jüdische Allgemeine* draws parallels between Ginsberg and the German poet Stephan Hermlin, who died on the same weekend in 1997, in that both embody a flight from their Jewish heritage: Ginsberg, who chose Buddhism over Judaism; and Hermlin, committed communist rather than Jew.[12] All in all, the wide range of tributes is a testament to how the legacy of Ginsberg and the Beats has lived on in postwar Germany.

The popularity of the Beat poets in Germany has had a profound effect on the reception of American poetry, but not without its consequences. In fact one could argue that a fascination with the Beats has displaced or obscured a huge body of twentieth-century American poetry. Postwar German reception of American poetry appears to have leapfrogged from the Eliot-Pound era to that of Ginsberg and his cohorts. As a result a whole generation of American poets born in the first quarter of the twentieth century were, and remain to this day, largely ignored, a list including Theodore Roethke, Kenneth Rexroth, Robert Penn Warren, Allen Tate, Randall Jarrell, and John Berryman. Two exceptions, Robert Lowell

---

[9] Paul Ingendaay, "Das Geheul der Verlierer in freien Versen," *Frankfurter Allgemeine Zeitung*, 7 Apr. 1997; see also Linder, Oehlen, Schmidt, and Winkler.

[10] Thomas Rothschild, "Geheul," *Freitag*, 11 Apr. 1997; and "Nachruf. Allen Ginsberg. 1926 bis 1997," *Der Spiegel*, 14 Apr. 1997: 214.

[11] Peter Hughes, "Amerika als Traum und Wahn," *Neue Zürcher Zeitung*, 7 Apr. 1997; see also Ingendaay, Ohnemus, and Stiefele, *Stuttgarter Zeitung*.

[12] Stan Schneider, "Der Clown und der Claqueur," *Jüdische Allgemeine*, 17 Apr. 1997.

and Elizabeth Bishop, prove the rule; however, they, like William Carlos Williams, were slow to gain recognition in German circles.

In addition to the Beats, two other schools of American poetry have shown staying power. First, there are the Black Mountain poets and especially Robert Creeley and Charles Olson. Olson, important as much for his poetry as his poetics, remains vital as one of the first to use — and then exemplify — the term *postmodern* in its present-day context.[13] Second, we must acknowledge the New York school of the 1960s which lives on primarily through the poetry of Frank O'Hara and John Ashbery. O'Hara, though not with the standing of Ginsberg, is an icon in German literary circles, and his name remains synonymous with contemporary American poetry. Although long overlooked in Germany, Ashbery has grown in status in recent decades, and there are indications that he will be regarded as the leading American poet of the latter half of the twentieth century.

Who, then, since 1945 are the most important German figures with respect to America's role in German poetry? To begin, we must recognize Hans Hennecke and Rainer M. Gerhardt for setting standards and paving the way for subsequent poets, critics, editors, and translators. Walter Höllerer warrants special mention for advancing postwar American poetry. Although often in the role of provocateur, his efforts as mediator of the poetry of two continents was crucial for American poets to be recognized on a level with their European counterparts. As editor of *Akzente* and director of the *Literarische Colloquium Berlin* he literally brought American poets to German soil. It is noteworthy, however, that Höllerer's own poetry shows little of the American influences he so vigorously promoted. Even his poems written for American poets are more personal tributes than homage to any trademark style, and in this regard Höllerer the poet is more closely aligned with pre-1960s, European traditions.[14]

---

[13] See Olson's letter to Creeley on 20 Oct. 1951 in *Olson & Creeley* VIII, 79. See also the preface to Donald Allen and George R. Butterick, eds., *The Postmoderns: The New American Poetry Revised* (New York: Grove, 1982), 9–12, here 10; and the introduction to Paul Hoover, ed., *Postmodern American Poetry* (New York and London: Norton, 1994), xxv.

[14] See Höllerer, *Gedichte 1942–1982*, especially the poems "für Allen" (165), "für Robert Creeley (166), "für Frank O'Hara" (168), "für Charles Olson" (169).

Rolf Dieter Brinkmann is a decisive figure for a generation of writers and readers, especially those coming of age in the 1960s and 1970s. There is a certain Horace Greeley quality to his mystique in that he led many to look westwards to America for inspiration, subject matter, and style. The American influences on his own poetry, however strong they may be, are frequently misunderstood when not viewed in the proper proportion and perspective. Of the many American poets who helped shape Brinkmann's poetry all played a more fleeting than long-lasting role. In fact, Anglo-American pop music probably had a stronger, more ongoing impact than any one poet, and the only American writer whose style endured for Brinkmann is William S. Burroughs, in particular his cut-up prose method. The clearest and most abiding influences on Brinkmann were European, writers such as Gottfried Benn, Louis-Ferdinand Céline, and Hans Henny Jahnn. The American side of Brinkmann is best understood when viewed in the context of his editorial observations in *ACID* and *Silverscreen*, specifically the notion of the poem as a snapshot capturing a special moment in everyday life. *Westwärts 1 & 2* renders theory in praxis, especially such well-crafted poems as "Die Orangensaft Maschine," "Trauer auf der Wäschedraht im Januar," and "Einen jener klassischen." Moreover, the latter, perhaps the most frequently anthologized German poem of the 1970s, shows how Brinkmann's masterful use of German syntax not only extends but also raises that special moment to aesthetic heights.

Brinkmann did more than merely further the reception of American poetry; for him American poetry and poetics served as a glucose IV to invigorate postwar German verse. And even though Brinkmann himself may have turned his back on America, others continued to follow his lead. In retrospect we may ask: with regard to America, what was Brinkmann's most significant contribution to German poetry? The answer is twofold: first, by hyping the consumer component to reception he made Frank O'Hara a household name in German poetry;[15] and second, using an American model he thrust popular

---

[15] As to weight carried by his name in late-1960s Germany, see Jordan, "Dichtung unter Einfluß," 157 note 23, who points out that Frank O'Hara was listed on the book jacket blurb of the German edition of *Where is Vietnam?* even though this anthology contains no poem by O'Hara.

culture into literature.[16] For all of his positive contributions to America's place in German poetry since the late 1960s, there is, however, a down side to Brinkmann's role as intermediary. In introducing the "new American scene" he was extremely selective. It is not so much that he ignored much of what was not new — that is, established, mainstream, not counterculture — but he overlooked many important names then shaping American poetry, for example, Charles Simic and James Tate, two poets recognized in late-1960s America as noteworthy new voices. Perhaps these two poets were then too closely associated with the American Midwest, and Brinkmann's American anthologies have a definite predilection for East and West Coast contingents. As a result, Brinkmann did not so much shape but skew perceptions by presenting a very restricted picture of the American scene. Highlighting the overtly countercultural made it extremely difficult for any number of young voices to gain recognition in German circles. Moreover, it took years, indeed decades, for other poets and translators to broaden the vista. In the case of Simic and Tate, most German readers encounter them as established, mainstream American poets. The chance to read them in a more timely manner, that is, to experience their poetry during the formative years of the 1960s and 1970s before moving into the 1980s and 1990s, is long since past.

Before closing off our review of important German names in the field of reception, we must recognize the contribution of countless translators. Rudolf Hagelstange is worthy of special recognition for his translations of James Weldon Johnson. Not only are these poetic sermons documents of an era, when viewed in conjunction with his travel poem "Bei den schwarzen Baptisten" we can see how Hagelstange foreshadows the 1990s flood of tourists, predominantly European, inundating churches in Harlem. With charter buses clogging the avenues and white tourists lining the sidewalks in hopes of attending an authentic African-American church service, Sunday morning in Harlem has taken on the atmosphere of an "ecclesiastical theme park."[17] However, it is too easy to say Hagelstange anticipates this cu-

---

[16] See Jörgen Schäfer, *Pop-Literatur: Rolf Dieter Brinkmann und das Verhältnis zur Populärkultur in der Literatur der sechziger Jahre* (Stuttgart: M & P, 1998).

[17] See Frank Bruni, "At Harlem Churches, Flocks of Tourists; Drawn to Gospel, if Not Gospels, Foreigners Arrive by Busload," *New York Times*, 24 Nov. 1996, late ed., sec. 1:37.

rious phenomenon; his travel poems of the 1950s fed the European fascination with Black America in traditional fashion, indeed in the romantic mode of the modernist era. In a postmodern world with international travel a matter of fact, Hagelstange's role is superfluous as everyone is a travel poet. In addition to well-known poets who have served as translators — Celan, Enzensberger, Fried, and Brinkmann — we need to recognize Eva Hesse for her role not only in Eliot and Pound reception but also for promoting E. E. Cummings, Langston Hughes, Robinson Jeffers, James Laughlin and Marianne Moore. Carl Weissner deserves mention as the leading proponent of the American underground scene. And finally, there is Joachim Sartorius who, aside from advancing John Ashbery, has both set the standard and established the vision for taking the reception of American poetry into the twenty-first century.

An overview of America in German poetry since 1945 reveals as much an image of America as an imago America, that is, an idealized mental image of the land, its people (or better yet: peoples), and their respective ways. As a mental image an imago is more conceptual than concrete, more of the mind than of the real world. The imago America in postwar German literature has a two-tiered basis in history: one, the historically based myth existing since long before Columbus happened upon the Americas in 1492; and two, the historical realities developing since the end of the Second World War. The latter category takes on special dimensions in that America's place on the world stage between 1945 and 1990 reflects a world — as well as Germany itself — divided between two superpowers.

There is also an inescapable imago America with respect to reception. In other words, American poets are valued in terms of how they represent various ideals. For instance, the poetry of T. S. Eliot was an ideal complement to the conservative politics of the Adenauer era in West Germany, while later the underground poetry of the Beats served as an ideal balance to the influx of overground America on everyday West German life. However, the most multifaceted poet with regard to ideals in reception is Walt Whitman. After the Second World War Whitman once again stood as the paragon poet of democracy, and in this capacity he was extremely important for both postwar German states. Whitman carries universal appeal by personifying the ideals of the common folk and the potential for uniting the peoples of the world. Moreover, within the framework of early cold

war rhetoric East German critics saw Whitman's humanism as anti-
dote to the hysteria of the McCarthy era. Within the socio-political
sphere, Whitman is a poet of gay rights and sexual freedom. For others, he personifies an ideal beyond the world of politics and lifestyle,
for instance, Walter Höllerer, for whom Whitman represents a stylistic ideal, as the long lines and rolling rhythms of his poetry formed
the cornerstone for Höllerer's concept of the long poem. Similarly,
the reception of other American poets frequently hinges on the em-
bodiment of specific ideals. For instance, while Frank O'Hara is the
imago cosmopolitan poet, Charles Bukowski is the imago dirty old
man; likewise, Charles Olson serves as an imago advocate of poetic
theory, while Allen Ginsberg ("ich, ein schwuler, mit Drogen expe-
rimentierender Jude aus einem kommunistischen Elternhaus"[18]) is
the imago postwar antitype of National Socialist ideology.

Although German-American relations have changed drastically
during the twentieth century, the myth of America has remained
relatively unchanged over the ages. Jantz's four-part delineation of
the myth establishes both a frame and perspective. The first two
points highlight America's — from a European point of view —
primitive status: one, its golden primitivism; and two, the opposite
thereof, not merely less than sophisticated, but crude, harsh, and
oftentimes monstrous. Point three features America's place in the
westward migration of civilization and culture, while point four
celebrates America as the promised land of the future. Let us look
once again at select German poems with an eye for how the imago
America reflects specific aspects of the myth of America.

In the early postwar period we find numerous examples of the
ideal manifesting itself as real. Eich's "Pfannkuchenrezept," Kasper's
"Nachricht (Michigan)" and Waldinger's America poems all depend
in varying degrees on an idealized image, but more so, the ideal
finding its tangible counterpart. These various ideal images are closely
aligned with the myth of America; for instance, Eich presents the
United States as the promised land of abundant resources fulfilling its
prescribed ideal by means of the Marshall Plan. Kasper headlines the
ideal by taking the notion of Western civilization literally above and
beyond the terrestrial sense of humankind's westward migration. And

---

[18] See Jürgen Frey, "Der Dichter der Beat-Generation," *Badische Zeitung*, 7
Apr. 1997.

for Waldinger, the mythic ideal manifests itself within the context of the promised land as refuge for the émigré poet forced into westward migration. Arp's "Amerika," on the other hand, subverts the mythic ideal while highlighting the horrific in order to poke fun at both America and Europe. While Arp relies on the grotesque, other poets offer less than flattering portrayals by pitting the real against the ideal. Hagelstange's "Grand Canyon," for instance, places the crass, commercial side of tourism against the scenic backdrop of a natural wonderland. Similar negative portrayals can be found in the America poems of Benn and Brecht. Moreover, we should note how America — thematically speaking — is unique in uniting these polar opposites of twentieth-century German poetry in that their respective portraits of Broadway and Hollywood clearly agree on one aspect of the myth of America: primitive, yes; but golden, no.

If the main goal of German poets in the 1950s was to rejoin the world language of poetry, then for many German poets of the 1960s membership in this world body meant protest against the American military machine in Southeast Asia. While select poems from the 1950s raised questions regarding America's role in the nuclear arms race or social equality in the United States, by the 1960s poets had advanced beyond raising questions. Protest poems of the Vietnam era did not merely point out incongruities between professed American ideals and official governmental policy; the poets of this generation shouted out the contradictions and mocked the hypocrisy. Political poems about America likewise hold the real up against the ideal, either implicitly, as in Kaschnitz's "Hiroshima," or explicitly, as in Fried's "Amerika" or Karsunke's "Kilroy war hier." Much the same can be said of German poems about Black America. In the Harlem poems of Ausländer, Bachmann, and Gong, as well as the *Jazz* portraits of Gerlach, the reality of life in Black America is tacitly mirrored against the American ideals of freedom and equality. Such political poems portray the U.S.A. as a land where some are more free and equal than others, and thus ridicule the cold war rhetoric of America as leader of the Free World.

As Hartung shows with his anthology *Luftfracht*, the 1960s are a decade as much of politics as pop, and there is a definite imago concept with regard to how German poets address the notion of popular culture American style. The reception of American Beat writers in the early 1960s not only affected German attitudes toward American literature but also initiated long-lasting changes in both the form and content of contemporary German poetry. Poems such as Karsunke's "Frag mich nach Geno" and Meckel's "Jugend" illustrate the influence of counterculture America on a generation of German writers. Throughout the decade we encounter numerous examples of distinctively American culture finding expression in German poetry. Jazz, for example, plays a crucial part in establishing America's pre-eminent position in the world of twentieth-century music, a status celebrated in German poetry by Ernst Jandl in minimalist style and within the societal sphere by Volker Braun. Braun's "Jazz" transforms a uniquely American art form into a socio-political ideal — all the more bold from an East German perspective — and reveals the secret of jazz in terms of a democratic sense of teamwork and an improvisational style in which individual members of the ensemble perform solo songs of the self. In addition to jazz, German poetry has advanced other forms of music, especially the Anglo-American world of pop music, with Becker, Brinkmann, and Delius heading a list of those who established a niche for rock 'n' roll within serious literature. In similar fashion, poets such as Brinkmann and Handke extol Hollywood films and film stars, glorifying the ideals of a youth culture bent on displacing the staid values of generations past. With Brinkmann once again at the forefront, German poetry applauds the world of pop art for its whimsy, energy, and accessibility to the masses. Andy Warhol, of course, is the imago pop artist whose aesthetics span the various art forms, not just painting but also film, music, dance, and literature; moreover, Warhol encouraged a blending of art forms, a crossover concept reflected in the poetry of Becker and Brinkmann. Finally, Warhol hyped an aesthetic ideal in the packaging of commercial products, another notable feature in the pop phase of Brinkmann's poetry.

In addition to continuing the German fascination with pop music and culture, the 1970s are noteworthy as a decade of the American travel poem. Advancements in international travel coupled with an increase in educational exchanges brought more and more German-language writers to the United States. The travel poems of the 1970s follow traditions and styles of earlier decades, and if protest poems of the 1960s reveled in the clash between the real and ideal America, then German poets of the 1970s continued to highlight contradictions in the American way of life. For instance, Theobaldy's "Bilder aus Amerika" plays off discrepancies between the American dream and real life on Main Street America. If Kaschnitz's 1950s poem "Hiroshima" sardonically evokes Goethe's line "Amerika, du hast es besser," then Brinkmann's American travel poems of the 1970s, especially those in the posthumously published *Eiswasser in der Guadalupe Str.*, brazenly scoff at the notion that America has it better.[19] Brinkmann's firsthand experiences in the United States often stand in direct opposition to the America he had once praised, and in retrospect we can conclude that the real America he met face to face failed to match his imago America. While Brinkmann confronts contradictions bluntly, other travel poets such as Born, Kunert, and Kunze take a more subtle approach to idiosyncratic discrepancies characterizing America. Owing to its scope and depth, Martin Walser's "Versuch, ein Gefühl zu verstehen" is the most comprehensive travel poem of the decade. Walser provides a summary view of America, in effect a review of America in German poetry not only since 1945 but also since ages past. As with his compatriots, Walser focuses on disparities, the very contradictions that make his subject matter so inexplicable. His accomplishment is in giving us a composite picture marked by both approval and reproach, accolades and censure, and a good dose of nostalgia. Nevertheless, two main points remain paramount in Walser's attempt to capture and explain an elusive feeling: one, a steadfast view of America as the ultimate European colony, that westernmost outpost of civilization where the poet as social scientist can test theories on the westward migration of occidental culture; and two, with the line "Amerikaner kann man werden" Walser places the mythic notion of America as the promised land within constitutional parameters.

If 1975 is a turning point with regard to America's role in postwar German poetry, then one feature of the late 1970s and early 1980s is the lyric portrait of Native Americans. Heise's "Indianerreservation" reflects an age and attitude far removed from the days of celebrating the golden primitivism of proud nations once inhabiting North America. His message is not so much that the golden image has been tarnished, that Native American culture is confined to a reservation, and that a once noble race is beset by alcoholism and gambling. Within a greater context this poem, as well as others by Herburger and Delius, reminds us of the horrific side to the westward migration of Western civilization. Indeed, these poems ask

---

[19] See also Brinkmann, *Briefe an Hartmut* (Reinbek bei Hamburg: Rowohlt, 1999).

how civilized is Western civilization if its advance is at the expense of the very existence of indigenous people. Even if the 1980s are devoid of any pronounced issue or movement in German poetry, this decade is significant for confirming the respect gained by America since 1945. Perhaps the most unique poem of the entire postwar era is Hartung's "Wann lasen Sie den Plato Mr. Hopper." Hartung's depiction of Edward Hopper is in many ways a portrait of the artist as America. Significant is how the poet holds his subject up to an ideal distinctly non-American, that is, a classical European ideal. And here neither Hopper nor America pales in comparison.

At the end of the twentieth century we look for signs of changes in America's standing in Germany after reunification. Delius and his "Selbstporträt mit Luftbrücke" punctuate America's post-reunification role in everyday German life as more historical than current. Even though Delius pushes America into the background, Kling's "taunusprobe. lehrgang im hessischn" clearly shows American culture leading the way within specific strata of German society. Here we see the monstrous side of the myth of America embraced, commandeered, and transplanted on German soil. Furthermore, there is an eerie echo to the "heavy metal sounzz" captured by Kling. Within the overall context of changes in German poetry since 1965 and especially the mass appeal of certain forms of popular culture, these ominous sounds remind us of Walser's warnings "Über die Neueste Stimmung im Westen" or Becker's reflections on how from a German perspective rock 'n' roll can become curiously "*faschistoid.*"

It may very well be that German poetry since the end of the Second World War has not expanded on Jantz's four categories to the myth of America. On the other hand, German poets have certainly amplified the monstrous element at work in the myth. Indeed, postwar German poetry has redefined this monstrous element as not merely the flip side of golden primitivism, but a harsh power capable of supplanting other categories of the myth. Adding a cruel ingredient to the mix creates a force with the power to dash all sense of hope associated with the promised land. Truly mythic in proportion, the horrific side to the postwar myth of America the superpower is especially menacing, a threat to halt the advance if not the existence of Western civilization. Over the ages German poetry has confirmed America as the land of contradictions, but since 1945 German poets more than ever before have thrived on those contradictions that are America.

Works Cited

Primary Literature

Works by Individual Authors

Arp, Hans. *Auf einem Bein*. Wiesbaden: Limes, 1955.

———. *Gesammelte Gedichte II: Gedichte 1939–1957*. Zürich: Schifferli; Wiesbaden: Limes, 1974.

Ashbery, John. *The Double Dream of Spring*. New York, NY: Dutton, 1970.

———. *Selbstporträt in einem konvexen Spiegel*. Trans. Christa Cooper and Joachim Sartorius. Munich and Vienna: Hanser, 1980.

———. *Eine Welle*. Trans. Joachim Sartorius. Munich and Vienna: Hanser, 1986.

Astel, Arnfrid. *Notstand*. Wuppertal: Hammer, 1968.

Auden, W. H. *Zeitalter der Angst: ein barockes Hirtengedicht*. Trans. Kurt Heinrich Hansen. Wiesbaden: Limes, 1952.

Ausländer, Rose. *Die Sichel mäht die Zeit zu Heu: Gedichte 1957–1965*. Ed. Helmut Braun. Frankfurt am Main: Fischer, 1984. Vol. 2 of *Gesammelte Werke in sieben Bänden*. 7 Vols.

———. *Hügel aus Äther unwiderruflich: Gedichte und Prosa 1966–1975*. Vol. 3 of *Gesammelte Werke*.

Bachmann, Ingeborg. *Gedichte, Hörspiele, Libretti, Übersetzungen*. Ed. Christine Koschel, Inge von Weidenbaum, and Clemens Münster. Munich and Zürich: Piper, 1982. Vol. 1 of *Werke*. 4 vols.

Becker, Jürgen. *Bilder Häuser Hausfreunde: Drei Hörspiele*. Frankfurt am Main: Suhrkamp, 1969.

———. *Das Ende der Landschaftsmalerei: Gedichte*. Frankfurt am Main: Suhrkamp, 1974.

———. *Erzähl mir nichts vom Krieg: Gedichte*. Frankfurt am Main: Suhrkamp, 1977.

———. *Erzählen bis Ostende.* Frankfurt am Main: Suhrkamp, 1981.

———. *Gedichte 1965–1980.* Frankfurt am Main: Suhrkamp, 1981.

———. "Momente · Ränder · Erzähltes · Zitate." *Kursbuch* 10 (1967): 164–77.

———. *Schnee: Gedichte.* Berlin: LCB, 1971.

Benn, Gottfried. *Gedichte 1.* Ed. Gerhard Schuster. Stuttgart: Klett-Cotta, 1986. Vol. 1 of *Sämtliche Werke.* 6 vols.

———. *Prosa 4.* Vol. 6 of *Sämtliche Werke,* 1994.

Berrigan, Ted. *Guillaume Apollinaire ist tot. Und anderes.* Trans. Rolf Dieter Brinkmann. Frankfurt am Main: März, 1970.

Berryman, John. *Huldigung für Mistress Bradstreet.* Trans. Gertrude C. Schwebell. Hamburg: Hoffmann und Campe, 1967.

Bienek, Horst. *Vorgefundene Gedichte: Poèmes trouvés.* Munich: Hanser, 1969.

Biermann, Wolf. *Die Drahtharfe: Balladen Gedichte Lieder.* Berlin: Wagenbach, 1965.

Borchardt, Rudolf. *Gesammelte Werke in Einzelbänden: Prosa III.* Ed. Marie Luise Borchardt and Ernst Zinn. Stuttgart: Klett, 1960.

Born, Nicolas. *Das Auge des Entdeckers: Gedichte.* Reinbek bei Hamburg: Rowohlt, 1972.

———. *Gedichte 1967–1978.* Reinbek bei Hamburg: Rowohlt, 1978.

———. *Marktlage: Gedichte.* Cologne: Kiepenheuer & Witsch, 1967.

———. *Wo mir der Kopf steht: Gedichte.* Cologne: Kiepenheuer & Witsch, 1970.

Braun, Volker. *Provokation für mich.* Halle an der Saale: Mitteldeutscher, 1965.

———. *Wir und nicht sie: Gedichte.* Halle an der Saale: Mitteldeutscher, 1970.

Brecht, Bertolt. *Gedichte 3.* Vol. 10 of *Gesammelte Werke in 20 Bänden.* Frankfurt am Main: Suhrkamp, 1967. 20 vols.

———. *Schriften zur Literatur und Kunst 2.* Vol. 19 of *Gesammelte Werke in 20 Bänden.* Frankfurt am Main: Suhrkamp, 1967. 20 vols.

Brinkmann, Rolf Dieter. "Angriff aufs Monopol: Ich hasse alte Dichter." *Christ und Welt,* 15 November 1968.

———. *Briefe an Hartmut: 1974–1975.* Reinbek bei Hamburg: Rowohlt, 1999.

———. "Brief an Hermann Peter Piwitt, 22.7.1972." *Literaturmagazin* 36. Ed. Maleen Brinkmann. 92–101.

———. *Eiswasser an der Guadelupe Str.* Reinbek bei Hamburg: Rowohlt, 1985.

———. *Erkundungen für die Präzisierung des* Gefühls *für einen Aufstand: Reise/ Zeit/ Magazin (Tagebuch).* Reinbek bei Hamburg: Rowohlt, 1987.

———. *Der Film in Worten: Prosa, Erzählungen, Essays, Hörspiele, Fotos, Collagen 1965–1974.* Reinbek bei Hamburg: Rowohlt, 1982.

———. *Keiner weiß mehr.* Cologne: Kiepenheuer & Witsch, 1968.

———. *Rom, Blicke.* Reinbek bei Hamburg: Rowohlt, 1979.

———. *Standphotos: Gedichte 1962–1970.* Reinbek bei Hamburg: Rowohlt, 1980.

———. "Ein unkontrolliertes Nachwort zu meinen Gedichten." *Literaturmagazin* 5. Ed. Hermann Peter Piwitt and Peter Rühmkorf. Reinbek bei Hamburg: Rowohlt, 1976. 228–48.

———. "Vanille." *März Texte 1.* Darmstadt: März, 1969. 106–44.

———. *Westwärts 1 & 2: Gedichte.* Reinbek bei Hamburg: Rowohlt, 1975.

Bukowski, Charles. *Flinke Killer: Gedichte.* Trans. Carl Weissner and Rolf-Eckart John. Cologne: Palmenpresse, 1977.

———. *Gedichte die einer schrieb bevor er im 8. Stockwerk aus dem Fenster sprang.* Trans. Carl Weissner. Gersthofen: Maro, 1974.

———. *Western Avenue: Gedichte aus über 20 Jahren 1955–1977.* Trans. Carl Weissner. Frankfurt am Main: Zweitausendeins, 1979.

Burroughs, William S. "Die literarischen Techniken der Lady Sutton-Smith." Trans. Peter Behrens and Katharina Behrens. *Akzente* 11.5–6 (1964): 420–24.

———. *Naked Lunch.* Paris: Olympia, 1959.

Ciardi, John. *How Does a Poem Mean?* Boston: Houghton Mifflin, 1959. Vol. 3 of *An Introduction to Literature.* Gen. Ed. Gordon N. Ray. 4 vols.

Cleaver, Eldridge. *Seele auf Eis.* Trans. Céline Bastian and Heiner Bastian. Munich: Hanser, 1969.

Corso, Gregory. "Dichter und Gesellschaft in Amerika." Trans. Erika Gilbert. *Akzente* 5.2 (1958): 101–12.

———. *Gasoline and The Vestal Lady on Brattle.* San Francisco, CA: City Lights, 1958.

———. *In der flüchtigen Hand der Zeit.* Trans. Anselm Hollo. Wiesbaden: Limes, 1963.

Crane, Hart. *The Collected Poems of Hart Crane.* Ed. Waldo Frank. 2nd ed. New York, NY: Liveright, 1946.

———. *Weisse Bauten: Gedichte.* Trans. Joachim Uhlmann. Berlin: Henssel, 1960.

Creeley, Robert. *The Collected Poems of Robert Creeley: 1945–1975.* Berkeley and Los Angeles, CA: U of California P, 1982.

———. *For Love: Poems 1950–1960.* New York, NY: Scribner's, 1962.

———. *Gedichte.* Trans. Klaus Reichert. Salzburg and Vienna: Residenz, 1988.

———. *Gedichte: amerikanisch und deutsch.* Trans. Klaus Reichert. Frankfurt am Main: Suhrkamp, 1967.

———. *Words.* New York, NY: Scribner's, 1967.

Cummings, E. E. *Gedichte.* Trans. Eva Hesse. Ebenhausen bei München [Munich]: Langewiesche-Brandt, 1958.

Dauthendey, Max. *Die geflügelte Erde: Ein Lied der Liebe und der Wunder um sieben Meere.* Munich: Langen, 1910.

Delius, F[riedrich]. C[hristian]. *Ein Bankier auf der Flucht: Gedichte und Reisebilder.* Berlin: Rotbuch, 1975.

———. *Kerbholz: Gedichte.* Berlin: Wagenbach, 1965.

———. *Selbstporträt mit Luftbrücke: Ausgewählte Gedichte 1962–1992.* Reinbek bei Hamburg: Rowohlt, 1993.

———. *Die unsichtbaren Blitze: Gedichte.* Berlin: Rotbuch, 1981.

———. *Wenn wir, bei Rot: Achtunddreißig Gedichte.* Berlin: Wagenbach, 1969.

Derschau, Christoph. *So hin und wieder die eigene Haut ritzen. . .: Ausgewählte Gedichte.* Frankfurt am Main: Fischer, 1986.

Dickinson, Emily. "Acht Gedichte." Trans. Paul Celan. *Die Neue Rundschau* 72.1 (1961): 36–39.

———. *Der Engel in Grau: Aus dem Leben und Werk der amerikanischen Dichterin Emily Dickinson.* Trans. Maria Mathi. Mannheim: Kessler, 1956.

———. *Gedichte.* Trans. Lola Gruenthal. Berlin: Henssel, 1959.

———. *Ten Poems.* Trans. Rosey E. Pool. Amsterdam: Balkema 1944.

Dove, Rita. *Die gläserne Stirn der Gegenwart: Gedichte, amerikanisch und deutsch.* Trans. Fred Viebahn. Eisingen: Heiderhoff, 1989.

———. *Die morgenländische Tänzerin: Gedichte.* Trans. Karin Graf. Reinbek bei Hamburg: Rowohlt, 1988.

Droste-Hülshoff, Annette von. *Sämtliche Werke in zwei Bänden.* Ed. Günther Weydt and Winfried Woesler. 3rd ed. Vol. 1. 1973. Munich: Winkler, 1989. 2 vols.

Eich, Günter. *Abgelegene Gehöfte.* Frankfurt am Main: Schauer, 1948.

———. *Werke I: Die Gedichte.* Ed. Horst Ohde. Frankfurt am Main: Suhrkamp, 1973. Vol. 1 of *Gesammelte Werke.* 4 vols.

Eliot, T. S. *Ausgewählte Gedichte: englisch und deutsch.* Trans. Klaus Günther Just. Frankfurt am Main: Suhrkamp, 1951.

———. *Collected Poems, 1909–1962.* New York, NY: Harcourt, 1963.

———. *Gesammelte Gedichte 1909–1962.* Trans. Eva Hesse, Erich Fried, Hans Magnus Enzensberger, et al. Ed. Eva Hesse. Frankfurt am Main: Suhrkamp, 1988.

———. "Goethe der Weise." Trans. Wolfgang Clemen. *Merkur* 9.8 (1955): 701–23.

———. *Old Possums Katzenbuch.* Trans. Werner Peterich, Erich Kästner, et al. Frankfurt am Main: Suhrkamp, 1952.

———. *On Poetry and Poets.* New York: Farrar, 1957. 240–64.

———. "Shelley and Keats." *The Use of Poetry and the Use of Criticism.* 1933. Cambridge: Harvard UP, 1986. 78–94.

———. *Vier Quartette.* Trans. Nora Wydenbruck. Vienna: Amandus, 1948.

———. "Von Poe zu Valéry." Trans. Hans Heinrich Schaeder, *Merkur* 4.12 (1950): 1252–67.

———. *Das wüste Land.* Trans. Ernst Robert Curtius. *Die Neue Schweizer Rundschau* 20.4 (1927): 348–77. Rpt. in *Die Neue Rundschau* 61.3 (1950): 327–45.

Enzensberger, Hans Magnus. *blindenschrift: gedichte.* Frankfurt am Main: Suhrkamp, 1964.

———. "Dunkle Erbschaft, tiefer Bayou." Gong, *Interview mit Amerika,* 256–87.

———. *Einzelheiten.* Frankfurt am Main: Suhrkamp, 1962.

———. *landessprache: gedichte.* Frankfurt am Main: Suhrkamp, 1960.

———. *verteidigung der wölfe: gedichte.* Frankfurt am Main: Suhrkamp, 1957.

Fauser, Jörg. *Die Harry Gelb Story: Gedichte.* Gersthofen: Maro, 1973.

Fels, Ludwig. "Black Spirit Brevier." *Dimension* (1983): 118–45.

———. "Ich war nicht in Amerika." Krischker, *Overseas call*, 297.

Ferlinghetti, Lawrence. *Ausgewählte Gedichte*. Trans. Alexander Schmitz. Zürich: Diogenes, 1972.

———. *Ein Coney Island des inneren Karussells*. Trans. Erika Güttermann. Wiesbaden: Limes, 1962.

———. "Where is Vietnam." *Kursbuch* 6 (1966): 1–2.

Fried, Erich. *Anfechtungen: Fünfzig Gedichte*. Berlin: Wagenbach, 1967.

———. *Befreiung von der Flucht: Gedichte und Gegengedichte*. Hamburg: Claassen, 1968.

———. *Die Beine der größeren Lügen: Gedichte*. Berlin: Wagenbach, 1969.

———. *Die bunten Getüme: Siebzig Gedichte*. Berlin: Wagenbach, 1977.

———. *Die Freiheit den Mund aufzumachen: 48 Gedichte*. Berlin: Wagenbach, 1971.

———. *Es ist was es ist: Liebesgedichte, Angstgedichte, Zorngedichte*. Berlin: Wagenbach, 1983.

———. *Gegengift: 49 Gedichte und ein Zyklus*. Berlin: Wagenbach, 1974.

———. *100 Gedichte ohne Vaterland*. Berlin: Wagenbach, 1978.

———. *und Vietnam und: Einundvierzig Gedichte mit einer Chronik*. Berlin: Wagenbach, 1966.

———. *Unter Nebenfeinden: Fünfzig Gedichte*. Berlin: Wagenbach, 1970.

———. *Warngedichte*. Munich: Hanser, 1964.

Frost, Robert. *Gesammelte Gedichte*. Trans. Alexander von Bernus. Mannheim: Kessler, 1952.

———. "Stopping by Woods on a Snowy Evening." Trans. Joachim Maass. *Die neue Rundschau* 57.3 (1946): 340–41.

Fuhrmann, Joachim. "Guam." Brunner, Juhre, and Kulas, *Wir sind Kinder von Marx und Coca-Cola*, 15.

George, Stefan. *Das Jahr der Seele*. Vol. 4 of *Gesamt-Ausgabe der Werke: Endgültige Fassung*. Berlin: Biondi, 1928. 18 vols.

———. *Das Neue Reich*, vol. 9 of *Gesamt-Ausgabe der Werke*.

Gerhardt, Rainer M. *Umkreisung*. Karlsruhe: fragmente, 1952.

Gerlach, Jens. *Jazz: Gedichte*. 2nd ed. Berlin: Aufbau: 1967.

Ginsberg, Allen. *Das Geheul und andere Gedichte*. Trans. Wolfgang Fleischmann and Rudolf Wittkopf. Wiesbaden: Limes, 1959.

——. *Herzgesänge: Gedichte 1974–1980*. Trans. Michael Mundhenk, Klaus Feiten, Jürgen Schmidt, and Eckhard Rhode. Hamburg: Loose Blätter, 1981.

——. *Howl and Other Poems*. San Francisco, CA: City Lights, 1956.

——. *Indische Tagebücher, März 1962-Mai 1963: Notizhefte, Tagebuch, Leere Seiten, Aufzeichnungen*. Trans. Carl Weissner. Munich: Hanser, 1972.

——. *Jukebox Elegien: Gedichte aus einer Vierteljahrhundert 1953–1978*. Trans. Bernd Samland. Munich: Heyne, 1981.

——. *Kaddisch: Gedichte*. Trans. Anselm Hollo. Wiesbaden: Limes, 1962.

——. *Planet News*. Trans. Heiner Bastian. Munich: Hanser, 1969.

——. *Reality Sandwiches*. San Francisco, CA: City Lights, 1963.

——. *Überlegungen zur Poesie*. Trans. Jürgen Schmidt. Hannover: Apartment Edition, 1988.

——. *Der Untergang Amerikas*. Trans. Carl Weissner. Munich: Hanser, 1975.

Giorno, John. *Cunt: Gedichte*. Trans. Rolf-Eckart John, Rolf Dieter Brinkmann et al. Darmstadt: März, 1969.

Gong, Alfred, *Early Poems: A Selection from the Years 1941–1945*. Ed. Jerry Glenn, Joachim Herrmann, and Rebecca S. Rodgers. Columbia, SC: Camden House, 1987.

——. *Gras und Omega: Gedichte*. Ed. Joachim Herrmann. Aachen: Rimbaud, 1997.

——. *Israels letzter Psalm: Gedichte. Mit einer Auswahl aus dem Nachlaß*. Ed. Joachim Herrmann. Aachen: Rimbaud, 1995.

Grass, Günter. *Ausgefragt*. Neuwied and Berlin: Luchterhand, 1967.

——. *Gedichte und Kurzprosa*. Ed. Volker Neuhaus and Daniela Hermes. Göttingen: Steidl, 1997. Vol.1 of *Werkausgabe*. 16 vols.

——. *Theaterspiele*. Neuwied: Luchterhand, 1970.

Hagelstange, Rudolf. *Gast der Elemente: Zyklen und Nachdichtungen 1944–1972*. Cologne: Kiepenheuer & Witsch, 1972.

——. *How do you like America? Impressionen eines Zaungastes*. Munich: Piper, 1957.

Handke, Peter. *Deutsche Gedichte*. Frankfurt am Main: euphorion, 1969.

——. *Die Innenwelt der Außenwelt der Innenwelt*. Frankfurt am Main: Suhrkamp, 1969.

————. *Der kurze Brief zum langen Abschied.* Frankfurt am Main: Suhrkamp, 1972.

Hartung, Harald. *Traum im Deutschen Museum: Gedichte 1965–1985.* Munich: Piper, 1986.

————. "Zechenkolonie." Hamm, *Aussichten,* 59.

Haufs, Rolf. *Vorstadtbeichte: Gedichte.* Neuwied and Berlin: Luchterhand, 1967.

Haushofer, Albrecht. *Moabiter Sonette.* 4th ed. Berlin: Blanvalet, 1953.

Heise, Hans-Jürgen. *Gedichte und Prosagedichte 1949-2001.* Göttingen: Wallstein Verlag, 2002.

Herburger, Günter. "Des Dichters Brinkmanns Tod." *Die Zeit,* 13 June 1975.

————. "Dogmatisches über Gedichte." *Kursbuch* 10 (1967): 150–61.

————. *Makadam: Gedichte.* Darmstadt and Neuwied: Luchterhand, 1982.

————."soso Vietnam aha." *Kursbuch* 10 (1967): 162–63.

————. *Training: Gedichte.* Neuwied and Berlin: Luchterhand, 1970.

Hermlin, Stephan. *Nachdichtungen.* 2nd ed. Berlin and Weimar: Aufbau, 1987.

Höllerer, Walter. *Der andere Gast: Gedichte.* Munich: Hanser, 1952.

————. *Gedichte 1942–1982.* Frankfurt am Main: Suhrkamp, 1982.

————. *Systeme: Neue Gedichte.* Berlin: LCB, 1969.

————. "Thesen zum langen Gedicht." *Akzente* 12.2 (1965): 128–30. Rpt. in Bender and Krüger, *Was alles hat Platz?* 7–9.

Hübsch, Paul-Gerhard. *Ausgeflippt.* Neuwied: Luchterhand, 1971.

————. "tagesschau & wetterkarte, das war der überblick." Piontek, *Deutsche Gedichte seit 1960,* 264.

Hughes, Langston. *Gedichte.* Trans. Eva Hesse and Paridam von dem Knesebeck. Ebenhausen bei München [Munich]: Langewiesche-Brandt, 1960.

————. *Selected Poems of Langston Hughes.* 1959. New York, NY: Vintage, 1990.

Jandl, Ernst. *poetische werke.* Ed. Klaus Siblewski. Munich: Luchterhand Literaturverlag, 1997. Vols. 2 (*Laut und Luise & verstreute gedichte 2*) and 6 (*übung mit buben &serienfuss & wischen möchten*). 10 vols.

Jedamus, Erwin. "Detroit, Sommer '67." *kürbiskern* 2 (1968): 247–48.

Johnson, James Weldon. *Gib mein Volk frei: Acht Negerpredigten.* Trans. Rudolf Hagelstange. Gütersloh: Mohn, 1961

Karsunke, Yaak. "Frag mich nach Geno." Hamm, *Aussichten,* 94–96.

———. *Kilroy & andere: Gedichte.* Berlin: Wagenbach, 1967.

Kaschnitz, Marie Luise. *Neue Gedichte.* Hamburg: Claassen, 1965.

Kasper, Hans. *Nachrichten und Notizen.* Stuttgart: Goverts, 1957.

Kerouac, Jack. "Belief & Technique for modern Prose: List of Essentials." *Evergreen Review* 8 (1959): 57.

———. *On the Road.* 1957. New York, NY: Viking, 1971.

Kirsch, Rainer, and Sarah Kirsch. *Gespräch mit dem Saurier: Gedichte.* Berlin: Neues Leben, 1965.

Kiwus, Karin. Afterword. *39 Gedichte.* By Kiwus. Stuttgart: Reclam, 1981. 62–70.

———. *Angenommen später: Gedichte.* Frankfurt am Main: Suhrkamp, 1979.

———. *39 Gedichte.* Stuttgart: Reclam, 1981.

———. *Von beiden Seiten der Gegenwart: Gedichte.* Frankfurt am Main: Suhrkamp, 1976.

Kleist, Heinrich von. *Werke und Briefe in vier Bänden.* Ed. Siegfried Streller. 2nd ed. 4 vols. Berlin: Aufbau, 1984.

Kling, Thomas. *brennstabm: Gedichte.* Frankfurt am Main: Suhrkamp, 1991.

Koch, Kenneth. *Vielen Dank: Gedichte und Spiele.* Trans. Nicolas Born. Reinbek bei Hamburg: Rowohlt, 1976.

Krechel, Ursula. *Nach Mainz! Gedichte.* Darmstadt and Neuwied: Luchterhand, 1977.

Kunert, Günter. *Der ungebetene Gast.* Berlin and Weimar: Aufbau, 1965.

———. *Verlangen nach Bomarzo: Reisegedichte.* Munich: Hanser, 1978.

Kunze, Reiner. *auf eigene hoffnung: gedichte.* Frankfurt am Main: Fischer, 1981.

———. *Die wunderbaren Jahre.* Frankfurt am Main: Fischer, 1977.

Laughlin, James. *Die Haare auf Großvaters Kopf.* Trans. Eva Hesse. Zürich: Arche, 1966.

Leifert, Arnold. "weißer Riese." Brunner, Juhre, and Kulas, *Wir sind Kinder von Marx und Coca-Cola,* 54.

Leisegang, Dieter. *Hoffmann am Fenster.* Frankfurt am Main: Heiderhoff, 1968.

———. *Lauter Letzte Worte: Gedichte und Miniaturen.* Ed. Karl Corino. Frankfurt am Main: Suhrkamp, 1980.

———. *Überschreitungen.* Darmstadt: Bläschke, 1965.

Levertov, Denise. "O Taste and See." Trans. Christa Langenscheidt. *Akzente* 11.5–6 (1964): 385.

Longfellow, Henry Wadsworth. *Evangeline.* Trans. August Vezin. Heidelberg: Meister, 1947.

Lowell, Robert. *Day by Day.* New York, NY: Farrar, 1977.

———. *The Dolphin.* New York, NY: Farrar, 1973.

———. *Ein Fischnetz aus teerigem Garn zu knüpfen: Gedichte.* Trans. Karl Heinz Berger. Ed. Joachim Krehayn. Berlin: Volk und Welt, 1975.

———. Foreword. *Ariel.* By Plath. New York: Harper, 1966. vii–ix.

———. *Für die Toten der Union.* Trans. Curt Meyer-Clason. Frankfurt am Main: Suhrkamp, 1969.

———. *Gedichte.* Trans. Manfred Pfister. Stuttgart: Klett, 1982.

———. *Life Studies.* New York, NY: Farrar, 1959.

———. *Notebooks, 1967–68.* 1969. New York, NY, Farrar, 1970.

MacLeish, Archibald. *Groß und tragisch ist unsere Geschichte: Gedichte.* Trans. Kurt Heinrich Hansen. Düsseldorf: Schwann, 1950.

———. *Journey Home.* Trans. Hans-Jürgen Heise. Darmstadt: Bläschke, 1965.

Mailer, Norman. *The White Negro.* San Francisco, CA: City Lights, 1957.

Malanga, Gerard. *Selbstporträt eines Dichters.* Trans. Rolf Dieter Brinkmann. Frankfurt am Main: März, 1970.

Masters, Edgar Lee. *Die Toten von Spoon River.* Trans. Hans Rudolf Rieder. Bad Wörshofen: Drei Säulen, 1947.

McClure, Michael. *Dunkelbraun: Gedichte.* Trans. Heiner Bastian. Frankfurt am Main: März, 1970.

Meckel, Christoph. "Landschaften, die sie durchfahren." *Akzente* 22.4 (1975): 289.

———. *Liebesgedichte.* Berlin: Anabis, 1977.

———. *Suchbild: Über meinen Vater.* 1980. Frankfurt am Main: Fischer, 1983.

———. *Wen es angeht: Gedichte.* 1974. Munich: Heyne, 1979.

Mensching, Steffen. *Tuchfühlung: Gedichte.* Halle an der Saale and Leipzig: Mitteldeutscher, 1986.

Millay, Edna St. Vincent. "April," "Zu S. M.," and "Das fröhliche Mäd-chen." Trans. Rudolf Borchardt. *Die Neue Rundschau* 62.1 (1951): 80–81.

———. "Kindheit ist das Reich, worin niemand dir stirbt." Trans. Rudolf Borchardt. *Die Neue Rundschau* 62.4 (1951): 80–81.

Moore, Marianne. *Gedichte: Eine Auswahl.* Trans. Eva Hesse and Werner Riemerschmid. Wiesbaden: Limes, 1954.

Oates, Joyce Carol. "Edward Hopper's *Nighthawks*, 1942." In *Transforming Vision: Writers on Art.* Ed Edward Hirsch. Boston: Little, 1994. 64.

———. "Ekstase von Langeweile an der Berliner Mauer." Trans. Renate Lasker-Harpprecht. *Akzente* 30.2 (1983): 188–89.

Oberländer, Harry. "Das Achtundsechziger-Sonett." *Luchterhand Jahrbuch der Lyrik 1987/88.* Ed. Christoph Buchwald and Jürgen Becker. Darmstadt and Neuwied: Luchterhand, 1987. 23

———. "orte." Brunner, Juhre, and Kulas, *Wir sind Kinder von Marx und Coca-Cola.* 14.

O'Hara, Frank. *The Collected Poems of Frank O'Hara.* Ed. Donald Allen. New York, NY: Knopf, 1971.

———. *Early Writing.* Ed. Donald Allen. Bolinas, CA: Grey Fox, 1977.

———. *Lunch Poems und andere Gedichte.* Trans. Rolf Dieter Brinkmann. Cologne: Kiepenheuer & Witsch, 1969.

———. *Standing Still and Walking in New York.* Ed. Donald Allen. Bolinas, CA: Grey Fox, 1975.

Olson, Charles. *The Collected Poems of Charles Olson: Excluding the* Maximus *Poems.* Ed. George F. Butterick. Berkeley, CA: California UP, 1987.

———. *Gedichte.* Trans. Klaus Reichert. Frankfurt am Main: Suhrkamp, 1965.

———. *Proprioception.* San Francisco, CA: Four Seasons, 1964.

———. *Selected Writings of Charles Olson.* Ed. Robert Creeley. New York, NY: New Directions, 1966.

———. *West.* Trans. Klaus Reichert. Berlin: LCB, 1969.

Olson, Charles, and Robert Creeley. *Charles Olson & Robert Creeley: The Complete Correspondence.* Ed. George F. Butterick and Richard Blevins. Santa Barbara, CA: Black Sparrow, 1980–1990. 9 vols.

Padgett, Ron. *Grosse Feuerbälle: Gedichte, Prosa, Bilder.* Trans. Rolf-Eckart John. Reinbek bei Hamburg: Rowohlt, 1973.

Piwitt, Hermann Peter. *Deutschland. Versuch einer Heimkehr*. Hamburg: Hoffmann und Campe, 1981.

Plath, Sylvia. *Ariel*. New York, NY: Harper, 1965.

———. *Ariel: Gedichte, englisch und deutsch*. Trans. Erich Fried. Frankfurt am Main: Suhrkamp, 1974.

———. *Das Bettbuch*. Trans. Eva Demski. Frankfurt am Main: Frankfurter Verlagsanstalt, 1989.

———. *Die Bibel der Träume: Erzählungen, Prosa aus den Tagebüchern*. Trans. Julia Bachstein and Sabine Techel. Frankfurt am Main: Frankfurter Verlagsanstalt, 1987.

———. *Briefe nach Hause 1950–1963*. Trans. Iris Wagner. Ed. Aurelia Schober Plath. 1981. Frankfurt am Main: Fischer, 1992.

———. *Drei Frauen: Ein Gedicht für drei Stimmen*. Trans. Friederike Roth. Frankfurt am Main: Frankfurter Verlagsanstalt, 1991.

———. *Die Glasglocke: Roman*. Trans. Christian Grote. Frankfurt am Main: Suhrkamp, 1968.

———. *Die Glasglocke: Roman*. Trans. Reinhard Kaiser. Frankfurt am Main: Suhrkamp,1997.

———. *Die Tagebücher*. Trans. Alissa Walser. Ed. Frances McCullough. Frankfurt am Main: Frankfurter Verlagsanstalt, 1997.

———. *Zungen aus Stein: Erzählungen*. Trans. Julia Bachstein and Susanne Levin. Frankfurt am Main: Frankfurter Verlagsanstalt, 1989.

Poe, Edgar Allan. *Der Rabe und andere Gedichte*. Trans. Johannes von Guenther. Hannover: Hahn, 1947.

———. *Vom Ursprung des Dichterischen*. Trans. Albrecht Fabri. Cologne: Staufen, 1947.

Pollak, Felix. *Vom Nutzen des Zweifels*. Ed. Reinhold Grimm. Frankfurt am Main: Fischer, 1989.

Pound, Ezra. *ABC des Lesens*. Trans. Eva Hesse. Frankfurt am Main: Suhrkamp, 1963.

———. *Dichtung und Prosa*. Trans. Eva Hesse. Zürich: Arche, 1953.

———. *Fisch und Schatten und andere Dichtungen*. Trans. Eva Hesse. Zürich: Arche, 1954.

———. *Lesebuch: Dichtung und Prosa*. Trans. Eva Hesse. Zürich: Arche, 1985.

———. *Die Pisaner Gesänge*. Trans. Eva Hesse. Zürich: Arche, 1956.

——. *Das Testament des Confucius: Die grosse Unterweisung, oder das Erwachsenenstudium.* Trans. Rainer M. Gerhardt. Karlsruhe: fragmente, 1953.

——. *Wie lesen.* Trans. Rainer M. Gerhardt. Karlsruhe: fragmente, 1953.

Pynchon, Thomas. *Slow Learner: Early Stories.* Boston: Little, 1984.

Reed, Ishmael. "diese gedicht anthologie/ die ich gerade lese." Krischker, *Overseas call*, 296.

——. *New and Collected Poems.* New York, NY: Atheneum, 1988.

Ritter, Roman. "Der Krieg ist anderswo." *kürbiskern* 3 (1967): 112.

Rühmkorf, Peter. *Irdisches Vergnügen in g: 50 Gedichte.* Reinbek bei Hamburg: Rowohlt, 1959.

——. *Die Jahre die Ihr kennt: Anfälle und Erinnerungen.* Reinbek bei Hamburg: Rowohlt, 1972.

——. *Über das Volksvermögen: Exkurse in den literarischen Untergrund.* Reinbek bei Hamburg: Rowohlt, 1967.

Sandburg, Carl. *Guten Morgen, Amerika: Ausgewählte Gedichte.* Trans. Alfred Czach. Berlin: Herbig, 1948.

——. *The People, Yes / Das Volk, jawohl.* Trans. Helmut Heinrich. Berlin: Aufbau, 1964.

Scharpenberg, Margot. "Kind deiner Zeit." *The German Quarterly* 65.3.4 (1992): 265–66.

Schenk, Johannes. "Wir sind alle verrückt." *Dimension* Special Issue (1983): 432–35.

——. *Zittern.* Berlin: Wagenbach, 1972.

Seale, Bobby. *Seize the Time: The Story of the Black Panther Party and Huey Newton.* New York, NY: Random House, 1970.

——. *Wir fordern Freiheit: Der Kampf der Black Panther.* Trans. Regine Wolf. Frankfurt am Main: Fischer, 1971.

Sexton, Anne. *All meine Lieben / Lebe oder Stirb.* Trans. Silvia Morawetz. Ed. Elisabeth Bronfen. Frankfurt am Main: Fischer, 1996.

——. *Buch der Torheit. Das ehrfürchtige Rudern hin zu Gott: Gedichte.* Trans. Silvia Morawetz. Ed. Elisabeth Bronfen. Frankfurt am Main: Fischer, 1998.

——. *Liebesgedichte.* Trans. Silvia Morawetz. Ed. Elisabeth Bronfen. Frankfurt am Main: Fischer, 1995.

Simic, Charles. *Ein Buch von Göttern und Teufeln: Gedichte.* Trans. Hans Magnus Enzensberger. Munich: Hanser, 1993.

————. *Die Fliege in der Suppe: Gedichte.* Trans. Rudolf von Bitter. Munich: Hanser, 1997.

Stevens, Wallace. *Menschen, aus Worten gemacht.* Trans. Karl Heinz Berger, Kurt Heinrich Hansen, and Klaus-Dieter Sommer. Ed. Klaus-Dieter Sommer. Berlin: Volk und Welt, 1983.

————. *Der Planet auf dem Tisch: Gedichte und Adagia.* Ed. and trans. Kurt Heinrich Hansen. Hamburg: Claassen, 1961. Rev. ed. Stuttgart: Klett, 1983.

Techel, Sabine. *Es kündigt sich an: Gedichte.* Frankfurt am Main: Suhrkamp, 1986.

Theobaldy, Jürgen. "Die Freiheit für Bobby Seale." *kürbiskern* 3 (1970): 492–94.

————. *Zweiter Klasse: Gedichte.* Berlin: Rotbuch, 1976.

Timm, Uwe. *Widersprüche.* Hamburg: Neue Presse, 1971.

Wagner, Richard. *Rostregen: Gedichte.* Darmstadt and Neuwied: Luchterhand, 1986.

————. *Schwarze Kreide: Gedichte.* Frankfurt am Main: Luchterhand Literaturverlag, 1991.

Waldinger, Ernst. *Gesang vor dem Abgrund.* Graz and Vienna: Stiasny, 1961.

————. *Die kühlen Bauernstuben.* New York, NY: Aurora, 1946.

————. *Noch vor dem jüngsten Tag: Ausgewählte Gedichte und Essays.* Ed. Karl Markus Gauß. Salzburg: Müller, 1990.

————. *Zwischen Hudson und Donau: Ausgewählte Gedichte.* Vienna: Bergland, 1958.

Walker, Alice. *Ihr blauer Körper: Gedichte I.* Trans. Gerhard Döhler. Reinbek bei Hamburg: Rowohlt, 1993.

————. *Ihre braune Umarmung: Gedichte II.* Trans. Gerhard Döhler. Reinbek bei Hamburg: Rowohlt, 1995.

Walser, Martin. "Osterpflicht '68." *elan* 4 (1968): 26.

————. "Versuch, ein Gefühl zu verstehen." *Tintenfisch* 8 (1975): 27–30.

————. *Versuch, ein Gefühl zu verstehen und andere Versuche.* Stuttgart: Reclam, 1982.

Weisenborn, Günther. "Mekong-Ballade." In *Denkzettel: Politische Lyrik aus den sechziger Jahren der BRD und Westberlins.* Ed. Annie Voigtländer and Hubert Witt. Leipzig: Reclam, 1976. Röderberg: Frankfurt am Main, 1977. 401–2.

Wenders, Wim. "Der Amerikanische Traum." In *Overseas call: Eine USAnthologie*. Ed. Gerhard Krischker. Eggingen: Isele, 1989. 12–27.

Whitman, Walt. *Auf der Brooklyn Fähre*. Trans. Hans Reisiger. Berlin: Suhrkamp, 1949.

———. *Demokratische Ausblicke*. Trans. Hans Reisiger. Berlin: Suhrkamp, 1948.

———. *Gesang von mir selbst*. Trans. Hans Reisiger. Berlin: Suhrkamp, 1946.

———. *Gesang von der offenen Landstraße*. Trans. Hans Reisiger. Lauenburg/Elbe: Saal, 1922.

———. *Grashalme*. Trans. Johannes Schlaf. 1907. Leipzig: Reclam, 1948.

———. *Grashalme*. Trans. Elisabeth Serelman-Küchler and Walter Küchler. Erlangen: Dipax, 1947.

———. *Grashalme*. Trans. Georg Goyert. Berlin: Blanvalet, 1948.

———. *Grashalme*. Trans. Hans Reisiger. Berlin: Aufbau, 1957.

———. *Grashalme: Neue Auswahl*. Trans. Hans Reisiger. Berlin: Fischer, 1919.

———. *Hymnen für die Erde*. Trans. Franz Blei. Leipzig: Insel, 1947.

———. *Salut au monde*. Trans. Hans Reisiger. Berlin: Suhrkamp, 1946.

———. *Tagebücher 1862–1864, 1876–1882*. Trans. Hans Reisiger. Berlin: Suhrkamp, 1946.

———. *Walt Whitmans Werk*. Trans. Hans Reisiger. Hamburg: Rowohlt, 1956.

Wilbur, Richard. "The Genie in the Bottle." In *Mid-Century American Poets*. Ed. John Ciardi. New York: Twayne, 1950. 1–7.

Williams, William Carlos. *The Autobiography of William Carlos Williams*. New York, NY: New Directions, 1951.

———. *The Collected Earlier Poems*. New York, NY: New Directions, 1938.

———. *The Collected Later Poems*. New York, NY: New Directions, 1950.

———. *endlos und unzerstörbar: amerikanisch und deutsch*. Trans. Christine Koller et al. Walbrunn: Heiderhoff, 1983.

———. *Gedichte*. Trans. Hans Magnus Enzensberger. Frankfurt am Main: Suhrkamp, 1962.

————. *Der harte Kern der Schönheit: ausgewählte Gedichte, amerikanisch und deutsch.* Trans. Joachim Sartorius. Munich and Vienna: Hanser, 1991.

————. *Kore in der Hölle: frühe Schriften.* Trans. Joachim Sartorius, Walter Fritzsche, and Jürg Laederach. Leipzig: Kiepenheuer, 1988.

————. *Neue Orte.* Trans. Gertrude C. Schwebell. Darmstadt: Bläschke, 1966.

————. *Paterson.* New York, NY: New Directions, 1963.

————. *Paterson.* Trans. Karin Graf and Joachim Sartorius. Munich: Hanser, 1998.

————. *Paterson.* Trans. Anselm Hollo and Josephine Hollo. Stuttgart: Goverts, 1970.

————. *Selected Poems: Enlarged Edition.* New York, NY: New Directions, 1985.

Wondratschek, Wolf. *Chuck's Zimmer: Gedichte/Lieder.* Frankfurt am Main: Zweitausendeins, 1974.

————. "Er war too much für Euch, Leute." *Die Zeit,* 13 June 1975.

————. *Männer und Frauen.* Frankfurt am Main: Zweitausendeins, 1978.

Wüstefeld, Michael. "Noch knistert." In *Berührung ist nur eine Randerscheinung: Neue Literatur aus der DDR.* Ed. Sascha Anderson and Elke Erb. Cologne: Kiepenheuer & Witsch, 1985. 81–82.

Anthologies, Magazines, and Omnibus Volumes

Allen, Donald, ed. *The New American Poetry: 1945–1960.* New York, NY: Grove, 1960.

Allen, Donald, and George R. Butterick, eds. *The Postmoderns: The New American Poetry Revised.* New York, NY: Grove, 1982.

Anderson, Sascha and Elke Erb, eds. *Berührung ist nur eine Randerscheinung: Neue Literatur aus der DDR.* Cologne: Kiepenheuer & Witsch, 1985.

Becker, Jürgen and Wolf Vostell, eds. *Happenings, Fluxus, Pop Art, Nouveau Réalisme: Eine Dokumentation.* Reinbeck bei Hamburg: Rowohlt, 1965.

Bender, Hans, ed. *In diesem Land leben wir: Deutsche Gedichte der Gegenwart.* Munich: Hanser, 1978.

————, ed. *Mein Gedicht ist mein Messer: Lyriker zu ihren Gedichten.* Heidelberg: Rothe, 1955.

———, ed. *Was sind das für Zeiten: Deutschsprachige Gedichte der achtziger Jahre.* Munich and Vienna: Hanser, 1988.

———, ed. *Widerspiel: Deutsche Lyrik seit 1945.* Munich: Hanser, 1962.

Bender, Hans, and Michael Krüger, eds. *Was alles hat Platz in einem Gedicht? Aufsätze zur deutschen Lyrik seit 1965.* Munich: Hanser, 1977.

Brinkmann, Rolf Dieter, ed. *Silverscreen: Neue amerikanische Lyrik.* Cologne: Kiepenheuer & Witsch, 1969.

Brinkmann, Rolf Dieter, and Ralf-Rainer Rygulla, eds. *ACID: Neue amerikanische Szene.* 1969. Reinbek bei Hamburg: Rowohlt, 1983.

Brunner, Frank, Arnim Juhre, and Heinz Kulas, eds. *Wir Kinder von Marx und Coca-Cola: Gedichte der Nachgeborenen: Texte von Autoren der Jahrgänge 1945–1955 aus der Bundesrepublik, Österreich und der Schweiz.* Wuppertal: Hammer, 1971.

Bukowski, Charles and Carl Weissner, eds. *Terpentin on the Rocks: Die besten Gedichte aus der amerikanischen Alternativpresse 1966–1977.* Trans. Carl Weissner. Augsburg: Maro, 1978.

Ciardi, John, ed. *Mid-Century American Poets.* New York, NY: Twayne, 1950.

Corso, Gregory, and Walter Höllerer, eds. *Junge amerikanische Lyrik.* Munich: Hanser, 1961.

Domin, Hilde, ed. *Nachkrieg und Unfrieden: Gedichte als Index 1945–1970.* Neuwied: Luchterhand, 1970.

Enzensberger, Hans Magnus, ed. *Museum der modernen Poesie.* Frankfurt am Main: Suhrkamp, 1960.

Gerhardt, Rainer M., ed. *fragmente* 1 (1951).

———, ed. *fragmente* 2 (1952).

Gomringer, Eugen, ed. *konkrete poesie: deutschsprachige autoren.* Stuttgart: Reclam, 1972.

Gong, Alfred, ed. *Interview mit Amerika: 50 deutschsprachige Autoren in der neuen Welt.* Munich: Nymphenburger, 1962.

Hage, Volker, ed. *Lyrik für Leser: Deutsche Gedichte der siebziger Jahre.* Stuttgart: Reclam, 1980.

Hamm, Peter, ed. *Aussichten: Junge Lyriker des deutschen Sprachraums.* Munich: Biederstein, 1966.

Hans, Jan, Uwe Herms, and Ralf Thenior, eds. *Lyrik Katalog Bundesrepublik: Gedichte, Biographien, Statements.* Munich: Goldmann, 1978.

Hansen, Kurt Heinrich, ed. and trans. *Gedichte aus der neuen Welt: amerikanische Lyrik seit 1910.* Munich: Piper, 1956.

Hartung, Harald, ed. *Luftfracht: Internationale Poesie 1940 bis 1990.* Frankfurt am Main: Eichborn, 1991.

Heldt, Uwe, ed. *Amerika, wie bist du? Deutschsprachige Texte aus USA ausgewählt von Irmgard Elsner.* Special issue *Litfass* 13.47 (1989).

Hermlin, Stephan, ed. and trans. *Auch ich bin Amerika: Dichtungen amerikanischer Neger.* Berlin: Volk und Welt, 1948.

Hirsch, Edward, ed. *Transforming Vision: Writers on Art.* Boston: Little, 1994.

Höllerer, Walter, ed. *Ein Gedicht und sein Autor: Lyrik und Essay.* Berlin: LCB, 1967.

———, ed. *Theorie der modernen Lyrik: Dokumente zur Poetik.* Reinbek bei Hamburg: Rowohlt, 1965.

Hoover, Paul, ed. *Postmodern American Poetry: A Norton Anthology.* New York, NY and London: Norton, 1994.

Kahn, Lisa, ed. *In her Mother's Tongue: Women Authors in the U.S. Who Write in German 1938–1983.* Denver: Emerson, 1983.

Krischker, Gerhard C., ed. *Overseas call: Eine USAnthologie.* Eggingen: Isele, 1989.

Lowenfels, Walter, ed. *Where is Vietnam? American Poets Respond.* New York, NY: Doubleday, 1967.

———, ed. *Wo ist Vietnam? 89 amerikanische Dichter gegen den Krieg in Vietnam.* Darmstadt: Melzer, 1968.

März Texte 1. Darmstadt: März, 1969.

McCormick, John O., ed. *Amerikanische Lyrik der letzten fünfzig Jahre.* Trans. Herta Elizabeth Killy and Walter Killy. Göttingen: Vandenhoeck & Ruprecht, 1957.

Meurer, Kurt Erich, ed. and trans. *Das goldene Zeitalter.* Heidelberg: Meister, 1948.

———, ed. and trans. *Nordamerikanische Lyrik des 19. Jahrhunderts.* Heidelberg: Meister, 1949.

Monroe, Harriet and Alice Corbin Henderson, eds. *The New Poetry.* New York, NY: Macmillan, 1923.

———. eds. *Amerikanische Lyrik des XX. Jahrhunderts.* Trans. Rolf Göhring. Waibstadt: Kemper, 1948.

Paetel, Karl O., ed. *Beat: Eine Anthologie.* Reinbek bei Hamburg: Rowohlt, 1962.

Piontek, Heinz, ed. *Deutsche Gedichte seit 1960: Eine Anthologie.* Stuttgart: Reclam, 1972.

Rohrer, Max, ed. *Amerika im deutschen Gedicht.* Stuttgart: Röhm, 1948.

Rygulla, Ralf-Rainer, ed. *Fuck you! Underground Gedichte: englisch und deutsch.* 1968. Frankfurt am Main: Fischer, 1980.

———, ed. *Untergrund Gedichte: Letzte amerikanische Lyrik.* Berlin: Oberbaumpresse, 1967.

Sartorius, Joachim, ed. *Atlas der neuen Poesie.* Reinbek bei Hamburg: Rowohlt, 1995.

Schmidt, Jürgen, ed. *Lines of Feeling.* Trans. Jürgen Schmidt. N.p. [Germany]: Altaquito, 1987.

Theobaldy, Jürgen, ed. *Und ich bewege mich doch: Gedichte vor und nach 1968.* Munich: Beck, 1977.

tode, riewert qu., ed. *gegen den krieg in vietnam: eine anthologie.* Berlin: amBEATion, 1968.

Voigtländer, Annie, and Hubert Witt, eds. *Denkzettel: Politische Lyrik aus den sechziger Jahren der BRD und Westberlins.* Leipzig: Reclam, 1976. Röderberg: Frankfurt am Main, 1977.

Weyrauch, Wolfgang, ed. *Expeditionen: Deutsche Lyrik seit 1945.* Munich: List, 1959.

———, ed. Tausend Gramm: *Sammlung neuer deutscher Geschichten.* Hamburg: Rowohlt, 1949.

Secondary Literature

Alves, Eva Maria. "Das Leben gedichtet, auf daß es erträglich werde." Rev. of Plath, *Ariel*, trans. Fried; *Glasglocke*, trans. Grote; *Drei Frauen*, trans. Roth; and Wagner-Martin, *Sylvia Plath: Eine Biographie*, trans. Techel. *Deutsches Allgemeines Sonntagsblatt*, 26 July 1991.

Arnheim, Rudolf. *Entropy and Art: An Essay on Disorder and Order.* Berkeley, CA: U of California P, 1971.

Arnold, Heinz Ludwig, ed. *Geschichte der deutschen Literatur aus Methoden: Westdeutsche Literatur von 1945–1971.* 3 vols. Frankfurt am Main: Athenäum, 1972.

Bauschinger, Sigrid, Horst Denkler, and Wilfried Malsch, eds. *Amerika in der deutschen Literatur: Neue Welt — Nordamerika — USA.* Stuttgart: Reclam, 1975.

Bender, Hans. Afterword. Bender, *Was sind das für Zeiten*, 243–46.

———. "Die Entwicklung der Lyrik seit 1945 in der Bundesrepublik." Weissenberger, *Die deutsche Lyrik 1945–1975*, 25–37.

Blöcker, Günter. "Im Kreislauf der Zerstörung." Rev. of Plath, *Ariel*, trans. Fried. *Frankfurter Allgemeine Zeitung*, 5 Oct. 1974.

Borchardt, Rudolf. "Die Entdeckung Amerikas: Die Poesie von Edna St. Vincent Millay." *Die neue Rundschau* 62.4 (1951): 81–104. Rpt. in Borchardt, *Gesammelte Werke: Prosa III*, 429–72.

Bormann, Alexander von. "Ein Dichter, den Worte zusammenfügen: Versöhnung von Rhetorik und Poesie bei Erich Fried." *Text + Kritik* 91 (1986): 5–23.

Born, Nicolas and Jürgen Manthey, eds. *Literaturmagazin 7*. Reinbek bei Hamburg, Rowohlt, 1977.

Bratfisch, Rainer. "Und vergeßt nicht den Wahnsinn: Allen Ginsberg starb 70jährig in New York." *Berliner Zeitung*, 7 Apr. 1997.

Braune-Steininger, Wolfgang. "Porträt des Künstlers als alternder Leser. Zu Harald Hartungs Gedicht *Wann lasen Sie den Plato Mr. Hopper.*" Hinck, *Gegenwart II*, 301–09.

Brinkmann, Maleen, ed. *Literaturmagazin 36. Sonderheft Rolf Dieter Brinkmann*. Reinbek bei Hamburg: Rowohlt, 1995.

Brinkmann, Rolf Dieter. "Die Lyrik Frank O'Haras." Afterword. *Lunch Poems und andere Gedichte*. By Frank O'Hara. Rpt. in Brinkmann, *Der Film in Worten*, 207–22.

Bruni, Frank. "At Harlem Churches, Flocks of Tourists; Drawn to Gospel, if Not Gospels, Foreigners Arrive by Busload." *New York Times*, 24 Nov. 1996, late ed., sec. 1:37.

Buschmann, Christel. "Gegen feinsinnigen Hokuspokus." Rev. of *Die Piloten*, by Brinkmann. *Die Zeit*, 6 June 1969.

Buselmeier, Michael. "Das alltägliche Leben: Versuch über die neue Alltagslyrik." Buselmeier and Grzimek, *Neue deutsche Lyrik*, 4–34.

Buselmeier, Michael, and Martin Grzimek, eds. *Neue deutsche Lyrik: Beiträge zu Born, Brinkmann, Krechel, Theobaldy, Zahl u.a.* Heidelberg: Arbeitskreis linker Germanisten, 1977.

Calas, Nicolas. *Art in the Age of Risk*. New York, NY: Dutton, 1968.

Canby, H. S. *Walt Whitman: Bildnis eines Amerikaners*. Trans. Georg Goyert. Berlin: Blanvalet, 1946.

Chotjewitz, Peter O. "Trivialmythen." Matthaei, *Trivialmythen*, 115–27.

Christadler, Martin. "Autobiographen — Essayisten — Lyriker," in Frenz and Lang, *Nordamerikanische Literatur*, 111–36.

Cosentino, Christine and Wolfgang Ertl. *Zur Lyrik Volker Brauns*. Hanstein: Forum Academicum, 1984.

Curtius, Ernst Robert. "T. S. Eliot." *Merkur* 3.1 (1949): 1–23.

Cwojdrak, Hans G. *Walt Whitman, Dichter und Demokrat: ein Lebensbild.* Hamburg: Christen, 1946.

Demetz, Peter. "Ezra Pounds Pisaner Gesänge." Rev. of Pound, *Pisaner Gesänge,* trans. Hesse. *Merkur* 12.1 (1958): 97–100.

———. *Postwar German Literature: A Critical Introduction.* New York, NY: Pegasus, 1970.

Detering, Heinrich. "Lauter kleine Wunder." Rev. of Plath, *Drei Frauen,* trans. Roth. *Frankfurter Allgemeine Zeitung,* 28 Sept. 1991.

Divers, Greg. "Noch ein 'Geheimnis des Jazz': Saying 'oja' to Afro-German Studies." *Die Unterrichtspraxis* 28.2 (1995): 124–31.

Drews, Jörg. "Antwort auf Jürgen Theobaldy." *Akzente* 24.4 (1977): 379–82.

———. "Nach der »Neuen Sensibilität« — Überlegungen zur jüngsten Lyrik." Jordan, Marquardt, and Woesler, *Von allen Seiten,* 159–80.

———. "Selbsterfahrung und Neue Subjektivität in der Lyrik." *Akzente* 24.1 (1977): 89–95.

Durzak, Manfred. *Das Amerika-Bild in der deutschen Gegenwartsliteratur: Historische Voraussetzungen und aktuelle Beispiele.* Stuttgart: Kohlhammer, 1979.

———. "Perspektiven des Amerika-Bildes, historisch und gegenwärtig: Reisen in der Zeitmaschine." *Sprache im technischen Zeitalter* 56 (1975): 297–310.

———, ed. *Deutsche Gegenwartsliteratur: Ausgangspositionen und aktuelle Entwicklungen.* Stuttgart: Reclam, 1981.

Emig, Günther, ed. *Verzeichnis deutschsprachiger Literaturzeitschriften.* Heilbronn: Emig, 1981.

Enzensberger, Hans Magnus. "Gemeinplätze, die Neueste Literatur betreffend." *Kursbuch* 15 (1968): 187–97.

———. Afterword. *Gedichte.* By William Carlos Williams. 172–99.

Fiedler, Leslie. *Collected Essays.* 2 vols. New York, NY: Stein, 1971.

———. "Cross the Border, Close the Gap: The Case for Post Modernism." *Playboy* 12 (1969): 151, 230, 252–58.

———. "Das Zeitalter der neuen Literatur. Die Wiedergeburt der Kritik." *Christ und Welt* 13 Sept. 1968.

————. "Das Zeitalter der neuen Literatur. Indianer, Science Fiction und Pornographie: die Zukunft des Romans hat schon begonnen." *Christ und Welt* 20 Sept. 1968.

Fischer, Ludwig. "Vom Beweis der Güte des Puddings: Zu Jörg Drews' und Jürgen Theobaldys Ansichten über neuere Lyrik." *Akzente* 24.4 (1977): 371–79.

Fleischmann, W. B. "Amerikanische Dichtkunst und deutsche, 1945–1965." Frenz and Lang, *Nordamerikanische Literatur*, 65–78.

Frenz, Horst. "Die Reception of Thornton Wilder's Plays in Germany." *Modern Drama* 3.1 (1960): 123–37.

Frenz, Horst, and John Hess. "Die nordamerikanische Literatur in der Deutschen Demokratischen Republik." Frenz and Lang, *Nordamerikanische Literatur*, 171–99.

Frenz, Horst, and Hans Joachim Lang, eds. *Nordamerikanische Literatur im deutschen Sprachraum seit 1945: Beiträge zu ihrer Rezeption*. Munich: Winkler, 1973.

Frey, John R. "America and Her Literature Reviewed by Postwar Germany." *American-German Review* 20.5 (1954): 4–6, 31.

————. "Postwar German Reactions to American Literature." *Journal of English and Germanic Philology* 54.2 (1955): 173–94.

————. "Postwar Germany: Enter American Literature." *American-German Review* 21.1 (1954): 9–12.

Frey, Jürgen. "Der Dichter der Beat-Generation: Allen Ginsberg starb mit 70 Jahren an Leberkrebs." *Badische Zeitung*, 7 Apr. 1997.

Friedrich, Hugo. *Die Struktur der modernen Lyrik: Von Baudelaire bis zur Gegenwart*. Hamburg: Rowohlt, 1956.

Galinsky, Hans. *Amerikanisch-deutsche Sprach- und Literaturbeziehungen: Systematische Übersicht und Forschungsbericht 1945–1970*. Frankfurt am Main: Athenäum, 1972.

————. "Deutschlands literarisches Amerikabild: Ein kritischer Bericht zu Geschichte, Stand und Aufgabe der Forschung." Ritter, *Deutschlands literarisches Amerikabild*, 4–27.

Gehring, Hansjörg. "Literatur im Dienst der Politik. Zum Re-education Programm der amerikanischen Militärregierung in Deutschland." Born and Manthey, *Literaturmagazin* 7, 252–70.

Gemünden, Gerd. "The Depth of the Surface, or What Rolf Dieter Brinkmann Learned from Andy Warhol." *The German Quarterly* 68.3 (1995): 235–50.

Ginsberg, Allen. "Das war eine Befreiung des Worts." 1996 Interview with Werner Stiefele. *die tageszeitung*, 7 Apr. 1997.

Glenn, Jerry. "What is German-American Literature?" *Monatshefte* 86.3 (1994): 350–53.

Gnüg, Hiltrud. "Die Aufhebung des Naturgedichts in der Lyrik der Gegenwart." Jordan, Marquardt, and Woesler, *Von allen Seiten*, 264–83.

———. "Was heißt »Neue Subjektivität«?" *Merkur* 32.1 (1978): 60–75.

———. "Wolf Wondratschek — Erfolg eines Lyrikers." Rev. of *Männer und Frauen*, by Wondratschek. *Neue Zürcher Zeitung*, 27 March 1979.

Grimm, Reinhold. "Die problematischen 'Probleme der Lyrik.'" Eds. Heinz Otto Burger and Klaus von See. *Festschrift Gottfried Weber*. Bad Homburg: Gehlen, 1967. 299–328.

Grimm, Reinhold, and Jost Hermand, eds. *Basis: Jahrbuch für deutsche Gegenwartsliteratur*. Vol. 1. Frankfurt am Main: Athenäum, 1970.

Grzimek, Martin. "Über den Verlust der Verantwortlichkeit: Zu Rolf Dieter Brinkmanns poetischen Texten." Buselmeier and Grzimek, *Neue deutsche Lyrik*, 98–129.

Gutzschhahn, Uwe-Michael. *Prosa und Lyrik Christoph Meckels*. Cologne: Oberbaum, 1979.

Härtling, Peter. "Gegen rhetorische Ohnmacht: Kann man über Vietnam Gedichte schreiben?" Rev. of *und Vietnam und*, by Fried. *Der Monat* 19.5 (1967): 57–61.

Hage, Volker. "Zu Wondratscheks *In den Autos.*" Hinck, *Gedichte und Interpretationen*, 395–402.

Hahn, Ulla. *Literatur in der Aktion: Zur Entwicklung operativer Literaturformen in der Bundesrepublik*. Wiesbaden: Athenaion, 1978.

Hartung, Harald. "Die eindimensionale Poesie: Subjektivität und Oberflächigkeit in der neuen Lyrik." *Neue Rundschau* 89.2 (1978): 222–41.

———. *Experimentelle Literatur und konkrete Poesie*. Göttingen: Vandenhoeck & Ruprecht, 1975.

———. "Lyrik als Warnung und Erkenntnis: Zur Zeitlyrik Erich Frieds." Rev. of *Warngedichte*, by Fried. *kürbiskern* 3 (1966): 182–87. Rpt. in Arnold, *Geschichte der deutschen Literatur aus Methoden*, 71–77.

———. "Poesie und Vietnam: Eine Entgegnung." *Der Monat* 19.7 (1967): 76–79.

———. "Pop als 'postmoderne' Literatur: Die deutsche Szene: Brinkmann und andere." *Neue Rundschau* 82.4 (1971): 723–42.

———. "Pop-Lyrik am Beispiel von Brinkmanns 'Piloten.'" *Replik* 4–5 (1970): 57–62.

Hartung, Rudolf. "Selbstmörderisch eins mit dem Ritt." Rev. of Plath, *Ariel*, trans. Fried. *Süddeutsche Zeitung*, 8 Feb. 1975.

Heise, Hans-Jürgen. *Ein Galgen für den Dichter: Stichworte zur Lyrik.* Weingarten: Drumlin, 1986.

———. "Einer nennt es Sprache: Pop-Poesie mit Klischees aus zweiter Hand." Rev. of *Standphotos*, by Brinkmann. *Rheinischer Merkur*, 5 Dec. 1980.

Hennecke, Hans. *Dichtung und Dasein: Gesammelte Essays.* Berlin: Henssel, 1950.

———. *Kritik: Gesammelte Essays zur Modernen Literatur.* Gütersloh: Bertelsmann, 1958.

Hermand, Jost. *Pop International: Eine kritische Analyse.* Frankfurt am Main: Athenäum, 1970.

———. "Pop oder die These vom Ende der Kunst." Grimm and Hermand, *Basis* 1, 94–115.

Hetmann, Frederik. *So leicht verletzbar unser Herz: Die Lebensgeschichte der Sylvia Plath.* Weinheim: Beltz & Gelberg, 1988.

Hinck, Walter. "Erich Fried, der rasende Verworter." Rev. of *Es ist was es ist*, by Fried. *Frankfurter Allgemeine Zeitung*, 14 Jan. 1982.

———, ed. *Gedichte und Interpretationen: Gegenwart.* Vol. 6. Stuttgart: Reclam, 1982. 7 vols.

———, ed. *Gedichte und Interpretationen: Gegenwart II.* Vol. 7. Stuttgart: Reclam, 1997. 7 vols.

———. "Die offene Schreibweise Jürgen Beckers." Kreutzer, *Über Jürgen Becker*, 119–89.

Hinderer, Walter. "Form ist eine Ausdehnung vom Inhalt: Zu Nicolas Borns Gedicht *Da hat er gelernt was Krieg ist sagt er.*" Hinck, *Gedichte und Interpretationen*, 374–85.

Hohendahl, Peter Uwe, ed. *A History of German Literary Criticism 1730–1980.* Lincoln, NB and London: U of Nebraska P, 1988.

———. "Introduction." Hohendahl, *A History of German Literary Criticism*, 1–11

Höllerer, Walter. Afterword. Höllerer, *Theorie der modernen Lyrik*, 419–39.

———. "Anmerkungen zur Autorenpoetik." Jordan, Marquardt, and Woesler, *Von allen Seiten*, 13–31.

———. "Gedichte in den sechziger Jahren." *Akzente* 13.4 (1966): 375–83. Rpt. in Bender and Krüger, *Was alles hat Platz?*, 29–38.

———. "Junge amerikanische Literatur." *Akzente* 6.1 (1959): 29–43.

———. "Veränderung." *Akzente* 11.5–6 (1964): 386–98.

Holthusen, Hans Egon. "Anmerkungen zu einem 'Museum der modernen Poesie.'" Rev. of *Museum der modernen Poesie*, ed. Enzensberger. *Merkur* 15.11 (1961): 1073–84.

———. "Der Dichter im eisernen Käfig." Rev. of Ezra Pound, *Dichtung und Prosa*, trans. Eva Hesse. *Merkur* 9.1 (1955): 77–94.

———. "Sie bekämpfen den Hunger am Schreibtisch." Rev. of *und Vietnam und*, by Fried. *Christ und Welt*, 4 Aug. 1967.

Hopkins, Leroy. "'Black Prussians': Germany and African American Education from James W. C. Pennington to Angela Davis." McBride, Hopkins, and Blackshire-Belay, *Crosscurrents*, 65–81.

Hübsch, Hadayatullah. "Allen Ginsbergs Echo zieht weiter." *Der Literat* 39.5 (1997): 18.

Hughes, Langston. *Das Buch von Jazz*. Trans. Paridam von dem Knesebeck. Munich: Domino, 1965.

Hughes, Peter. "Amerika als Traum und Wahn: Zum Tod des Lyrikers Allen Ginsberg." *Neue Zürcher Zeitung*, 7 Apr. 1997.

Ingendaay, Paul. "Das Geheul der Verlierer in freien Versen. Dichter, Sänger, Wanderprediger: Zum Tod von Allen Ginsberg, dem Begründer der amerikanischen Beatnik-Bewegung." *Frankfurter Allgemeine Zeitung*, 7 Apr. 1997.

Jacobs, Steffen. "Überall weinen die Leute." Rev. of Walker, *Ihre braune Umarmung*, trans. Döhler. *Frankfurter Allgemeine Zeitung*, 21 Dec. 1995.

Jansen, Peter W. "Dann und wann das Empire State Building." Kreutzer, *Über Jürgen Becker*, 86–90.

Jantz, Harold. "Amerika im deutschen Dichten und Denken." *Deutsche Philologie im Aufriß*. Gen. ed. Wolfgang Stammler. 2nd ed. 3 vols. Berlin: Schmidt, 1962. 3: col. 309–72.

———. "The Myth about America: Origins and Extensions." Ritter, *Deutschlands literarisches Amerikabild*, 37–49.

Jordan, Lothar. *Bibliographie zur europäischen und amerikanischen Gegenwartslyrik im deutschen Sprachraum: Sekundärliteratur 1945–1988*. Tübingen: Niemeyer, 1996.

————. "Eine Dichtung unter Einfluß: Zur amerikanischen Wirkung auf westdeutsche Lyrik seit 1965." Jordan, Marquardt, and Woesler, *Blick über die Grenzen,* 139–58.

————. *Europäische und nordamerikanische Gegenwartslyrik im deutschen Sprachraum 1920–1970: Studien zu ihrer Vermittlung und Wirkung.* Tübingen: Niemeyer, 1994.

Jordan, Lothar, Axel Marquardt, and Winfried Woesler, eds. *Lyrik — Von allen Seiten: Gedichte und Aufsätze des ersten Lyrikertreffens in Münster.* Frankfurt am Main: Fischer, 1984.

————. *Lyrik — Blick über die Grenzen: Gedichte und Aufsätze des zweiten Lyrikertreffens in Münster.* Frankfurt am Main: Fischer, 1981.

Jungwirth, Nicolaus, and Gerhard Kromschröder. *Die Pubertät der Republik: Die 50er Jahre der Deutschen.* Frankfurt am Main: Fricke, 1978.

Just, K[laus] G[ünther]. "Zur amerikanischen Literaturkritik: Ezra Pound und R. P. Blackmur." *Merkur* 10.12 (1956): 1230–33.

Karsunke, Yaak. "Ins Gras gebissen." Rev. of *Gras,* by Brinkmann. *Frankfurter Rundschau,* 27 June 1970.

Kenner, Hugh. *The Poetry of Ezra Pound.* Norfolk, CT: New Directions, 1951.

Kneerich-Woerner, Marianne. *Der Selbstmord: eine psychoanalytische Untersuchung am Material eines Schriftstellers und einer Schriftstellerin, die sich selbst getötet haben.* Frankfurt am Main: Lang, 1988.

Knörrich, Otto. *Die deutsche Lyrik seit 1945.* 2nd ed. Stuttgart: Kröner, 1978.

Koch, Hans. "Unsere soziale Wirklichkeit im Spiegel der Literatur." *Neues Deutschland,* 26–27 July and 2–3 Aug. 1966.

Koch, Steven. *Stargazer: The Life, World and Films of Andy Warhol.* 3rd ed. 1973. New York, NY and London: Boyars, 1991.

Koebner, Thomas, ed. *Tendenzen der deutschen Literatur seit 1945.* Stuttgart: Kröner, 1971.

Koepke, Wulf. "German-American and Exile Studies: Still a Divided Stream?" *Monatshefte* 86.3 (1994): 361–66.

Krättli, Anton. "Ganz leer sein, um zu begreifen." Rev. of *Standphotos,* by Brinkmann. *Neue Zürcher Zeitung,* 10 Apr. 1981.

Krätzer, Anita. *Studien zum Amerikabild in der neueren deutschen Literatur: Max Frisch, Uwe Johnson, Hans Magnus Enzensberger und das "Kursbuch."* Bern and Frankfurt am Main: Lang, 1982.

Kramer, Jane. "Letter from Europe." *The New Yorker,* 25 May 1992: 40–64. Rpt. as "Stasi" in Kramer, *Politics of Memory,* 153–212.

———. *The Politics of Memory: Looking for Germany in the New Germany.* New York, NY: Random, 1996.

Kreutzer, Leo, ed. *Über Jürgen Becker.* Frankfurt am Main: Suhrkamp, 1972.

Krolow, Karl. "Angst, daß Genet nur Spaß macht." Rev. of *ACID*, eds. Brinkmann and Rygulla. *Die Tat*, 14 June 1969.

———. *Aspekte zeitgenössischer deutscher Lyrik.* Gütersloh: Mohn, 1961.

———. "Das Problem des langen und kurzen Gedichts — heute." *Akzente* 13.3 (1966): 271–87. Rpt. in Bender and Krüger, *Was alles hat Platz?* 10–28.

Kruse, Sabine. *Ted Hughes' Birthday Letters vor dem Hintergrund der Plath-Hughes-Kontroverse.* Essen: Die Blaue Eule, 1999.

Kühlmann, Wilhelm. "Die klare Sicht des Wahns." Rev. of Plath, *Glasglocke*, trans. Kaiser. *Frankfurter Allgemeine Zeitung*, 15 Apr. 1997.

Künzler, Hanspeter. "Die Tote und die Lebenden: Janet Malcolms Studie über die Biographien der Sylvia Plath." Rev. of Malcolm, *Die schweigende Frau*, trans. Levin. *Neue Zürcher Zeitung*, 8/9 July 1995.

Kuhlbrodt, Detlef. "Hallo Nikita, hier ist Gott! Allen Ginsberg ist am Samstag 70jährig gestorben." *die tageszeitung*, 7 Apr. 1997.

Lampe, Gerhard. *Ohne Subjektivität: Interpretationen zur Lyrik Rolf Dieter Brinkmanns vor dem Hintergrund der Studentenbewegung.* Tübingen: Niemeyer, 1983.

Leonhardt, Rudolf Walter. "Sie sind aus Wasser." Rev. of Plath, *Drei Frauen*, trans. Roth. *Die Zeit*, 30 Aug. 1991.

Levin, Gail. *Edward Hopper: An Intimate Biography.* New York, NY: Knopf, 1995.

———. *Edward Hopper, 1882–1967: Gemälde und Zeichnungen.* Trans. Karin Stempel. Munich: Schirmer-Mosel, 1981.

Linder, Christian. "Sänger der Beatniks: Dichter Allen Ginsberg starb 70jährig in New York." *Rheinische Post*, 7 Apr. 1997.

Link, Franz H., ed. *Amerika Vision und Wirklichkeit: Beiträge deutscher Forschung zur amerikanischen Literaturgeschichte.* Frankfurt am Main and Bonn: Athenäum, 1968.

Lohner, Edgar. "Gottfried Benn und T. S. Eliot." *Neue Deutsche Hefte* 3 (1956/57): 100–107.

Lützeler, Paul Michael. *Zeitgeschichte in Geschichten der Zeit: Deutschsprachige Romane im 20. Jahrhundert.* Bonn: Bouvier, 1986.

Lützeler, Paul Michael, and Egon Schwarz, eds. *Deutsche Literatur in der Bundesrepublik seit 1965: Untersuchungen und Berichte.* Königstein/Ts.: Athenäum, 1980.

MacLeish, Archibald. *Elemente der Lyrik: Leitfaden für Leser.* Trans. Bazon Brock and Reinhold Grimm. Ed. Reinhold Grimm. Göttingen: Sachse & Pohl, 1963.

Malcolm, Janet. *Die schweigende Frau: Die Biographien der Sylvia Plath.* Trans. Susanne Friederike Levin. Hamburg: Kellner, 1994.

Malsch, Wilfried. "Einleitung. Neue Welt, Nordamerika und USA als Projektion und Problem." Bauschinger, Denkler, and Malsch, *Amerika in der deutschen Literatur,* 9–16.

Masata, Holger. "Die Befreiung des Gedankens." Rev. of *ACID*, eds. Brinkmann and Rygulla. *Die Publik* 31, 1 Aug. 1969: 20.

Matthaei, Renate, ed. *Trivialmythen.* Frankfurt am Main: März, 1970.

McBride, David, Leroy Hopkins, and C. Aisha Blackshire-Belay, eds. *Crosscurrents: African Americans, Africa, and Germany in the Modern World.* Columbia, SC: Camden House, 1998.

Mennemeier, Franz Norbert. "Die Anti-Gedichte des Rolf Dieter Brinkmann." Rev. of *Was fraglich ist wofür,* by Brinkmann. *Neues Rheinland* 2 (1968): 37.

———. "Gedichte in Pop: Zu Editionen von R. D. Brinkmann." *Neues Rheinland* 3 (1970): 30.

Middell, Eike, ed. *Exil in den USA.* Leipzig: Reclam, 1979. Vol. 3 of *Zu Kunst und Literatur im antifaschistischen Exil 1933–1945 in sechs Bänden.* Gen. ed. Werner Mittenzwei. 6 vols.

Mönnig, Richard. *Amerika und England im deutschen, österreichischen und schweizerischen Schrifttum der Jahre 1945–1949: Eine Bibliographie.* Stuttgart: Kohlhammer, 1951.

Mohr, Peter. "Beat-Poet Ginsberg gestorben." *Saarbrücker Zeitung,* 7 Apr. 1997.

"Nachruf. Allen Ginsberg. 1926 bis 1997." *Der Spiegel,* 14 Apr. 1997: 214.

Nettelbeck, Uwe. "Generalthema 'Trivialmythen.'" Matthaei, *Trivialmythen,* 151–79.

Nolte, Jost. "Aufstand gegen die Grammatik?" Rev. of *ACID*, eds. Brinkmann and Rygulla. *Die Welt,* 8 Jan. 1970.

Oehlen, Martin. "Im Rausch der Worte. Zum Tode des US-Dichters Allen Ginsberg. Von der Beat-Generation zur Hippie-Bewegung." *Kölner Stadt-Anzeiger,* 7 Apr. 1997.

Office of the United States High Commissioner for Germany, Education and Cultural Relations Division. *Verzeichnis amerikanischer Bücher in deutscher Übersetzung: Erschienen in Deutschland seit 1945.* Frankfurt am Main: Information Centers Branch, 1951.

Ohff, Heinz, ed. *Pop und die Folgen: Oder die Kunst, Kunst auf der Straße zu finden.* Düsseldorf: Droste, 1968.

Ohnemus, Günter. "Hungrig, hysterisch, nackt: Zum Tod von Allen Ginsberg." *Die Zeit,* 11 Apr. 1997.

O'Pray, Michael, ed. *Andy Warhol: Film Factory.* London: British Film Institute, 1989.

Osterle, Heinz D., ed. *Bilder von Amerika: Gespräche mit deutschen Schriftstellern.* Münster: Englisch Amerikanische Studien, 1987.

Paulsen, Wolfgang, ed. *Die USA und Deutschland: Wechselseitige Spiegelungen in der Literatur der Gegenwart.* Bern: Francke, 1976.

Paulus, Rolf, and Ursula Steuler. *Bibliographie zur deutschen Lyrik nach 1945: Forschung — Autoren — Anthologien.* 2nd. ed. Wiesbaden: Athenaion, 1977.

Perloff, Marjorie. *Frank O'Hara: Poet Among Painters.* Austin, TX: U of Texas P, 1979.

Platschek, Hans. "Tautologie der Gegenstände." *Merkur* 18.1 (1964): 33–42.

Platzeck, Wolfgang. "Am Puls der Zeit: Zum Tod des Lyrikers Allen Ginsberg." *Westdeutsche Allgemeine Zeitung,* 7 Apr. 1997.

Pollak, Felix. "The Popeye Papers." *The Smith* 5 (1965): 4–15.

Priessnitz, Reinhard. "Meinetwegen, fuck you!" Rev. of *ACID,* eds. Brinkmann and Rygulla. *Neues Forum* 3 (1970): 257–58.

Räther, Helmut. "Die 'Beat Generation' verlor ihren Begründer. Revolution und Resignation: Allen Ginsberg starb 70jährig." *Westfälische Rundschau,* 7 Apr. 1997.

Reichart, Manuela. "Spaßwunderbetten." Rev. of Plath, *Bettbuch,* trans. Demski. *Die Zeit,* 20 Apr. 1990.

Reich-Ranicki, Marcel. "Die Leiden des Dichters Erich Fried: Aus Anlaß seiner neuen Lyrikbände." *Frankfurter Allgemeine Zeitung,* 23 Jan. 1982.

———. "Wolf Wondratschek oder Poesie in Jeans." *Frankfurter Allgemeine Zeitung,* 25 July 1981.

Ribbat, Ernst. "Subjektivität als Instrument? Zu Jürgen Becker und Nicolas Born." Jordan, Marquardt, and Woesler, *Von allen Seiten,* 485–501.

Richter, Hansjürgen. *Ästhetik der Ambivalenz: Studien zur Struktur "postmoderner" Lyrik — exemplarisch dargestellt an Rolf Dieter Brinkmanns Poetik und dem Gedichtband "Westwärts 1 & 2."* Frankfurt am Main: Lang, 1983.

Ritter, Alexander. "Amerika-Literatur 1945–1976: Eine Bibliographie zum literarischen Amerikabild und zu verwandten Themen." Ritter, *Deutschlands literarisches Amerikabild*, 562–615.

———, ed. *Deutschlands literarisches Amerikabild: Neuere Forschungen zur Amerikarezeption der deutschen Literatur.* Hildesheim and New York, NY: Olms, 1977.

Rothschild, Thomas. "Geheul: Zum Tod von Allen Ginsberg." *Freitag*, 11 Apr. 1997.

Rühmkorf, Peter. "Die Mord- und Brandsache." Rev. of *und Vietnam und*, by Fried. *Der Spiegel*, 24 Apr. 1967: 166–67.

———. "Haben wir zu viele Vietnam Gedichte?" *Konkret* 5 (1967): 36.

Ruland, Richard. *America in Modern European Literature: From Image to Metaphor.* New York, NY: New York UP, 1976.

Rusch, Heinz. "Dichter der Zukunft." *Börsenblatt für den Deutschen Buchhandel* 121.22 (1954): 487–88.

Ryan, Judith. "'Your life jacket is under your skin.' Reflections on German poetry of the seventies." *The German Quarterly* 55.3 (1982): 296–308.

Salzinger, Helmut. "Pop mit Ra-ta-ta-ta." Rev. of *Die Piloten*, by Brinkmann. *Der Tagesspiegel*, 23 Feb. 1969.

Sartorius, Joachim. "Die Oberfläche des Sommers oder Was Brinkmann mit Ashbery machte." *Akzente* 32.3 (1985): 196–98.

———, ed. *Der Mann mit dem roten Handkarren: Über William Carlos Williams.* Munich: Hanser, 1987.

Schader, Angela. "Mit reinerem Klang: Sylvia Plaths »Glasglocke« neu übersetzt." Rev. of Plath, *Glasglocke*, trans. Kaiser. *Neue Zürcher Zeitung*, 8 Aug. 1997.

Schäfer, Hans Dieter. "Dieter Leisegang." Weissenberger, *Die deutsche Lyrik 1945–1975*, 404–14.

———. Rev. of *Das Ende der Landschaftsmalerei*, by Becker. *Neue deutsche Hefte* 3 (1974): 585–91.

———. "Rolf Dieter Brinkmann." Weissenberger, *Die deutsche Lyrik 1945–1975*, 391–403.

———. "Zusammenhänge der deutschen Gegenwartslyrik." Durzak, *Deutsche Gegenwartsliteratur*, 166–203.

Schäfer, Jörgen. *Pop-Literatur: Rolf Dieter Brinkmann und das Verhältnis zur Populärkultur in der Literatur der sechziger Jahre.* Stuttgart: M & P, 1998.

Scheidgen, Ilka. "Afroamerikanische Lyrik." Rev. of Dove, *Die gläserne Stern,* trans. Viebahn. *Der Literat* 32.6 (15 June 1990): 172–73.

Schlüter, Hermann. *Grundkurs der Rhetorik: Mit einer Textsammlung.* 1974. Munich: dtv, 1985.

Schlütter, Hans-Jürgen, ed. *Lyrik — 25 Jahre: Bibliographie der deutschsprachigen Lyrikpublikationen 1945–1970.* Vol. 2. *Bibliographie zur deutschen Literatur.* Hildesheim, Zürich, New York, NY: Olms, 1983.

Schmidt, Thomas E. "Geheul — und andere politische Aktivitäten: Zum Tode des Beat-Lyrikers Allen Ginsberg." *Frankfurter Rundschau,* 7 Apr. 1997.

Schmitter, Elke. "Karriere auf schiefer Ebene." Rev. of Stevenson, *Sylvia Plath: Eine Biographie,* trans. Ohl and Sartorius; and Wagner-Martin, *Sylvia Plath: Eine Biographie,* trans. Techel. *Der Spiegel,* 17 Dec. 1990: 193, 196–99.

———. "Ein Panther stellt mir lauernd nach." Rev. of Stevenson, *Sylvia Plath: Eine Biographie,* trans. Ohl and Sartorius. *Die Weltwoche,* 1 Feb. 1990.

Schmitz, Alexander. "Am Vater verzweifelt." Rev. of Plath, *Ariel,* trans. Fried. *Die Welt,* 21 Nov. 1974.

———. "Geträller." Rev. of Dove, *Die gläserne Stirn,* trans. Viebahn. *Die Welt,* 24 March 1990.

Schneider, Stan. "Der Clown und der Claqueur. Zwei Dichterleben auf der Flucht vor dem eigenen Judentum: Allen Ginsberg und Stephan Hermlin sind tot." *Jüdische Allgemeine,* 17 Apr. 1997.

Schöfer, Erasmus. "Demokratisierung der Künste." *kürbiskern* 2 (1969): 292–97.

Schröder, Jörg. "Interview mit einem Verleger." *März Texte 1.* Darmstadt: März, 1969. 283–96.

Schütz, Erhard. "»Dichter der Gesellschaft«. Neuer deutscher Journalismus oder Für eine erneuerte Asphaltliteratur." *Text + Kritik* 113 (1992): 63–71.

Schuhmann, Klaus. Foreword. Voigtländer and Witt, *Denkzettel,* 5–27.

———. *Weltbild und Poetik: Zur Wirklichkeitsdarstellung in der Lyrik der BRD bis zur Mitte der siebziger Jahre.* Berlin and Weimar: Aufbau, 1979.

Schulz, Bernhard. "Der Untergang Amerikas: Zum Tod von Allen Ginsberg, dem Dichter der Beat Generation." *Der Tagesspiegel*, 7 Apr. 1997.

Schwarz, Egon. "Die sechste Schwierigkeit beim Schreiben der Wahrheit: Zum Gruppendenken in Leben und Literatur." Paulsen, *Die USA und Deutschland*, 11–26.

Sontag, Susan. "Anmerkungen zu »Camp«." *Akzente* 13.6 (1966): 501–21.

———. *Kunst und Anti-Kunst: 24 literarischen Analysen*. Trans. Mark W. Rien. Reinbek bei Hamburg: Rowohlt, 1968.

———. "Die pornographische Phantasie." *Akzente* 15.1 (1968): 77–95 and 15.2 (1968): 169–90.

Späth, Sibylle. *"Rettungsversuche aus dem Todesterritorium": Zur Aktualität der Lyrik Rolf Dieter Brinkmanns*. Frankfurt am Main: Lang, 1986.

———. *Rolf Dieter Brinkmann*. Stuttgart: Metzler, 1989.

Staiger, Emil. "Ein Briefwechsel mit Martin Heidegger." Staiger, *Die Kunst der Interpretation*, 34–39.

———. *Die Kunst der Interpretation: Studien zur deutschen Literaturgeschichte*. Zürich: Atlantis, 1955.

Staudacher, Cornelia. "Eine späte Würdigung." Rev. of Dove, *Die morgenländische Tänzerin*, trans. Graf. *Der Tagesspiegel*, 9 Apr. 1989.

Steinert, Monika. *Mythos in den Gedichten Sylvia Plaths*. Frankfurt am Main: Lang, 1995.

Stephan, Peter M. "Das Gedicht in der Marktlücke: Abschließende Marginalien zur Diskussion über die »Neue Subjektivität« in der Lyrik." *Akzente* 24.6 (1977): 493–504.

Stevenson, Anne. *Sylvia Plath: Eine Biographie*. Trans. Manfred Ohl and Hans Sartorius. Frankfurt am Main: Frankfurter Verlagsanstalt, 1989.

Stiefele, Werner. "Nein, zornig war er nicht! Der Beat hört auf zu schlagen — Zum Tod des Dichters Allen Ginsberg." *Stuttgarter Zeitung*, 7 Apr. 1997.

Stromberg, Kyra. "Das existentielle Wagnis: Leben und Dichtung der amerikanischen Lyrikerin Sylvia Plath." *Frankfurter Allgemeine Zeitung*, 7 Feb. 1976.

Theobaldy, Jürgen. "Begrenzte Weiten: Amerika-Bilder in der westdeutschen Lyrik." *Akzente* 22.5 (1976): 402–17.

———. "Literaturkritik, astrologisch: Zu Jörg Drews' Aufsatz über Selbsterfahrung und Neue Subjektivität in der Lyrik." *Akzente* 24.2 (1977): 188–91.

————. "Schreckensbilder aus Wörtern." Rev. of *Westwärts 1 & 2*, by Brinkmann. *Frankfurter Rundschau*, 24 May 1975.

————. "Wie und warum ich Benzin herausgab." Emig, *Verzeichnis deutschsprachiger Literaturzeitschriften*, 7–13.

Theobaldy, Jürgen, and Gustav Zürcher. *Veränderung der Lyrik: Über westdeutsche Gedichte seit 1965*. Munich: Text + Kritik, 1976.

Thomas, R. Hinton, and Keith Bullivant. *Literature in Upheaval: West German Writers and the Challenges of the 1960s*. Manchester: Manchester UP, 1974.

Tolzmann, Don Heinrich, ed. *German-American Literature*. Metuchen, NJ and London: Scarecrow, 1977.

Trommler, Frank. "Realismus in der Prosa." Koebner, *Tendenzen der deutschen Literatur*, 179–275.

Tschapke, Reinhard. "Vom ekstatischen Hippi zum sanften Buddhisten. Erfinder von 'Flower Power,' Sänger der Beat-Generation und König der Subkultur: der amerikanische Lyriker Allen Ginsberg ist gestorben." *Die Welt*, 7 Apr. 1997.

Updike, John. "Hopper's Polluted Silence." Rev. of Edward Hopper Exhibition at the Whitney Museum of American Art. *New York Review of Books*, 10 Aug. 1995: 19–21.

Urbe, Burglind. *Lyrik, Fotographie und Massenkultur bei Rolf Dieter Brinkmann*. Frankfurt am Main: Lang, 1985.

Volckmann, Silvia. "Ausflüge in die Romantik. F. C. Delius — *Selbstporträt mit Luftbrücke*." Hinck, *Gegenwart II*, 261–69.

Vollmann, Rolf. "Wie man vielleicht besser leben könnte." Rev. of Plath, *Ariel*, trans. Fried. *Stuttgarter Zeitung*, 10 Oct. 1974.

Vordtriede, Werner. "Der Weg des Todes." Rev. of Plath, *Ariel*, trans. Fried. *Die Zeit*, 25 Oct. 1974.

Vormweg, Heinrich. "Bilder aus dem Leben der Armen." Rev. of Dove, *Die morgenländische Tänzerin*, trans. Graf. *Süddeutsche Zeitung*, 5/6 Aug. 1989.

Wagner-Martin, Linda. *Sylvia Plath: Eine Biographie*. Trans. Sabine Techel. Frankfurt am Main: Insel, 1990.

Wallman, Jürgen Peter. "Jedermann-Gedichte." Rev. of *Gras*, by Brinkmann. *Nürnberger Nachrichten*, 6 Jan. 1971. Rpt. in *Rheinische Post*, 27 Feb. 1971.

———. "Ein wüster, alltäglicher Alptraum." Rev. of *Westwärts 1 & 2*, by Brinkmann. *Die Tat*, 3 Oct. 1975. Rpt. in *Neue Deutsche Hefte* 22 (1975): 597–603.

Walser, Martin. "Über die Neueste Stimmung im Westen." *Kursbuch* 20 (1970): 19–41.

Wehdeking, Volker. "Eine deutsche *Lost Generation*? Die 47er zwischen Kriegsende und Währungsreform. Born and Manthey, *Literaturmagazin* 7, 145–66.

Weinreich, Harald. "Gegen die Musterschüler, Schönfärber und Falschspieler." Rev. of *Die bunten Getüme*, by Fried. *Frankfurter Allgemeine Zeitung*, 26 March 1977.

Weissenberger, Klaus. "Die Voraussetzung der Gegenwartslyrik." Introduction. Weissenberger, *Die deutsche Lyrik*.

———, ed. *Die deutsche Lyrik 1945–1975: Zwischen Botschaft und Spiel*. Düsseldorf: Bagel, 1981.

Werth, Wolfgang. *Ikonographie des Entsetzens: die Todeslyrik der Sylvia Plath*. Trier: Wissenschaftlicher Verlag, 1990.

Weyrauch, Wolfgang. Preface. Weyrauch, *Tausend Gramm*.

Willson, A. Leslie. "Perspective: The Image of America." *Dimension* Special Issue (1983): 13–17.

Winkler, Willi. "Wutgeheul als Gassenhauer: Zum Tod des Beat-Poeten Allen Ginsberg." *Süddeutsche Zeitung*, 7 Apr. 1997.

Winter, Helmut. "Hölderlin auf der Veranda." Rev. of Dove, *Die morgenländische Tänzerin*, trans. Graf. *Frankfurter Allgemeine Zeitung*, 21 Jan. 1989.

———. "Der Hund im Blumenbeet." Rev. of Dove, *Die gläserne Stirn*, trans. Viebahn. *Frankfurter Allgemeine Zeitung*, 13 Feb. 1990.

Wintjes, Joseph, and J. Gehret, eds. *Ulcus Molle Info-Dienst: Jahrgänge 1969–1974*. Amsterdam: Azid, 1979.

Wirzberger, Karl-Heinz. "Einhundert Jahre 'Leaves of Grass.'" *Zeitschrift für Anglistik und Amerikanistik* 4.1 (1956): 77–87.

Wolff, Rudolf, ed. *Erich Fried: Gespräche und Kritiken*. Bonn: Bouvier, 1986.

Wollen, Peter, "Raiding the Icebox." O'Pray, *Andy Warhol*, 14–27.

Wüllner, Jochen. "R. D. Brinkmann— Der Autor als Kameramann." *Guckloch* 4 (1985): 121–23.

Wysocki, Gisela von. "Das Leben. Ein hektisches Dabeigewesensein." Rev. Plath, *Glasglocke*, trans. Kaiser. *Die Zeit*, 4 Apr. 1997.

Zimmer, Dieter E. "Weltausstellung der Lyriker: Eine Veranstaltungsreihe des Literarischen Colloquiums Berlin." *Die Zeit*, 10 Feb. 1967.

Zimmermann, Bernhard. "Literary Criticism from 1933 to the Present." Trans. Franz Blaha. Hohendahl, *A History of German Literary Criticism*, 359–437.

Zimmermann, Hans Dieter. "Die mangelhafte Subjektivität." *Akzente* 24.3 (1977): 280–87.

Zorach, Cecile Cazort and Charlotte Melin. "The Columbian Legacy in Postwar German Lyric Poetry." *The German Quarterly* 65.3–4 (1992): 267–93.

Copyrights and Permissions

Index